Vera Lex

Journal of the International Natural Law Society

New Series Volume 10, Numbers 1&2   Winter 2009

Copyright © 2010
Pace University Press
1 Pace Plaza
New York, NY 10038

ISBN 1-935625-02-0
ISBN-13 978-1-935625-02-5
ISSN 0893-4851

Contributors
Address all submissions and correspondence to The Editor, VERA LEX, Pace University, Department of Philosophy & Religious Studies, 1 Pace Plaza, New York, NY 10038. Please send two copies of the paper submitted. Include adequate margins, double space everything (text, notes, works cited, quotations). Use U.S. spelling and punctuation style, (e.g. periods inside quotation marks; "double quotes" for opening and closing quotations). The University of Chicago Manual of Style, 13th Edition, is to be consulted regarding matters of style. Notes are to be numbered consecutively (in Arabic numerals) and placed at the bottom of the page.

Subscribers
VERA LEX is published annually by Pace University Press, 41 Park Row, Room 1510, New York, NY 10038. Subscription price: $40. Please send all subscription inquiries to: PaceUP@pace.edu

Indexing and Abstracting
VERA LEX is indexed in Philosopher's Index.
Copyright © 2010 by Pace University Press. Permission is required to reprint an article or part of an article.

VERA LEX, the journal of the International Natural Law Society, was established to communicate and dialogue on the subject of natural law and natural right, to introduce natural law philosophy into the mainstream of contemporary thought, and to strengthen the current revived interest in the discussion of morals and law and advance its historical research.

Robert Chapman
Editor
Virginia Black
Editor Emerita

Editorial Board

Harold Brown
Department of Philosophy & Religious Studies, Pace University
Mark Gossiaux
Department of Philosophy, Loyola University, New Orleans
Gregory J. Kerr
Department of Philosophy & Theology, DeSales University
John Krummel
Department of Religion, Temple University
Thomas O'Sullivan
Department of Philosophy & Religious Studies, Pace University
Alice Ramos
Department of Philosophy, St. John's University
Lisa Sideris
Department of Religious Studies, Indiana University
Peter Widulski
Loyola University School of Law, New Orleans

Why do we use a shell (*Nautilus pomplilus Linnaeus*) to symbolize vera lex? The logarithmic spiraling and overlapping chambers of the shell are endless. They suggest a patterned development and evolution that, by its radial and circular design, never comes to an end. This means that the shell is at once specific and real, while its form, like law, is abstract and ideal.

The pattern of a shell is, like good law, uniform, regular and reliable. It can therefore be anticipated and known. The pattern of a shell is balanced, like justice. Una iustitia.

A shell is a biological being. Like law, it has life and dynamic. It grows. (There is an average of thirty growth lines per chamber, one for every day in the lunar cycle, suggesting that a new chamber is put down each lunar month and a new growth line each day, thus recording two different natural rhythms, lunar and solar.)

The shell is a universal and common object known to everyone. A shell is not soft tissue easily destroyed. And yet, like liberty, it is fragile in certain respects if stepped on with an iron boot. It has to be guarded with vigilance or it is crushed.

In every shell lives a nautilus. If the shell is law, the nautilus (snail) is a person—it is alive—person and law. Their destinies, like person and law, are interdependent.

Vera Lex
leges innumerae, una iustitia

CONTENTS
NEW SERIES VOLUME 10, NUMBERS 1&2   **WINTER 2009**

Editorial	Robert L. Chapman	1

FEATURED ARTICLES

Prescriptive Realism and the Limits of International Human Rights Law	Laura S. Johnson	7
Finding Footing in a Postmodern Conception of Laws	Bryan Druzin	27
The Architecture of Law: Building Law on a Solid Foundation— The Eternal and Natural Laws	Brian M. McCall	47
Law Without Disgust: A Fetid Freedom	Matthew Jordan Cochran	103
Questioning Authority: Just War Theory, Sovereign Authority and the United Nations	Michael P. Boulette	145
Revisiting Fuller's Cave: A Spelunker and His Lawyers	Jason Isbell	169

Persuasive Reasoning and the Praxis of Virtue	Jeffrey J. Maciejewski	197
CONTRIBUTORS		235
CALL FOR PAPERS		239

EDITORIAL

It has been both a pleasure and a challenge editing *Vera Lex* these last ten years. The pleasures were many and varied, from the opportunity to review cutting-edge scholarship to the many encouraging comments on the journal; I will miss these. As for the challenges, well, some you overcome and others remain elusive; this issue should have been completed four months ago. But I leave knowing the journal is in capable hands and wish the incoming editor and colleague, Professor Richard Connerney, all possible success.

As we change editors we are also changing the style and content of the journal to allow for a broader range of submissions. Although *Vera Lex* will continue to feature articles on "traditional" and "new classical natural law" theories, we will encourage articles from other traditions often critical of natural law and accept law-review articles. In short, the journal will transition to a more generalized venue for philosophy of law and jurisprudence, keeping in mind, of course, that natural law theory continues to remain important for moral theory, especially in times of social and cultural upheaval.

The articles collected here are representative of the move to introduce a variety of legal and philosophical approaches to moral issues in law that in some cases apply natural law theories and in others take a different approach. We do this to encourage an ongoing dialogue between various philosophical and legal traditions with the hope that a better understanding of the variant positions will lead to a more robust conversation. We believe the articles featured in this issue will act as a catalyst for this end.

Laura Johnson's lead article, "Prescriptive Realism and the Limits of International Human Rights Law," argues for a reconciliation or middle ground between two theories of international law, realism and idealism. Realists take the position that states act out of their own self-interest and international law only serves to subvert the interests of states. Idealists claim that international law matters and has the authority to act as a constraint on states' behavior—consider the United Nations as an institution modeled on idealist principles of international law. Johnson's suggestion is "prescriptive realism." Prescriptive realism differs from earlier realism by conceding that international law matters and compliance with it can be conceptualized as an instance of mutual self-interest, where *mutual* is the prescriptive/normative component. The challenge, of course, is to avoid the strong cultural relativism of standard realists' theories. Johnson concludes that prescriptive realism accommodates realism in being sensitive to the need for coercion, like economic sanctions, but sees these sanctions as providing a normative influence on state behavior and thus over time becoming universal, which skirts the claim to relativism.

Bryan Druzin grapples with the relativism inherent in postmodern legal concepts of law and argues that it can be countered by a return to basics, that is, moral objectivity grounded in the individual experience of suffering. In his "Finding Footing in a Postmodern Conception of Laws," Druzin challenges the relativist position to account for the ongoing activity of the creation and enforcement of laws; granted law changes but it would be a fool's errand to continue such an activity without some objective rationale. Druzin locates that rationale in the experience of human suffering: "When suffering comes into being, morality comes into being." To claim that value systems are subjective and culturally constructed misses the point. It is the experience of suffering that is value; the experience itself is an objective fact, part of nature itself. It doesn't matter that the suffering is caused by an irrational fear of "unwashed grapes," it is the utter fear he/she experiences that provides the ground for moral stability. Thus to intentionally subject someone to such a fear is morally wrong. If this is the case for irrational fears what about rational ones—death, sickness, torture, etc.? Can these be so easily dismissed as arbitrary by postmodern theorists? Druzin's response is, of course, no.

In "The Architecture of Law: Building Law on a Solid Foundation: The Eternal and Natural Laws," Bryan McCall returns us to more familiar territory with his detailed analysis of Thomistic Natural Law theory. Critical of the recent interpretations of natural law, particularly those that abandon or minimize the concept of Eternal Law, like that of John Finnis for example, McCall argues that you cannot separate Eternal Law [ET] from Natural Law [NL] without significant loss of coherence and efficacy. NL is anchored to ET by reason and volition. If NL rested on volition alone we end up back in book 1 of Plato's *Republic* on the side of Thrasymachusean power struggle where "what pleases the prince has the force of law." But according to traditional NL, law is the product of reason and reason orders positive law—the will of the people or sovereign—yet it derives its justification by participating in EL. So how does EL fit in and what are the consequences for NL theories of Grotius, Finnis and the like? McCall defends the need for EL for without it human actions are merely arbitrary. EL defines the end of human action; man has no choice over ends, they are established by divine law and guided by EL. Thus EL is distinguished from positive law and certain theories of natural law, wherein man can make laws about what men can do, but cannot make man as man or a man a man. It is EL that determines what human nature is; the role of EL is to explain the end of things, the way they ought to be. In this sense EL is not a set of precepts, whereas NL is. But once you deny EL as a foundation for NL, you are left with only a groundless set of precepts based on biology and psychology that, at times, resembles utilitarianism. NL theory for Aquinas was part of a comprehensive metaphysical system that was structured in a descending hierarchy from Divine Law-EL-NL-Positive Law. So to the question "Is the Natural Law of any practical relevance to one who does not acknowledge God's existence?" yes, because man is rational and necessarily participates in EL even without realizing it.

Is disgust an extra-political source in support of human dignity? Are laws based on repugnance necessary to promote human well-being? Michael Cochran's article "Laws Without Disgust: A Fetid Freedom," compares the contrasting positions of Martha Nussbaum and Leon Kass and finds Nussbaum's lacking in consistency. Whereas Nussbaum claims that the reaction of disgust is really a departure from human dignity and as such undermines liberal political principles, Kass argues that "the wisdom of repugnance" is a rational response and needed for an expression of human dignity. Although Nussbaum will permit emotional defenses as reasonable—anger, and other primal emotions that support current nuisance laws—yet there are some emotions that are "repositories of unreasonableness" and disgust is among them. At bottom, Nussbaum's rejection of disgust as a healthy emotion is the fear that it can be used as an excuse for discrimination, resulting in hierarchies inimical to liberal principles. Kass, on the other hand, claims that repugnance is an expression of a deep wisdom beyond reason's ability to fully articulate it; part of what it means to be human, part of human nature. And it is dangerous to leave it "to the vagaries of culture" as Nussbaum is willing to do. According to Kass (and Cochran) full human dignity resides in our "Godlike" qualities—reason, judgment, freedom, and moral consciousness, not in a set of acquired human capabilities that if left undeveloped could lead to what Nussbaum wishes to avoid and would indignantly scorn, political discrimination. This is just one of the inconsistencies Cochran identifies in his critique of Nussbaum's capability theory. Other shortcomings include Nussbaum's understanding of irrationality and her over reliance on Mill's harm principle.

Traditional and contemporary just war theory has tended to favor "just cause" in discussions of the legality of war and relegating "right intention" and, especially, "sovereign authority" to a secondary statue. In a recent debate between George Weigel and Rowan Williams, Archbishop of Canterbury, the Archbishop chose to emphasize sovereign authority. It is the soundness of the Archbishop's argument that is the topic of Michael Boulette's article "Questioning Authority: Just War Theory, Sovereign Authority, and the United Nations." Boulette addresses the question: "Has the United Nations supplemented traditional states as the central unit of concern for just war theory?" After reviewing Aquinas' position on sovereign authority, Boulette compares it with the Archbishop's strong "internationalist" position, and against Weigel's critique claims the Archbishop's argument is defensible. He rests his claim on the analogy between individuals in a state and nations within the international community. Aquinas argued that sovereign authority can never be held by individuals and (by analogy) nations, since neither has the charge to protect the common good. Today the only entity with such responsibility is the United Nations; hence sovereign authority rests with it.

There is a mythic quality attached to Lon Fuller's law review article "The Case of the Speluncean Explorers." The article has been called "the greatest fictitious law case of all time." Jason Isbell's article "Revisiting Fuller's Cave: A Spelunker and His Lawyers," reminds us of how timeless the piece is as he adds a twist of his own to the decisions reached by the Supreme Court of the Commonwealth of Newgrath. In the original story, the trapped Spelunker cave explorers had the opportunity to consult with the rescue engineers and an on-site medical team. In Isbell's retelling they also consult with members from a legal firm. For those of you unfamiliar with the case, I won't divulge the story here, but only add that the case raises the perennial philosophical issue, "whether a person may save himself at the expense of another." Enjoy Isbell's version.

Aristotle's three types of rhetoric—judicial, deliberative, epideictic—provide no obvious connection to praxis, the praxis of virtuous action. Jeffrey Maciejewski's article, "Persuasive Reasoning and the Praxis of Virtue," fills this gap by offering a *natural rhetoric* in conformity with Aristotle's theory of action. Since the goal of virtue is to integrate the various aspects of human consciousness, especially when conflicted, Maciejewski argues that there is a need for a "discursive mechanism" to convince the actor to choose virtue. This discursive praxis differs from other rhetorics in that it has a particular ontology with certain dispositional properties and first and second order functions. The first order employment of natural rhetoric is to move the individual toward personal self-integration, while the second order functions to externalize this integrity to promote social harmony, thus the making of a citizen and the creation of *societas*.

FEATURED ARTICLES

PRESCRIPTIVE REALISM AND THE LIMITS OF INTERNATIONAL HUMAN RIGHTS LAW

Laura S. Johnson

I. INTRODUCTION

Rethinking public international law requires moving past the debate as to whether international law exists or matters to a discussion of how it matters, under what conditions, and why.[1] This article will attempt to discern ways in which international law can be of importance in today's world by focusing the lens of realism on the international human rights regime. In asking what realism can tell us about our available choices among ideal positions in international law with regard to human rights,[2] I argue that realism can be used to provide a prescriptive approach to international law[3] and is therefore

---

[1] The "arduous" task of rethinking international law was the goal of the seminar for which I originally wrote this article. See Alexander Somek, "Seminar: Rethinking Public International Law 1-4" (Nov. 8, 2008) (unpublished introduction to course packet, on file with author arguing that public international law is in a crisis, and challenging students in the course to confront both the "incoherence of the current system *and* its potential inaccuracy with regard to what it has been designed to regulate"). In their review of *The Limits of International Law* by Goldsmith and Posner, Oona A. Hathaway and Ariel N. Lavinbuk state that my generation of scholarship must "move past stale, dichotomous debates over whether international law exists or whether it matters, to instead address *how* it matters, *under what conditions*, and *why*." Oona A. Hathaway & Ariel N. Lavinbuk, "Book Review: Rationalism and Revisionism in International Law," 119 *Harvard Law Review* 1404, 1407 (2006). This article does not purport to solve the crisis of public international law, but instead aims to further international law scholarship by assuming that international law exists and matters, and shedding light on the predicaments that international law faces in the current world through examining and conflating two conflicting views of the role of law in the international system.

[2] Kenneth Anderson asks what realism will tell us about our available choices among ideal positions in international law and relations in a discussion of Goldsmith and Posner's book. See Kenneth Anderson, "Remarks by an Idealist on the Realism of the Limits of International Law," 34 *Ga. J. Int'l & Comp. L.* 253, 261 (2006) (asking what realism can offer in bringing about the ideal).

[3] The question of how realism can be used to "prescribe international law – to suggest

a means to counterbalance not only the limits of international law,[4] but also the limits of idealism.[5] In other words, realism can provide jurisprudential principles that, when incorporated into international human rights law, could affect a normative pull on states and in so doing, end up encouraging idealism.

I first lay the foundation for a discussion of the relationship between realism and idealism by briefly reviewing the separate characteristics and development of the two theories in international law scholarship in Part II. Compounding realism and idealism, this article distinguishes between a discussion of the validity of international law and my focus on a discussion of compliance in asking how realism can make international law matter. Tracing the permutations of realism, I consider if what this article proposes falls into the jurisprudential conceptualization developed by Richard Falk and other exponents of world order.

Turning to the human rights regime in Part III, I then consider the challenges cultural relativism poses to a system based on universalism. Theorizing that realism offers the most culturally relative approach to international law-making, this article argues that using a realist approach to suggest useful functions for international law could create a system where international law matters because states comply with international human rights law—because it is in their rational best interest to do so. Specifically I examine sanctions and humanitarian intervention as examples of "realism in action." From a realist perspective, I argue that human rights (at least Western conceptions of human rights) can and do matter

---

jurisprudential principles and bases for building international institutions" was posed to a panel at the ninety-sixth annual meeting of the American Society of International Law in 2002. See Richard H. Steinberg, "Overview: Realism in International Law," 96 *Am. Soc'y Int'l L. Proc.* 260 (2002) (outlining the goals of the panel including exploring a range of realist views and considering the relationship between realism and legalism).

[4] The title of the critical book on realism cited extensively in this article: Jack L. Goldsmith & Eric A. Posner, *The Limits of International Law* (Oxford University Press 2005).

[5] The title of a thought-provoking article on realism and idealism that first sparked my interest in this subject: Jack Goldsmith & Stephen D. Krasner, "The limits of idealism," *Daedalus,* Winter 2003.

and therefore the defense of international human rights norms can occur. Thus in the international human rights context, Part III puts forward a normative defense of realism. Concluding Part III with the unavoidable discussion of hegemony, I pose the question: who benefits from prescriptive realism?

Part IV closes with an inquiry into whether prescriptive realism is really possible. Again this article takes a softer realist position, moving away from the structural-realist extreme (which asserts that international law has no independent meaning or validity),[6] and draws a distinction between considering the validity of international law versus considering compliance with international law. With regards to compliance, this article asserts that realism provides legal concepts that, when incorporated into international human rights law, can affect a normative pull on states and in so doing, resolve the problems of idealism.

II. REALISM AND IDEALISM

In this article I work with the understanding of realism presented by Jack Goldsmith and Eric Posner: "international law emerges from states acting rationally to maximize their interests, given their perceptions of the interests of other states and the distribution of state power."[7] This concept of international law started its development with realists working in the field of international relations, such as E.H. Carr and Hans Morgenthau, in the first half of the twentieth century.[8] Realist international relations scholars developed their theories in reaction to idealism (the "legalist-moralist" tradition in American foreign policy) "which presumed that the combination of democracy and international organization could vanquish war

---

[6] Steinberg, supra note 3 at 261.
[7] Goldsmith & Posner, supra note 4, at 3.
[8] Hathaway & Lavinbuk, supra note 1, at 1408 (citing E.H. Carr, *The Twenty Years' Crisis, 1919-1939: An Introduction to the Study of International Relations* [Palgrave 2001(1939)] and Hans Morgenthau, *Politics Among Nations: The Struggle for Power and Peace* [5th ed. 1973 (1948)].

and power politics."[9] Realists argued that law had no place in the world, and that states would only act in their own interest.[10] With Kenneth Abbott's work in the late twentieth century, international law scholarship and international relations theory began to converge and realism became a theory of international law – law understood with reference to politics.[11] Realists challenged international lawyers to establish the relevance of international law and efforts to answer that challenge resulted in the growth of realism as a theory of international law.[12]

A comprehensive history of the development of realism is beyond the scope of this article; suffice to say, realism has undergone many incarnations and a range of realist theory exists.[13] This article's characterization of realism admittedly is very simplistic, returning to the realist/idealist debate that Morgenthau, Carr and others engaged in after World War I.[14] Alexander Somek defines realism as a theory that views the world of international relations as being composed of

---

[9] Anne-Marie Slaughter Burley, "International Law and International Relations Theory: A Dual Agenda," 87 *Am. J. Int'l L.* 205, 207 (1993).
[10] Ibid.
[11] Hathaway & Lavinbuk, supra note 1, at 1408-1410.
[12] Slaughter Burley, supra note 9, at 208-209.
[13] For a more complete discussion of the development of realism and an excellent summary of the history of international law scholarship after World War I, see Slaughter Burley, supra note 9, at 205-220 (delineating the major features and modifications of international law and international relations scholarship from Morgenthau, Carr and George Kennan's realism to Kenneth Waltz's structural realism to Robert Keohane's functionalism/rationalism). Hathaway and Lavinbuk note that realism is often grouped with institutionalism and liberalism as categories of rationalist international relations theory. See Hathaway & Lavinbuk, supra note 1, at 1412 (arguing that international lawyers have not yet developed a strong understanding of the important differences between the various rationalist approaches to international law scholarship).
[14] This may be because I am using the understanding of realism offered by Goldsmith and Posner. Hathaway and Lavinbuk argue that Goldsmith and Posner fall into the trend of characterizing the debate between rationalism (which I am calling realism) and constructivism (which I am describing as idealism) "at the more simplistic level of interests versus norms" and that looking at the debate at the basic level of interests versus norms "threatens to send international law scholarship backward nearly half a century." Hathaway & Lavinbuk, supra note 1, at 1412.

states that seek their own advantages using scarce resources.[15] "The most essential ingredient of realism is the belief that international relations are a zero sum game, with each country seeking its gain at the expense of others."[16] For the purposes of this discussion, realism is a theory that views international law as subservient to state interests. As Stephen Krasner describes: "For realists, the defining characteristic of the international system is anarchy, and the most important empirical reality is that national power, including but not limited to the ability to wage war, matters more than anything else."[17]

This is in stark contrast to idealism, which theorizes that international law exercises constraint on state behavior. For the purposes of this article, idealism can be understood as a theory that international law "exerts a pull toward compliance," or wields normative influence on state behavior.[18] Idealism was the driving force behind the formation of the League of Nations in the interwar years and the same idealism arguably is informing international law today, particularly in the area of human rights,[19] as I will discuss in Part III. Jack Goldsmith and Stephen Krasner write that today's idealism – "international idealism" – is limited and suffers from four fundamental flaws.

> First, it assumes the utopian premise that a global consensus can be reached, not just on normative principles, but also on when and how they should be

---

[15] Alexander Somek, "Kelsen Lives" 11 n.30 (IILJ Working Paper 2006/4, 2006) (suggesting Jeffrey W. Legro & Andrew Moraycsik, "Is Anybody Still a Realist?," 24 *Int'l Sec.* 5 [1999] for further discussion of realism).
[16] Ibid.
[17] Stephen D. Krasner, "Realist Views of International Law," 96 *Am. Soc'y Int'l L. Proc.* 260, 265 (2002).
[18] Thomas M. Franck, *The Power of Legitimacy among Nations* 24-25 (Oxford University Press 1990), quoted in Goldsmith & Posner, supra note 4, at 15.
[19] See Goldsmith & Krasner, supra note 5, at 2 (mentioning the creation of the International Criminal Court and recurring demands for humanitarian intervention as reflections of a renewed commitment to international idealism).

applied. Second, it minimizes considerations of power, and assumes that norms of right behavior can substitute for national capabilities and material interests. Third, it neglects political prudence...Fourth; it consistently slights the value of democratic accountability.[20]

The authors argue that idealism can only be effectively achieved if lawmakers take into account the distribution of power, national interests and the consequences of their policies in the international arena.[21]

The Chicken or the Egg?

This is precisely what this article aims to initiate: a way of thinking about international law that asks international lawmakers to take state interests into account; for international lawmakers to acknowledge that depending on international law to control the behavior of states is flawed. But going a step further than this conservative outlook on international lawmaking,[22] this article posits that realism itself can be used to shape political reality and thereby inform international legal concepts. If realism is used to provide a prescriptive approach to international lawmaking (henceforth "prescriptive realism"), it is a means to fill the gaps of an idealistic approach.[23] At the heart of prescriptive realism is an inquiry into how to make law matter. This is a question of compliance.

---

[20] Ibid.
[21] Ibid.
[22] See Andreas Paulus, "Realism and International Law: Two Optics in Need of Each Other," 96 *Am. Soc'y Int'l L. Proc.* 260, 270 (2002) (claiming that for one of the two main strands of international legal theory – for "conservatives" or "traditionalists" – the primary function of international law is providing rules and principles to sustain a minimum of order in international relations and for these conservatives, "law can enhance order in international relations if it pays due regard to the reality of power relationships").
[23] As Goldsmith and Krasner aptly state: "Ideals can play an important and constructive role in international relations, but only if those promoting them take account of the power and interests of states in the design of international institutions." Goldsmith & Krasner, supra note 5, at 15.

Traditionally a question of compliance has no place in a discussion of realist theory, as realism understands international law to be solely a reflection of state self-interest. After all, if there is no independent international law, there can be no compliance with international law. Goldsmith and Posner write that what non-realist scholars view as compliance with international law driven by a sense of legal obligation is "a behavioral regularity that results from states pursuing their interests."[24] Goldsmith and Posner go as far as providing four models of strategic behavior that they argue comprise what other legal scholars have termed "compliance" with international law.[25]

However, the "straw-man" version of realism, which asserts that realists believe that international law does not matter, is not common to today's mainstream realists.[26] Realism is not necessarily a theory that denies any role for international law. In fact, "the contemporary mainstream realist view is that international law does perform some important functions."[27] So if the ideal function for international law is that it exercises a normative pull on state behavior, how can compliance with international law be ensured? To what extent can realism suggest ways to guarantee compliance with international law? I disagree with Goldsmith and Posner's suggestion that compliance can always be explained as one of four models of strategic behavior (coincidence, coordination, cooperation and coercion) but agree that when states act in compliance with international law, they are acting strategically. Expanding on what Goldsmith and Posner are suggesting, it seems that a state will act strategically to comply with international law when it is in the state's rational best interest to do so. Thus using realism to understand that states act according to

---

[24] Goldsmith & Posner, supra note 4, at 39.
[25] Ibid. at 11-13. See also Hathaway & Lavinbuk, supra note 1, at 1416-1417 (discussing the four models of strategic behavior posited by Goldsmith and Posner: coincidence, coordination, cooperation and coercion).
[26] Steinberg, supra note 3, at 261.
[27] Ibid.

their rational best interests, making conformity to international law in a state's best interest will ensure compliance.

Somek writes that it is currently "fashionable" to attempt to construct public international law from the vantage point of reasons for compliance.[28]

> Obviously, such theories [of compliance] are theories of validity in disguise, for what they are really concerned with are the good reasons to abide by international obligations. Their thrust is clearly at odds with legal positivism's insistence on norm-creating facts. Compliance theories, consequently, are confronted with a recurring dilemma. They are either empirically indeterminate or overcharged with idealisations, that is, attributions to agents of reasons that are taken to be "the right reasons."[29]

So if the reason for compliance is that it is in a state's best interest to comply with international law, perhaps that is merely an empty idealization hiding a proposition that international law is valid. But, if I am approaching this conundrum as a legalist looking at the chances of legal prescriptions in the real world, perhaps seeking an answer as to how to ensure compliance with international law from a realist perspective is legitimate. If realism is used to *prescribe*, and not merely to describe international laws and institutions, then "we need a realism mitigated by regard to the influence of international legal concepts on political actors, on the constitution of power, and on the definition of interests."[30] If we desire law to guide state behavior in the international system, then I posit we can use the jurisprudential principles of realism to do the same.

---

[28] Somek, supra note 15, at 67.
[29] Ibid.
[30] Paulus, supra note 22, at 272.

Prescriptive Realism and the World Order Model

In the 1970s, Richard Falk, Saul Mendlovitz and Burns Weston developed a theory to establish the relevance of international law that mixed legal realism and global idealism.[31] Within the World Order Model framework that they developed:

> ...law could be conceived either as rules or as process, either as an "international code of conduct" formulated in response to "the living needs of international society," or as a flow of authoritative and effective decisions made by a hypothetical "supranational" decision maker. The result was the same, a transcendent order that served to "advance the values and interests of the overall world community rather than to promote the more special and diverse interests and values of national actors who are components of that system."[32]

Falk de-emphasized the constraining capacity of international law and instead recognized that international legal norms can perform a host of other functions in international relations, functions that may be in the rational self-interest of states.[33] If legal norms can perform a host of other functions in international relations, and if those functions are in the rational self interest of states, under the World Order Model framework, we can ask to what extent realism may suggest useful functions for legal norms.

---

[31] Slaughter Burley, supra note 9, at 211-212.
[32] Richard A. Falk, *The Status of Law in International Society* (1970), quoted in Slaughter Burley, supra note 9, at 212.
[33] See Slaughter Burley, supra note 9, at 212-213 (noting that included among the host of functions that international legal norms can perform in international relations, Falk recognized: (1) specifying the basic rules of international relations, defining boundaries of acceptable action even when violated; (2) providing a process of communication in crisis; (3) providing rules for bureaucracies to follow to create stable expectations for routine transactions; (4) enabling regimes of cooperation in technical areas; and (5) providing criteria for states to act reasonably if so inclined).

In exploring how realism can balance the limits of idealism, this article is seeking to advance an idealistic viewpoint, which can be understood as advancing the values and interests of the overall world community. I am seeking to intertwine realism and idealism, and in this I am exercising jurisprudential thinking similar to the World Order Model theory. But rather than conceding the constraining power of international law, as Falk, Mendlovitz and Weston did, I am seeking such constraint using prescriptive realism. By inquiring how realism can be used to suggest principles that ensure compliance with international law, I am arguing that international law can exercise constraint on state behavior, when it is in the rational best interest of states to comply with international law.

III. USING REALISM TO ACHIEVE IDEALISM: THE HUMAN RIGHTS CONTEXT

Using the human rights regime, we can examine how prescriptive realism can affect a normative pull on states, and in so doing pave the way for idealism. I am equating idealism with a view similar to the desired result of Falk's World Order Model, a view where the values of the world community are advanced over the values of the primary actors in the international system. In other words, the values and interests of the world community take precedence over individual state interests. Understanding from realism that states will act in their rational best interest, it must therefore be in the state's rational best interest to advance the values of the world community. This viewpoint leaves little room for cultural relativism.

Cultural relativism is the assertion that human values are not universal, but vary according to different cultural perspectives.[34] In the human rights context, where the international human rights regime is built on a definition of human rights as universal, cultural

---

[34] Diana Ayton-Shenker, "The Challenge of Human Rights and Cultural Diversity," *United Nations Background Note DPI/1627/HR* (March 1995), available at http://www.un.org/rights/dpi1627e.htm.

relativism undermines the effectiveness of the regime.[35] "If cultural tradition alone governs State compliance with international standards, then widespread disregard, abuse and violation of human rights would be given legitimacy."[36] An in-depth discussion of the debate over whether human rights *should* be universal is beyond the scope of this article, but cultural relativism is important to consider when turning to realism to inform the legal principles of the international human rights system.[37]

The current international human rights regime is a regime where human rights are taken to be universal. As I am considering how to make this regime effective (to attain idealism in constructing a system where human rights norms affect state behavior) I must consider the limits of such a system. By not incorporating cultural relativism into an idealist approach to making international human rights law, gaps are created where there is no normative force constraining state behavior. Goldsmith and Posner write, "There is no evidence that ratification of human rights treaties affects human rights practices."[38] Without recognizing that states will act according

---

[35] "The modern multilateral human rights regime consists primarily of treaties regulating genocide (1951), racial discrimination (1969), civil and political rights (1976), economic, social, and cultural rights (1976), discrimination against women (1981), torture (198), and the rights of children (1990)." Goldsmith & Posner, supra note 4, at 107-108.

[36] Ayton-Shenker, supra note 34.

[37] The debate over whether or not human rights are or should be considered universal swelled in the 1990s with the Asian Values Debates, where scholars and leaders in Asia asked if there is a distinctly Asian approach to human rights. See, e.g., Bilahari Kim Hee & P.S. Kausikan, "An East Asian Approach to Human Rights," 2 *Buff. J. Int'l L.* 263 (1996); Randall Peerenboom, "Beyond Universalism and Relativism: The Evolving Debates About 'Values in Asia,'" 14 *Ind. Int'l & Comp. L. Rev.* 1 (2003); Amartya Sen, "Human Rights and Asian Values: What Lee Kuan Yew and Le Peng Don't Understand About Asia," 217 *The New Republic* n.2-3 (1997); Surain Subramaniam, "The Asian Values Debate: Implications for the Spread of Liberal Democracy," 27 *Asian Affairs* 19 (2000).

[38] Goldsmith & Posner, supra note 4, at 121 (citing two studies that show no statistically significant relationship between accession to modern human rights treaties and the degree of respect for human rights covered by those treaties: Linda Camp Keith, "The United Nations International Covenant on Civil and Political Rights: Does It Make a Difference in Human Rights Behavior?," 36 *Journal of Peace Research* 95 (1999); Oona Hathaway, "Do Human Rights Treaties Make a Difference?," 111 *Yale Law Journal* 1935 [2002]).

to different interests, which are in turn generated by a great variation in cultural, ethnic and religious traditions, the international human rights regime is destined for breakdowns. Idealism, theorizing that international law wields normative influence on state behavior, does not work in the human rights context.

I propose that realism is the most culturally relative approach to international law. Describing a system where there are no norms aside from those reflecting states acting to further their own interests denies the possibility for universal norms. But if the goal is advancing the values of the world community over the values of individual states (an idealistic goal), what jurisprudential principles can realism provide to build a system that meets that goal? Realism recognizes that norms will not be universal—that there are no universal understandings of human rights. Yet if it were in a state's rational best interest to comply with the current agreed-upon international human rights standards (outlined in the Universal Declaration of Human Rights, for example), then realism tells us that human rights standards *could* have a normative effect on states. And if states act to comply with international human rights standards as outlined by the current regime, these standards can become universal as states are compelled to abide by them.

Coercive Human Rights Enforcement

Realism suggests that ensuring compliance with international human rights law requires what Goldsmith and Posner call "coercive human rights enforcement."[39] Coercion can ensure that it is in a state's rational best interest to abide by the current international human rights standards. To explore how this occurs, this article examines two examples of coercion in the human rights context: sanctions and humanitarian intervention. Sanctions, as I will discuss momentarily, can coerce states into complying with international human rights law, but sanctions can also play a larger role in *validating* international human rights law.

---

[39] Goldsmith & Posner, supra note 4, at 115-117.

In a discussion of Hans Kelsen's work, Alexander Somek writes that Kelsen characterized a legal norm as having two parts: a description of an unlawful act and the sanction that ought to be imposed as a consequence of that act.[40] Defining a sanction as a coercive act authorized by the legal system,[41] Somek argues that (at least for Kelsen) "the *onus explandandi* for what accounts for the normativity of a norm rests on the sanction and what it means to have authority to impose it."[42] Kelsen defined a sanction as the use of physical force, which differs from the conception of sanctions in today's international system.[43] Kelsen did not think of financial penalties, for example, as sanctions. But his framework is useful nonetheless in understanding that sanctions—understood as either physical force or financial intimidation for the purposes of this article—can validate international law by making international norms normative. Further, at the level of the discussion of compliance, sanctions can ensure that states follow norms.

Realism responds to idealism by positing that international law does not carry moral or legal obligation.[44] Where an idealist sees a concept of obligation to international law that has two components—both normative ("states *should* abide by international law") and descriptive (states do abide by international law because international law "has the power to shape state behavior")—realism rejects both components.[45] However, putting realism into action, both components can come into being. Sanctions are realism in

---

[40] Somek, supra note 15, at 42-43. Somek elaborates, writing: "As long as the international system speaks of unlawful acts and sanctions, it is a legal system, no matter how inefficiently the system may work in singular cases. In other words, if and when war and reprisals are conceived of, on the level of *discourse*, as sanctions for breaches of international norms, the system of public international law exists." Ibid. at 45.
[41] Somek points out that it is important to acknowledge that Kelsen did not have a moral conception of sanctions, in that Kelsen did not think of a sanction as being a "necessary evil." Somek, supra note 14, at 44.
[42] Ibid. at 43.
[43] Ibid. at 44.
[44] Hathaway & Lavinbuk, supra note 1, at 1426.
[45] Ibid.

action in that they are a form of coercion, and coercion is a behavior a state engages in to further its rational best interests. Sanctions create norms under Kelsen's structure (and under Goldsmith and Posner, as Somek observes that Goldsmith and Posner conceive of public international law only where it is backed up by force)[46] and taken further, provide both a normative and descriptive force to international law. Threatening another state with physical force or financial difficulty if that state violates a norm of international human rights will cause a state to evaluate what is in its rational best interest, complying with the norm or violating it and facing the consequences.

Humanitarian intervention is another example of coercive human rights enforcement. As a stronger version of the physical force threatened by sanctions, humanitarian intervention can confirm that states *should* abide by international human rights norms, and that states *will* abide by international human rights norms. Humanitarian intervention is perhaps the best example of prescriptive realism in the human rights context, as humanitarian intervention recognizes that states will do what they want when it comes to human rights, regardless of what treaties they have signed, and therefore humanitarian intervention acts to make it in the violating state's best interest to comply with international human rights law. Intervening in a violating state to ensure that it complies with international human rights law exercises a strong normative pull on the violating state. The threat of humanitarian intervention also exercises a normative pull on states that act in violation with international human rights law.

A Normative Defense of Realism

Goldsmith and Krasner write that recurring calls for humanitarian intervention in today's world reflect a "renewed commitment to

---

[46] Somek, supra note 15, at 67.

international idealism."[47] Is the normative pull that sanctions and humanitarian intervention create defensible? Prescriptive realism is normative in the sense that realist behaviors (coercive human rights enforcement) create a normative pull to comply with international human rights law. But is this defensible from an idealistic standpoint that takes morality into account? Obviously what prescriptive realism encourages in the human rights context is a hegemonic state coercing other states to comply with the hegemon's view of human rights norms. Prescriptive realism needs a hegemon. Prescriptive realism disregards cultural relativism and allows the strong state's definitions of human rights to become the universal definition. But arguably, at least in the context of human rights, this is not so morally reprehensible. Hegemony is not necessarily bad, not even in idealism, depending on the objective. If, as in the human rights context, the goal is to advance the values and interests of the world community rather than promoting individual state interests, then as long as the hegemon's interests correspond to the world community's, the system will work. Coercive human rights enforcement ensures that at least the "most important" human rights, from the coercer or hegemon's perspective, will be enforced.

Who benefits from prescriptive realism? Smaller, less powerful states that might have a different conception of human rights will find that their views are overruled. Recognizing cultural relativism—using realism as the most culturally relative descriptive approach to international law—may end up eliminating cultural relativism when realism becomes prescriptive. Coercive human rights enforcement imposes one view of human rights law. Smaller states lose out in this regard, but perhaps their citizens benefit in the long run. If the Universal Declaration of Human Rights, or other treaties making up the current international human rights regime, is considered to outline rights that are beneficial to all individuals, then citizens in all states benefit from coercive human rights enforcement or prescriptive realism.

[47] Goldsmith & Krasner, supra note 5, at 2.

IV. CONCLUSION

Is prescriptive realism really possible in the context of human rights? If I am proposing using realism to suggest jurisprudential principles to make up for the limits of idealism, then the desired end is compliance with international human rights law. However, coercive human rights enforcement could lead to further human rights violations if the individuals in the state being coerced are put at risk. Additionally there is no guarantee that the stronger states will enforce international human rights law, and this is perhaps the greatest challenge that prescriptive realism faces.

> There is little point to advocating sanctions if they will not achieve the desired end, especially if they will lead to more human rights violations and greater suffering on the part of those whom the sanctions are supposed to benefit. More controversially, states will also consider geopolitical factors and their own national interests when deciding what course of action to take. Humanitarian intervention is rare and occurs only when there is a consistent pattern of massive human rights violations.[48]

And even when there exists a consistent pattern of massive human rights violations, states "that possess the military muscle to make a difference" through humanitarian intervention or by threatening sanctions are often reluctant to engage in coercive human rights enforcement.[49]

The question is not so much whether or not states will be coerced by sanctions or humanitarian intervention—arguably they will be, as it will be more in a state's rational best interest to comply

---

[48] Peerenboom, supra note 37, at 21.
[49] Goldsmith & Krasner, supra note 5, at 12.

with human rights norms than to face economic hardship or to put sovereignty at risk. The question is how to make prescriptive realism in a state's best interest, or how to ensure that a hegemon will engage in coercive human rights enforcement. Coercive human rights enforcement happens, according to Goldsmith and Posner, when such behavior corresponds with other economic or political interests of the enforcing state.[50] How to ensure this correspondence is the challenge. A realist perspective is sensitive to the role of domestic politics in informing state behavior. Even Goldsmith and Posner argue that domestic political pressure can play a role in changing the behavior of states, but domestic politics are also informed by an array of varying factors and therefore are not reliable in consistently supporting coercive human rights enforcement.[51] Falk and other proponents of the World Order Model theory also argue that "dictates of the public conscience" inform international law and state behavior.[52] However, realism suggests that this is not enough to ensure states will engage in coercive human rights enforcement.

---

[50] Goldsmith & Posner, supra note 4, at 117. The authors consider the pattern of U.S. human rights enforcement, arguing that: "coercion is applied episodically and inconsistently," depending on economic and political interests. "The United States committed significant military and economic resources to redress human rights violations in Yugoslavia (where it had a strategic interest in preventing central European conflict and resolving NATO's crisis of credibility and purpose); Haiti (where turmoil was threatening a domestic crisis in Florida); and Iraq (where it had obvious strategic interests). But the United States has done relatively little in the face of human rights abuses in Africa, where it lacks a strong strategic interest, or in Saudi Arabia, China, and Russia, where its strategic interests conflict with enforcement of a human rights agenda, and where in any event the costs of enforcement are significantly higher." Ibid.

[51] Ibid. at 107-126. Stephen Krasner also comments on the role of domestic politics in influencing foreign policy choices. See Krasner, supra note 17, at 266 (arguing that human rights do matter to NGOs, legislators and voters in the U.S. and "other advanced industrialized democratic countries" and their initiatives can change the views of legislators and officials in the executive branch, as well as affecting electoral results).

[52] Burns H. Weston, Richard A. Falk and Saul H. Mendlovitz, "Introduction to the Draft Memorial in Support of Application of the World Health Organization for an Advisory Opinion by the International Court of Justice on the Legality of the Use of Nuclear Weapons Under International Law, Including the W.H.O. Constitution," 4. *Transnat'l L. & Contemp. Probs.* 709, 712 (1994).

This article has introduced the concept of prescriptive realism and suggested that international human rights law can have a normative effect if powerful states act to make compliance with international human rights law in the best interest of other states. Goldsmith and Krasner describe this as "a system of selective justice enforced by the powerful" and worry that a consequence of such a system "is effective immunity for the powerful."[53] There are certainly risks to relying on a hegemon to both validate international human rights law (as the hegemon's definitions of human rights will inform the norms) and to enforce compliance with international human rights law. Kenneth Anderson writes:

> If Goldsmith and Posner are right, the consequence of the rationalist project for idealism is, in effect, to leave only state interest standing. The best one can hope for – as a matter of values, morality, and ideology – is that state interest incorporate into itself notions of democratic and human rights morality, because international law cannot and will not as a matter of independent force.[54]

Prescriptive realism, alas, still comes back to a reliance on state interest. This article has attempted to offer a normative defense of realism in tracing how realism can offer principles to inform international law, thereby creating norms and validating international law. Further, in the international human rights context, I have attempted to examine how prescriptive realism could guide lawmaking to ensure compliance with international human rights law. This has been an exercise in rethinking international law. Hathaway and Lavinbuk argue: "For a theory to be useful, it must make particularized predictions about specific events. Such predictions necessarily create the possibility of being proven wrong (thereby rendering the claims 'falsifiable')."[55] I have attempted to

---

[53] Goldsmith & Krasner, supra note 5, at 12.
[54] Anderson, supra note 2, at 270.
[55] Hathaway & Lavinbuk, supra note 1, at 1424.

use prescriptive realism to make predictions, and I am certain that some of the claims made in this article are falsifiable. But if we don't take up the arduous challenge of rethinking international law, we will never discover how to make the current system coherent. In looking closer at how international law matters, under what conditions, and why, the limits of specific theories of international law can be addressed. Considering idealism through the lens of realism, for example, I found myself making a normative defense of realism.[56] This defense warrants further exploration in spite of its flaws, as realism could give rise to idealism—to the normative capacity of law—and could lead to prescriptions that *will* work.

---

[56] Credit must be given to Professor Alexander Somek for coining this phrase during a class discussion of a draft of this article.

FINDING FOOTING IN A POSTMODERN CONCEPTION OF LAW

Bryan Druzin

INTRODUCTION

To what extent are the basic principles that underlie our legal system universal? To what extent do they follow the dictates of human reason and appeal to an intuitive sense of what is fair, and are not simply the products of specific historical, economic, and cultural circumstances? If one believes they are in fact universal in character, one would expect to find general symmetry between the concepts that gird our legal systems. Criminal codes between legal cultures should mirror one another, as should other areas of law ranging from family law to constitutional law. The law of tort, for instance, where the chief aim is restitutio in integrum,[1] namely a remedy that is fair to all parties involved, a body of law founded upon an intrinsic sense of fairness applied to the mundane particularities of human interaction—should likewise exhibit homogeny between legal cultures.

Yet, we do not find this degree of uniformity.[2] Legal conceptions of what is fair are not always identical between legal systems, influenced significantly by religious, cultural, and arguably, economic factors. Not only do understandings of fair play sometimes differ between legal systems, even within a single unified system of law, such as the English common law, the concepts that underlie the law have changed over time. Wholly new principles, such as criminal insanity and negligence have been introduced. The law has transformed significantly over time, adapting to the trappings of its historical age. Conceptions of nuisance, trespass to land, and trespass to chattels have evolved in a fashion that seems inseparable from

---

[1] "Restoration to the original position." *Oxford Dictionary of Law* 464 (6th ed. 2006).
[2] As one justice opined, there is indeed "a jungle of separate, broadly based jurisdictions all over the world." Lord Goff in Airbus Industri GIE v Patel 1 AC 199 (1999).

principles of private property and economic necessity—concepts integrally linked to specific economic systems such as capitalism.[3] Many areas of tort such as economic torts are explicitly connected to certain economic positions that have emerged over time. This includes areas such as consumer protection, product liability, and restraint of trade. Even damages for intangible losses such as pain and suffering in the form of pure mental anguish reflects a certain cultural perspective. Family law, commercial law, and criminal law have all similarly undergone varying degrees of transformation. Thus, we do not find a static view of fairness as defined by law; rather, we have a shifting body of conceptions, in a state of subtle flux, continually experiencing change in reaction to general shifts in cultural attitudes.

What then are we left with when we consider the possibility that these legal principles are not extracted from immutable natural truths, but rather are largely subjective concoctions of the cultures that formulate them, specific to the values of that particular age? It is, in a sense, frightening. It strikes at the very heart of our sense of justice. It seems that upon the shifting sands of postmodern moral relativism, there is no firm footing on which to stand. So what are we left with? Does not the denial of objective truth ultimately undercut the premise that there is objective value –the very notion of justice? Are we left with only the prospect of uncertainty and moral anarchy? Is this Nihilism?[4] The argument of postmodernism is a powerful one.

[3] See Simon Deakin, Angus Johnston & Basil Markesinis, *Markesinis and Deakin's Tort Law* 113 (6th ed. 2008), writing on negligence in particular ("Its expansion, in particular in the course of the twentieth century, reflects the pressures that the rise of an industrial and urban society have brought to bear upon the traditional categories of legal redress for interference and protected interests. The growth and increasing sophistication of insurance have also contributed to this expansion. A doctrinal examination of negligence must not lose sight of this wider social and economic context within which the tort has developed, which is reflected in fluidity of the central legal concepts and the courts' ever-increasing recourse to 'policy' as an explanation of their decisions.") (footnotes omitted).

[4] The fact that most people find the possibility that our beliefs are not grounded upon any objectively valid criteria frightening, perhaps points to the very motivation for believing in the conventions we do. That is, there is a deep human need to affix certain moral truths to our systems of value as it provides a degree of emotional certainty that we are indeed

Its implications are profound, and thus, we must address it. This short paper will do just that, suggesting that, despite the absolute, all-consuming nihilism towards which postmodernism seems to lead in its most extreme form, the acceptance of postmodern relativism in fact in no way undermines the possibility of finding firm footing on which to stand, of finding moral certainty, and thus solid ground for our legal principles. To do this, the discussion that follows detours significantly from the conventional route of a law paper; I ask for the reader's patience in travelling this circuitous path through the terrain of philosophy. Notwithstanding this, however, the discussion's final destination indeed directly addresses the very foundations upon which our conceptions of law are typically constructed, the heart of law—our sense of what is just.

I. THE JETTISONING OF OBJECTIVE MORAL TRUTH

A. Subjectivity in The Law

To an extent, we already tacitly acknowledge a degree of moral relativism in the law. We establish legal standards to govern our society presumably founded upon moral imperatives, yet readily accept the validity of quite different legal standards within other cultures. I say to an extent because if the difference is too extreme, too egregious, we do not accept it. However, it is remarkable how high the threshold actually is for this measure of acceptance. It is

---

correct in our beliefs, and our beliefs are not simply subjective concoctions, but rather are out there, existing as objective moral truths. In a sense, our reaction to the argument of postmodernism goes far in explaining why we believe there is objective truth in the first place, i.e. we simply need to. To pose the question differently, do we need to believe in the value systems we do because they are true, or do we believe them to be true because we need to? Perhaps, there is a greater emotional compulsion lurking behind our beliefs than we are willing to acknowledge. A good example of this is religious belief. The vast majority of individuals who boast deeply held religious beliefs, subscribe to the very religion in which they were raised to believe. It is remarkable how this fact does not cause intelligent people to question at least the motivation behind their religious convictions.

astonishing how easily we can simply chalk the disparity up to a simple difference in cultural mores.

The age for sexual consent is a good example. In many jurisdictions the age is eighteen. However the age of consent under Danish law is fifteen.[5] While an adult engaging in sexual relations with a 15 year-old in the United States would be convicted of child molestation and seen generally by society as a paedophile, the exact same scenario would be tolerated by Danish society. And although this is the case, the rest of the world does not view the Danish legal system as sanctioning child molestation. But why not? How can this conform to the idea that our laws related to an issue of such importance as child molestation are grounded upon universal moral truths? Should not most Americans logically view Danish society as endorsing child molestation? Similarly, as British, French, German, Italian, Australian and Canadian law prohibits the use of execution in their respective legal systems, should these judiciaries, in the spirit of the law, not then view most U.S. nationals as being accessories to murder?[6] The Canadian Criminal Code, for instance, provides "that every one is a party to an offense who: does or omits to do anything for the purpose of aiding any person to commit it; or abets any person in committing."[7] Is not the whole of American society then culpable in that they fail to change these laws? The answer of course is no, and the mere mention of the idea seems absurd, as we feel each society is free to establish laws that are in line with their own moral standards. But again, how can this be reconciled with our notion that there is a fixed moral underpinning to the laws we enact? Clearly, we do tacitly acknowledge a degree of moral

---

[5] The Danish Penal Code 1995, s. 222 (1) states: "Any person who has sexual intercourse with any child under the age of 15 shall be liable to imprisonment for any term not exceeding 6 years"; See also Interpol, *Legislation Of Interpol Member States On Sexual Offences Against Children* (2009), http://www.interpol.int/public/Children/SexualAbuse/NationalLaws/csaDenmark.asp ("Age of consent for sexual activity: When a person is fifteen (15) years old s/he can consent to sexual intercourse").

[6] For an informative listing of abolitionist states, see Hugo Adam Bedau, *The Death Penalty in America: Current Controversies* 78-83 (1997).

[7] Canadian Criminal Code 1985, s. 21(1) *(a)*.

subjectivity beyond mere technical issues of jurisdiction. This is the deeper issue at play within the area of Conflicts of Law. On a purely practical level, our legal system often collides with other systems of law predicated on slightly differing notions of right and wrong. National laws at variance bring the issue of relativism to the fore in stark clarity.

B. Legal Positivism

Perhaps, it was as a result of a growing realization of the palpable disparity between our systems of law in the area of Conflicts of Law that legal positivism appeared within the margins of late nineteenth and early twentieth century jurisprudence, eventually replacing earlier natural law notions that held law as inextricably linked with a basic sense of justice and yes, morality. This separation of law and ethics is profoundly significant. With it, one could simply divorce law from morality, and leave legal regulation as a shallow vessel of legal positivism, bereft of ethical significance. One could bark out the separation thesis as espoused by many legal positivists, the idea that legal validity has no inherent connection with morality or a conception of justice, and be done with it.[8] However, anything short

---

[8] The Separation Thesis essentially posits the idea that there is "a conceptual separation between law and morality, that is, between what the law is, and what the law ought to be . . . Once again, the Separation Thesis, properly understood, pertains only to the conditions of legal validity. It asserts that the conditions of legal validity do not depend on the moral content of the norms in question. What the law is cannot depend on what it ought to be in the relevant circumstances. Many contemporary legal Positivists would not subscribe to this formulation of the Separation Thesis. A contemporary school of thought, called Inclusive Legal Positivism, endorses the Social Thesis, namely, that the basic conditions of legal validity derive from social facts, such as social rules or conventions which happen to prevail in a given community. But, Inclusive Legal Positivists maintain, legal validity is sometimes a matter of the moral content of the norms, depending on the particular conventions that happen to prevail in any given community. Those social conventions on the basis of which we identify the law may, but need not, contain reference to moral content as a condition of legality." See Andrei Marmor, *Stanford Encyclopedia Of Philosophy*, "The Nature Of Law" (2001), http://plato.stanford.edu/entries/lawphil-nature/. See also, Mark C. Murphy, *Natural Law in Jurisprudence and Politics* 20-26 (2006).

of absolute postmodern relativism must ultimately be grounded upon some form of overarching justification for a given system of law, be it some form of natural law, class struggle, or simple utilitarianism—there must be an underlying sense that it is correct and justified. Without this sense, why then would we even need to have it? Does not the fact that we still find it necessary to institute laws imply that there is an underlying justification and that this rationale is predicated on some semblance of objective truth offering at the minimum, pragmatic guidance if not moral direction?

Legal positivism, however, we should remember, is not wholly removed from an underlying idea of social control, or that maintaining a certain societal order, or simply the notion that staving off anarchy is a 'good thing.'[9] In a sense it replaces one rationale with another. But all rationales must be grounded upon an overarching notion of what is 'good' (for lack of a better word). Without this, the whole construction crumbles.[10] Carried to its extreme, the postmodern position, however, scratches mercilessly at this wound, thus threatening to undermine all possible constructions regardless of its rationale, by obliterating the idea of objective truth itself. Legal positivism, to be sure, is singularly important in that it is a stepping-stone towards the metastasising of postmodern thought within law. By snapping the tether that, for hundreds of years (arguably throughout all of human history), bound law to underlying bedrock of moral justice, it opens the door towards absolute relativism, and leaves us with a fundamental problem yet to be resolved: if law is

---

[9] See Marmor, op. cit. ("Legal Positivism can accept the claim that law is, by its very nature or its essential functions in society, something good that deserves our moral appreciation. Nor is Legal Positivism forced to deny the plausible claim that wherever law exists, it would have to have a great many prescriptions which coincide with morality. There is probably a considerable overlap, and perhaps necessarily so, between the actual content of law and morality").

[10] Indeed, the Law and Economics approach to legal study which flourished in the latter part of the twentieth century might be conceptualised as yet another attempt to ground law in some underlying rationale, this being the idea of economic efficiency, or the rationale of utility as borrowed from the discipline of economics. The rationale is certainly distinct from, for instance, natural law thinking, but they are in a sense similar in that the approach is pinned to an underlying explanatory justification of sorts.

not morality, what is it? Is the concept of justice, the shared human recognition of fairness—a grandiose historical myth? What is it, a social construction, a hastily written provision in our social contract, an internalised norm[11] born form an adaptive quality? To use a legal turn of phrase, the floodgates open.

C. Critical Legal Studies

The idea that there exists a relativist quality to law lingering just beneath our formalistic assumptions is expressed in the Critical Legal Studies (CLS) movement which emerged in the 1970s and 1980s as an independent subset of legal theory.[12] Influenced significantly by the ideas of the Frankfurt school (with the exception of Habermas) and French poststructuralism, CLS strove to expose as arbitrary the received social and political beliefs that underlie and shape our systems of law.[13]

Postmodern theorists, also known as "anti-foundationalists" and "critical legal students," claim "the law cannot have any foundation because there is no foundation for objective knowledge of any kind. They say we cannot objectively understand reality because all knowledge is contingent on social convention (especially language)."[14]

---

[11] In the social norm literature see, e.g., Robert C. Ellickson, *The Evolution of Social Norms: A Perspective from the Legal Academy* (Yale Law School, Program for Studies in Law, Economics and Public Policy, Working Paper No. 230, 1999); Robert C. Ellickson, "The Aim of Order Without Law," 97 *Journal of Institutional and Theoretical Economics* 150 (1994) Robert Cooter, "Expressive Law and Economics," 27 *Journal of Legal Studies* 585 (1998); Richard H. McAdams, "The Origin, Development, and Regulation of Norms," 96 *Michigan Law Review* 338 (1997); Mark J. Roe, "Chaos and Evolution in Law and Economics," 109 *Harvard Law Review* 641 (1996); Cass R. Sunstein, "Social Norms and Social Roles," 96 *Columbia Law Review* 903 (1996); Eric Posner, *Law and Social Norms*, (2000); Edna Ullmann-Margalit, *The Emergence of Norms* (1978).

[12] See Reza Banakar, and Max Travers, *An Introduction to Law and Social Theory* 119 (2002).

[13] See generally, Roberto Mangabeira Unger, "The Critical Legal Studies Movement" *Harv. Law Rev.* 561-675 (1983).

[14] Gary Saalman, *Postmodernism And You: Law* (1996), http://www.xenos.org/ministries/crossroads/dotlaw.htm

Thus, there are no foundational principles upon which to position the edifice of law. "Principles of law" these theorists go on to conclude "could never reflect universal truths . . . only allocations of power among social groups. According to these scholars, it is senseless to talk about whether a law is right or wrong or moral or amoral. Law is whatever the most powerful cultural group in society makes it."[15] Indeed, in the CLS perspective of law, all legal "truths" are mere mental constructs shaped by social convention. CLS boldly contends that objective ethical truth is a fiction, thus "consensus within a viable community is all we mean by the truth of ethical propositions . . . "[16] CLS theorists pointedly reject the notion that there is "good," or objective morality.[17] We are instead confronted by the subjective, cultural constructions that society erects to stand like ethical fortifications for us to retreat inside. Ultimately, anti-foundationalist theorists argue, these fortifications are arbitrary creations built upon a foundation of sand, the search for objective truth "misguided."[18]

D. The Flux of Mere Opinions

So how deep does this go? The postmodern method of deconstruction begins like peeling an onion. Layer after layer is pulled away to see what lies underneath, and layer by layer the onion is made smaller, until eventually one is left with only its empty core—nothing. Carried to its extreme, postmodernism deconstructs the very foundations on which the possibility of ever arriving at truth with a capital 'T' is built. Indeed, it puts forward the proposition that truth in this sense does not exist, that there is never indeed anything true apart from the values that arise from our own subjective constructions, or in the terminology of Foucault, that

---

[15] Ibid.
[16] Mark Kelman, *A Guide to Critical Legal Studies* 14 (1987).
[17] Ibid. at 70.
[18] Ibid. at 14.

we create entire belief structures through the 'discourses' through which we engage the world.[19] Apart from the very process itself of creating value, there does not exist any objective truth.

It is important for us to be clear; it is not that we can never achieve objectivity, but rather the whole notion of objectivity itself is an unreal concept. It is a figment of our imagination. It simply does not, nor ever has existed. This is not the denial of things in themselves. It is not solipsism.[20] No one is saying the chair is not there, or that fire does not burn. Rather, it is a complete denial of the objective validity of the value systems we construct around the external world. That is, the views that proliferate in relation to the objective world. Thus, as there is no 'real' in this sense, there is simply no hope of objectivity, only perspective. All we can ever know is one particular view as an alternative for another. And we are forever swimming in these perceptions. Whatever perspective the individual or culture engages in, takes on the illusion of truth for that individual or culture.

In a sense, one could argue that the very concept of truth is a by-product of view. Let us examine this idea by way of illustration using two mutually exclusive hypothetical opinions predicated on value: opinion A and opinion B. Opinion B necessitates that we see opinion A as implicitly wrong. We could never develop opinion B without doing so. It is important to understand that it is not that opinion A is necessarily wrong; it is that opinion B manifested itself, and thus made opinion A appear wrong. Thus, the moment we subscribe to opinion B, opinion A will seem erroneous. This is the consequence of believing opinion B is right; for opinion B to be right, opinion A must become wrong. It is a self-defining process. Likewise, when opinion C is adopted, opinions A and B will both appear to be wrong. And this is equally true when one goes on to adopt opinion D, E, F

---

[19] M. Foucault, *The History of Sexuality Volume I: An Introduction* 144 (1978).

[20] "The views that nothing exists outside one's own mind, or that nothing such can be known to exist, are called Solipsism (literally, 'only-oneself-ism')." Alan Robert Lacey, *Dictionary of Philosophy* 305 (3rd ed. 1996).

and so forth, and along we go. With each opinion there will be an underlying sense it is at last objectively correct, and this sense will persist until it is replaced by a new opinion, a new view.

On the surface of things, there will appear to a breaking away from previously held wrong notions—a general advance towards clarity. However, there is no reason to assume that in developing opinion B we have become any less deluded as before. There is no reason to believe that we are progressing through gradated levels of clarity. Instead, all we are left with, with any real certainty, is that there is change. Not progressive enlightenment, but mere change. And change does not imply that the new standpoint is any more inherently valid. Arguably, it will be "valid" precisely until one develops a new opinion. If the reader would honestly examine his or her own views, his or her own values, and note how they have changed over the course of his or her life, it becomes difficult to insist that one's present value system is definitively correct, and will not go on to change just as previously held viewpoints have done. Likewise, this is true for entire cultures, entire periods of human history.

II. FINDING OUR FOOTING

A. Bartley and Torture by Unwashed Grapes

So as asked at the beginning of this paper, where does that leave us? If our value systems are no more than subjective concoctions, none with any exclusive claim to truth, is not a value system that condones slavery equally as valid as one that condemns it? What about murder? What about genocide? In this wash of subjectivity, where is there the possibility for any moral compass? In the blind morass of moral relativism, do we not lose our only tether hold to truth, to value? The answer is no: we do not. But to understand why, we must examine the nature of our most basic conceptions of right and wrong.

To illustrate this point, let us examine a hypothetical situation involving a man, Bartley, who suffers from a very peculiar and unique condition: a crippling fear of unwashed grapes. For some inexplicable reason, the mere sight of unwashed grapes is enough to instill absolute terror into the heart of this man. There is no rational reason behind his fear. It is wholly arbitrary, without rhyme or reason. Now, what are we supposed to tell this man? Is Bartley's fear objectively valid? No. Does Bartley's reaction seem correct to us? No. Is Bartley's fear real? This is not as simple. Clearly, his fear, or let us refer to it as Bartley's value system, is real. While his value system may not reflect what we understand as real, his fear is very real. We cannot deny this fact, no more than we can tell a man who hears beauty in a particular piece of music that it is not beautiful.

Now, to torture Bartley by say locking him in a small room filled with crates of unwashed grapes would be, in very real sense, immoral. No sane person could make sense of, nor justify, Bartley's intense fear of unwashed grapes. Unquestionably, it presents itself as an arbitrary, subjective reaction, solely the product of Bartley's perception. However, equally there is no way to deny that as a result of his perception, this man is suffering, and therefore, it then becomes, in a very real sense, immoral to intentionally cause him to suffer in this way.[21] In the case of this man, to torture him with unwashed grapes *is* immoral. It is no longer a subjective view; it is an objective reality. There is suffering. When suffering comes into being, morality comes into being.[22] Likewise, there could not be morality without an act having at least the potential to cause suffering, or lessen it. Indeed, if the majority of human beings shared Bartley's value system, leaving unwashed grapes lying around might be seen as an unspeakable breach of moral behaviour. And it would be.

---

[21] Assuming no greater good could come of it.

[22] Here, and throughout the remainder of the paper, the term 'suffering' is used for lack of a better word. However, what is meant here by 'suffering' is any experience of that which we define as negative. This may not necessarily be as profound an experience as the word suffering implies. Indeed it may range from the mildest feeling of agitation, or discomfort, to the deepest depths of human anguish.

But we must go further and ask the question: why is Bartley's fear of unwashed grapes any less credible than our fears? Why should we not extend this same analysis to our fear of loneliness, cold, starvation, or even our fear of death? Equally, why should we not question our love of warmth, food, security, power, and beauty? To imagine these things may be totally arbitrary seems grossly counter-intuitive. They appear to be extracted from indelible truths prescribed by nature itself. One would of course reply that Bartley's fear is unfounded as nothing 'harmful' would result from contact with unwashed grapes, while our fear of cold is rational because our bodies may become sick as a result of overexposure to cold. But we must not stop here let us keep going. Well, if the body becomes sick, it may cease functioning. If it ceases functioning, we may die. And . . . if we die, this is a bad thing. And so there we have it: indisputable truth.

However, we must follow our analysis to its inevitable conclusion. How is the human fear of death itself unlike Bartley's fear of unwashed grapes? How is it any less arbitrary? Is it not only because these value determinations are so deeply embedded into our psyche, so necessitated by our physical state, and so pervasive and commonly held, that they seem beyond question—that they appear to us to possess categorical objectivity? These are value assumptions so entrenched into the nature of being alive, that it is inconceivable that, at the end of the day, they are not rooted in the real. And yet, they are not. If we could step beyond these patterns of belief that bind us to the blind acceptance that our values are self-evident truths, we would see clearly that, in the final analysis, our value system is wholly relative and no less arbitrary than Bartley's. But to put it mildly, this is a difficult thing to do. In fact, it is a virtually impossible thing to do, and our very inability to grasp this reality, speaks to how deeply rooted and powerful these perceptions really are. There is no difference between any of us and Bartley. All value is constructed, not intrinsic. Indeed the entire edifice of value itself—of any sense of value—is just the equivalent of unwashed grapes.

B. Bartley and Death by Vehicular Idiocy

Let us take another example involving Bartley, again illustrating the same point. In an effort to alleviate some of the anxiety brought about by his debilitating condition, Bartley's therapist recommends he take a vacation. Putting aside his paralysing fear of unwashed grapes, Bartley takes his trusted doctor's advice and takes a trip to London, England. He rents a car and plans a route through the English countryside, careful to avoid the few wineries that operate in the UK. As Bartley winds his way over the empty country roads of rural England, finally free of the oppressive terror of unhygienic grapes, he notices a tractor-trailer heading directly towards him. The massive truck is driving on the same side of the road as Bartley and refusing to change lanes. Bartley is bewildered. As Bartley frantically sounds his horn, the horn of the truck blares back at him, and the truck continues to barrel towards poor Bartley. Bartley panics yet again wishing he had never left home. And just at the point of impact, as Bartley's small car is about to be utterly crushed by the tractor trailer, we still the frame and notice (of course) that Bartley is driving on the right side of the road.

Clearly, if you will, we have here two conflicting value systems: a value system that deems driving on the right side of the road as correct and one that posits the left side of the road as correct. This highlights the postmodern dilemma in distinct terms. Driving on the right side of road is no more inherently valid than driving on the left. Certainly, this practice of driving on one side of the road or the other is no more than a mere cultural phenomenon, having no objective claim to being any truer than any other. What we have here are rules completely unrelated to any moral framework—a set of norms that show themselves as utterly subjective social constructions. That is fine enough, but what are we to tell Bartley who is about to be killed by oncoming traffic? Does it make a whit of difference? The rules do not have any objective reality to them in the sense that they are not grounded on any universal truth; however, the result (his impending death) is very real. That is to say, is there any question that traffic rules are arbitrary? But of what use is this insight when you are hit by a truck? If a man takes it upon himself (unlike Bartley) to intentionally drive on the right side of the road in a place where the rules dictate that traffic must drive on the left, is it not then a moral issue? People are going to get hurt; it does not matter that the rules are not founded upon objective truth. In a very real sense, they have become objective truths.

C. Pain and Moral Clarity

Let us now return to poor Bartley in the first example. How could subjecting this man to unwashed grapes be morally wrong? Let us get to the heart of the matter. It is wrong because in doing so we would cause Bartley to suffer, and it is precisely human suffering that is the yardstick with which to gauge right from wrong—the core underpinning to justice. Indeed, it is, and always has been, the only process through which "good" is defined; the whole of morality is grounded upon the extent to which an act creates suffering and the extent to which the act reduces suffering. This is all morality ever is. Although it may flower into systems of ethical complexity, it remains nothing more than just this. All sense of value is ultimately contingent upon this experience, and evolves from it. The experience of suffering physical or mental, is the very definition of "negative." *Negative has no meaning beyond this.*[23] "Negative" is the experience of suffering, and its inverse, "positive," is the cessation of this very same sense of suffering. It is a self-defining process that in no uncertain terms "reifies" itself. Once it is ushered into existence, it is "real." The experience of suffering is the root of good and bad. It

---

[23] Some might argue that human suffering is useful and has a function in life, in that it is conducive to great art, or human progress, but this is just semantics. What these advocates of suffering are really saying is that great art or human progress is worth the suffering. However, something can only be "worth it" if, in some way, it is a short-term sacrifice for a greater good. And what is "good" but ultimately reducing suffering? There is no way around this.

is its very core. Put simply, it is not the basis of right and wrong, it is the progenitor of right and wrong. Value is never anything more than the sum total of suffering and the lack of it. Human suffering is not the defining factor of value; it is not a mechanism through which to measure value—*it is value*.

An act in itself has no implicit moral character. It is the occurrence of suffering that provides a moral context through which an act becomes either right or wrong. To illustrate this point, let us return then to the question raised above regarding slavery. Imagine a situation in which the institution of slavery did not in any way create even a trace of human suffering—a situation where the slave did not experience pain (physical or emotional) as a result of his bondage. Even the master was not morally corrupted by this exploitive relationship, and does not mentally suffer as a result of his cruelty. Certainly, this kind of situation is not possible, but for argument's sake, let us supposes this is the case—absolutely no suffering is created for any parties, directly or otherwise. How could we then say that this situation is morally wrong? We could not. Once the element of suffering is taken out of the equation, the physical act of slavery ceases to possess any moral significance.[24] This does not seem to gel with our fundamental notions of right and wrong. It is, however, only because we intuitively recognize that this situation could never truly arise, that it appears so patently wrong. It is because we are aware that slavery as an institution is the cause of such misery that it is morally repugnant to us. However, let us not confuse the issue; it is not the act of slavery itself, it is the suffering it creates. The element of pain once introduced upon our emotional landscape imbues the world with a measure of moral reality. We construct entire value systems within which we then live, but the moment we react to these

---

[24] Kant though, and many other philosophers who view conforms to a Deontological ethics, would adamantly disagree. Kant for one places emphasis on the act itself, and not merely the consequences of the act, famously arguing that it would be even wrong to lie to a murderer asking the whereabouts of a potential victim. See C. Korsgaard, "Kant on Dealing With Evil" in James P. Sterba, *Ethics: The Big Questions* (1998).

constructions, all subjectivity ends. Our reactions are real. There is good and bad, right and wrong.

It is important to understand that what is being denied here is not that our belief systems and sense of value are largely determined by culture, economics etc., but rather that these subjective constructions preclude any possibility of clear moral guidance—just because they are subjective does not make them any less "real." Entire value systems are, as postmodernism contends, subjective creations. It is the very perception of value that creates value. Beyond the bonds of experience, value does not, nor ever has existed; when we speak of value and we speak of an individual's perception, we are speaking of one and the same thing. However, once it is created, it is very real. In that they ultimately create the experience of suffering or the lack of it, morality is thus reified. That is, the parameters are created through a wholly subjective process, but once created, we live and die within these very parameters. The postmodern argument fails to recognize this truth, and it is precisely this truth that no amount of postmodern relativism can undermine.

D. How This Is, and Is Not, Utilitarianism

This might be understood as Utilitarianism, or perhaps even a refined version of hedonism. To a certain extent this is true. The basic goal of utilitarianism is to offer a means with which to arrive at somehow valid normative propositions regarding what is "just" by positing the principle of maximizing individual's experience of happiness as a way to gauge what is right.[25] Similarly, we are here

[25] See Walter Sinnott-Armstrong, "Consequentialism," *Stanford Encyclopedia Of Philosophy*, (2003), http://plato.stanford.edu/entries/consequentialism/ ("The paradigm case of consequentialism is utilitarianism, whose classic proponents were Jeremy Bentham (1789), John Stuart Mill (1861), and Henry Sidgwick (1907). . . . Classic Utilitarians held hedonistic act consequentialism. *Act consequentialism* is the claim that an act is morally right if and only if that act maximizes the good, that is, if and only if the total amount of good for all minus the total amount of bad for all is greater than this net amount for any incompatible act available to the

positing "happiness" as having intrinsic value. However, although similar, there is a slight difference: the emphasis here is *not on maximizing utility, but on finding a stable underfooting of value on which to stand at all*. We can be said to be taking from utilitarianism only what is necessary to establish firm ground upon which to plant our footing upon the shifting sands of postmodern relativism. Issues of maximizing utility for the greatest good are purposively not brought into the discussion. The difference is: subjective reaction is not a tool with which to gauge the moral nature of an act, rather, *it is the moral nature of an act*—it is value. The point being made here is that subjective reaction is the very creation, or "reification" of value. There is simply no value outside of this phenomenon, regardless of whatever convoluted expression it assumes. Value does not exist in a vacuum; it is an interpretive process.

Bentham once famously decried the notion of natural law as "nonsense upon stilts."[26] Let us now carry it further: the notion of objective value at all is nonsense upon even higher stilts. Value is no more than an individual's subjective interpretation of events; an interpretation that can be enlarged to subsume entire cultures that have formed consensus around it. Thus, subjective reaction is not so much a mechanism through which we may quantify the moral nature of an act, rather, it is the very creation of value; value does not, nor ever has existed outside of this subjective process—as postmodernism suggests, it is solely a human construction. But, nevertheless, it is here in the core of this process of construction, that we can discover a degree of constancy.

---

agent on that occasion. *Hedonism* then claims that pleasure is the only intrinsic good and that pain is the only intrinsic bad. Together these claims imply that an act is morally right if and only if that act causes "the greatest happiness for the greatest number," as the common slogan says.") (footnotes omitted).

[26] Jeremy Bentham, "Anarchical Fallacies; Being An Examination of the Declarations of Rights Issued During the French Revolution" in John Bowring, *The Works of Jeremy Bentham* 501 (1843).

CONCLUSION

Our reasoning here accepts full throttle the inevitable conclusions to which postmodern thought leads us: value is the machinations of culture and subjective reaction. But at the end of the day, the measure of certainty implicit in these very reactions provides stability within this moral turmoil. Bartley's reaction to unwashed grapes constructs the possibility of value, and brings it into existence where otherwise it simply would not be present. As Bartley's reaction is what allows the possibility of value, we can turn to the very reaction for moral guidance. To bemoan the fact that value constructs are subjective is rather odd, if not irrelevant; it does not matter. We eventually come full circle. The reaction *is* value. Thus, once created, it is as real as anything, and is a point of stability that postmodern moral relativism cannot undercut. It does not matter what course we follow to stimulate those reactions. Subjective concoctions or not, they are real. And they are foundational principles.

The postmodern argument is a powerful one precisely because it reveals in unapologetic clarity the true magnitude of our ignorance. The subjective nature of our conceptions of the world is exposed for what they are. Nevertheless, this does not disenfranchise morality. On the contrary, in that the process of deconstruction sets our value systems in proper relief, the moral superstructure on which they are based becomes that much clearer, and thus reinvigorated. Our value systems are stripped of all claims to objective authority, but yet the end result remains the same—it makes no difference. There is right and wrong. Ultimately, all postmodernism does is force us to set aside the exterior expressions of "justice," and instead root our legal conceptions at this more fundamental level.

Value structures as reflected in the law may shift and change over time. As with all value systems, codified systems of law, and the principles they establish such as nuisance, trespass, and negligence, are highly determined by the particular cultural context from which they arise. However, it is in the intrinsically negative quality of suffering that we find firm footing on which to distinguish right from wrong—here we have a piece of "reality" on to which we can firmly clutch. It is here that the laws we formulate cease to be arbitrary fabrications and become rooted in fixed moral truth. It is a simple and familiar formula: the generation of suffering is inherently bad; conversely, the cessation of human suffering is good. It is logistically difficult to quantify, but is endowed with a quality of reality, of universal truth, more than capable of withstanding the nihilistic blows of moral relativism engendered by postmodern thought. The basis of law has credence only in so far as it conforms to this principle, and no more.

THE ARCHITECTURE OF LAW: BUILDING LAW ON A SOLID FOUNDATION—THE ETERNAL AND NATURAL LAWS
Brian M. McCall

"*Summum ius, summa iniuria.*"[1] "The greater the law the higher the injury."

With these words the great Roman orator Cicero warned against the exaltation of human law. His words take on a new poignancy in light of much contemporary jurisprudence. Not only have human positive laws grown exponentially in their number and scope but the dominant theory of Legal Positivism has exalted the place of human positive law by building an entire system of law on it alone. Human made law has become viewed as self-justifying and essentially self-restrained. Classical Natural Law theory placed human law within a grand hierarchical system of laws. This structure is held together by a foundation and a frame erected by its Creator and Artificer.

With the goal of reducing the greatness of human made law, this article examines part of the structure of law that should surround human made laws. It draws heavily on the jurisprudential writings of St. Thomas Aquinas and Gratian. Part I sets the stage for the discussion by describing how any legal jurisprudence not erected within this design of law reduces human law to a pure volitional act rooted in contests for power. Part II commences an examination of the blueprints for this legal edifice by examining the definition of law in general. Part III turns to the foundation of the structure, the Eternal Law. Part IV turns to the frame built up out of the foundation with the tool of man's rationality, the Natural Law. Part V draws some conclusions from the examination of these first two building blocks of law.

Various themes will weave through these first two levels of the artifice of the legal mansion. The hierarchical frame of Natural Law will be shown to be anchored to its foundation, the Eternal Law, by

---

[1] Cicero, *De officiis* 1.10.33

two pillars, reason and volition. Outside this structure, law balances precariously on the sole pillar of volition. The second theme centers on the interdependence of each level of the structure. Natural Law cannot survive if severed from its source and foundation, the Eternal Law. Otherwise it becomes a non-obligatory element floating by itself. The article concludes that it is futile to advocate a restoration of the Natural Law without restoring the foundation of Eternal Law and the hierarchical structure of Natural Law. By examining these themes, the article will bind together an overall schematic for the erection of the complete legal edifice which will encase and thereby reduce the greatness of human-made law.

PART I

The Power of Law: What Pleases the Prince Has the Force of Law

Much of the current attitude towards law making can be summarized in the ancient legal aphorism: "what pleases the prince has the force of law"[2] and "the prince is not bound by the law."[3] In the non-regal American political context, the principle has been abstracted to the more generalized "the intention of the lawgiver is the law."[4] The aphorism has become politically ambivalent. Whatever political system happens to be the reigning system for making law (a monarchy, an oligarchy, republic, democracy, totalitarian regime, *etc.*) is irrelevant. All that matters is that whatever the designated law giver decrees to be the law is the law without any other justification. All that matters is that the law givers comply with the reigning

---

[2] "*Quod principi placuit vigorem legis habet.*" Justinian, *Dig.* 1.4.1. To be fair to the ancient Roman legal theorists, this phrase was qualified by many other legal concepts, not least of which was the natural law. Thus, "what pleases the prince" was not always law but only what legitimately pleased the prince. Legal Positivism rejects all of these qualifications and accepts this principle as an absolute.

[3] "*Princeps legibus solutus est.*" Justinian, *Dig.* 1.3.31.

[4] Abraham Lincoln, "The Sacredness of Judicial Decisions," Speech of June 12, 1857, *Great Debates in American History*, Marion Mills Miller, ed., Vol. IV, 395-96, 398-99 (New York: Current Literature Publishing Company, 1913).

procedures for making and promulgating law. No higher criteria or foundation exists to make or judge or criticize human-made laws. In fact, this very procedure for making law itself is merely a creature of positive law. Law makers only have to comply with the "rule of law," meaning they comply with the way laws are made, until that rule of law itself is changed. In the words of the English poet Alexander Pope "[o]ne truth is clear, 'Whatever IS, is RIGHT'"[5]

To the original Legal Positivists such as John Austin, the act of the will and the threat of sanctions are what make a legal system. The established legislator decides what is to be law by no criteria other than its will and then uses the monopoly on violence which the State has claimed since the 16th century to make the law obeyed. In Austin's words: "every law properly so called is set by a superior to an inferior or inferiors: it is set by a party armed with might, to a party or parties to whom that might can reach."[6] Jeremy Bentham, a disciple of Austin defined law as "an assemblage of signs declarative of a volition conceived or adopted by the sovereign in a state. . . ."[7] Bentham's formulation indicates that politics has been transformed into the game of "capturing" the will of the sovereign (the levers of power). The sovereign need not even "conceive" of the new law or in fact desire it. If the sovereign can be made to "adopt" it, the new idea becomes law. Law making is the art of persuading the sovereign to adopt one's particular desire. Thomas Hobbes expands this notion of human control over law to the very idea of justice. Hobbes argues that justice and injustice can be demonstrated *a priori* because: "We ourselves make the principles—that is, the causes of justice (namely, laws and covenants)."[8]

Although later Positivists such as Hart and Raz, attempt to tone down the raw power element of this system by explaining how the sovereign (the dispute resolver) is bound by rules as to the way

---

[5] Alexander Pope, *An Essay on Man*, I. 1.294.
[6] John Austin, *The Province of Jurisprudence Determined* 350 (Prometheus Books 2000),
[7] Jeremy Bentham, *Of Laws in General*, 1 (ed. H.L.A. Hart 1970)
[8] Thomas Hobbes, *De Homine* X.5.

disputes are settled,[9] they never offer a criteria for establishing, evaluating and changing these primary or system rules which ultimate rest on the will of the sovereign.[10] The offspring of these theories is law as power politics. Pope Benedict XVI recently summarized the contemporary effect of the raw conception of power at the heart of modern law making:

> Today, a positivist conception of law seems to dominate many thinkers. They claim that humanity or society or indeed the majority of citizens is becoming the ultimate source of civil law. The problem that arises is not, therefore, the search for good but the search for power, or rather, how to balance powers.[11]

Politicians should really not be surprised at the lack of "bipartisanship" or "cooperation" in our political system. Under the tyranny of Positivism, politics is merely the combat to see who can control the "intention of the legislator." Law making and politics are about power not justification. The Democrats or Republicans, as the case may be, can pass whatever laws they want because they have a "mandate" to do so by conquering the will of the legislature by winning an election. This is no different from the victorious prince claiming the right to revise the laws of the vanquished territory according to "his" will. The principles of Legal Positivism apply equally to the "rule of law," the procedural system for controlling the will of the legislator. Thus, when a desired result is not obtained, the power seekers need only change the rules of the game or the existing "rule of law." Thus, when the proposed

---

[9] See e.g., H.L.A. Hart, *The Concept of Law* (1961) and J. Raz, *Practical Reason and Norms* (1975).

[10] For a discussion of how modern Positivism still retains an aspect of "might makes right," see Roger Berkowitz, *The Gift of Science: Leibnitz and the Modern Legal Tradition*, 5 (2007) (associating legal positivism with the view that law is "nothing but a willful decision" and with the idea that "might makes right").

[11] Benedict XVI, *Address to Members of the International Theological Commission*, October 5, 2007.

European Union constitution was voted down in several countries "the will of the people" is rejected as the rule of law. The will of the elected governments of the member states is substituted. The same constitution is redrafted as a treaty and the people who previously rejected these laws are told they have no right to vote anymore (with the exception of Ireland which did vote and reject the latest attempt). As Pope Benedict XVI has remarked: "It is necessary to go back to the natural moral norm as the basis of the juridic norm; otherwise the latter constantly remains at the mercy of a fragile and provisional consensus."[12]

This paradigm of law as power is not the only available paradigm. Other structures have and can be utilized. To elucidate the form of these structures it is necessary to begin with the most basic building material. It is necessary to begin with a thorough definition of law.

PART II

Surveying the Blueprint: What Is Being Built?

St. Thomas Aquinas provides the essential elements of a definition of law. First he defines law by its two functions; it is a rule (*regula*) and measure (*mensura*).[13] These two terms indicate that to be a law a thing must both direct an action and serve as a basis for evaluating an action. A rule directs or restricts action by binding or requiring actions to conform to a standard. St. Thomas in the same passage notes that one Latin word for law *lex, legis* is derived from *ligare* (meaning to bind). Law governs actions by directing them to an end. As a rule, a law has a dual function of proscribing and prescribing action furthering or hindering that end. As a measure, law serves as a way of evaluating or measuring acts to see to what extent they conform to the rule. The measure is not simply a binary

---

[12] Benedict XVI, *Message for the Celebration of the World Day of Peace*, January 1, 2008.
[13] St. Thomas Aquinas, *Summa Theologica* I-II q. 90 art. 1.

evaluation (it complies or not) but determines how far along the line formed by the directing rule an action lies.

St. Thomas goes on to define the essential elements of such a rule and measure: "*quae nihil est aliud quam quaedam rationis ordinatio ad bonum commune, ab eo qui curam communitatis habet, promulgata.*"[14] First, he begins by noting that anything which does not possess the following qualities is not a law—"nothing is [law] other than that which." There are definitional criteria, outside of the volition of the law giver, necessary to make something a law. These elements establish criteria for evaluating whether or not a command of the will qualifies as a law. It must be ordered of reason (*ordinatio rationis*). Law then is a product of reason. The primary criteria for something to be a law is that it must be "of reason" or reasonable. Gratian notes this requirement of law when he says that law *ratione consistat*,[15] which can be translated "consists in reason" or "stands with or agrees with reason." In the same section he points out that reason designates (with a connotation of entrusting) the law (*legem ratio commendat*) and that if law consists in reason then it will be all that may have already stood (or agreed) by reason (*si ratione lex constat lex erit omne, iam quod ratione constiterit*). The use of the perfect subjunctive in this last phrase is interesting. It expresses the temporal potentiality of law. Law arises after truths may have been constituted in reason. The tense of the phrase acknowledged the uncertainty of success in this first step—*may* have stood by reason. There is no certainty of complete success. This relationship between law and reason is a dramatic difference from Positivism which accepts as law anything which meets the currently reigning procedural requirements for making a law. For the Natural Law system, such is not sufficient; to be a law, the rule and measure must agree with or stand in the faculty of reason, not the will.

Next, law as a rule cannot be directed to any end but "toward the common good" (*ad bonum commune*). The concept of the common

---

[14] *Summa Theologica*, I-II q. 90 art. 4.
[15] Gratian, *Decretum* D.1, C.5.

good is an entire topic within itself. For purposes of this article, it is sufficient to establish that for something to be the common good it must be both *good* (i.e. objectively oriented to a good) and *common*. The concept of "good" will be developed *infra* when the contents of the Natural Law are discussed. Further, it must be a good that is not unique to one individual or group of individuals but it must be a good which is *common* to all in the relevant community.

Law may not be made by just anyone but only "by him who has care of the community" (*ab eo qui curam communitatis habet*). It is not someone merely in authority or in possession of power. The rule maker must have *care* of the community. Note that this formulation is not regime-type specific. It does not require the law be made by a king, or a legislative body or the people at large. The test of legitimacy (that which binds) is that the lawgiver has *care* of the relevant community. There must be a relationship of entrustment and responsibility between the community and the legitimate law giver.

The order of reason must not just exist in the mind of the law giver but must be externalized; it must become word; it must be publicly spoken or "promulgated" (*promulgata*). Although born of reason, law becomes an act of the will not just a product of speculation. Reason gives rise to the act of promulgation.

Having defined law, Aquinas considers the effects of law. Since the second prong of the definition of law is that it is directed towards the common good, the effect of law must be the common good of those subject to the law. Now the common good of man is his "proper virtue" or "that which makes its subject [Man] good."[16] In order to make Men good, law fixes punishment with respect to three kinds of human acts, those which are intrinsically good (*ex genere* having connotations of birth or generation), intrinsically evil (*ex genere*) or intrinsically indifferent (again *ex genere*). As to the first type of acts, the law orders or commands (*praecipere vel imperare*) these acts be done. With respect to the second the law prohibits (*prohibere*) them. As to those acts neither good nor evil in themselves, the law leaves

[16] *Summa Theologica* I-II Q. 92. Art. 1.

them alone (*permittere*) neither requiring nor forbidding them with the fear of punishment.

Placing together the elements of the definition and effects of law produces an understanding of law as a rule and measure of human acts ordained of reason towards the common good which is promulgated by one who has care of the community and which makes use of punishment to make men good by commanding good, forbidding evil and permitting neutral acts. This definition needs to be applied to the various stories of the house of law to see to what extent they conform. Before looking at individual levels, however, it is necessary to survey the design of the overall structure. How do the pieces fit together?

Gratian begins his *Treatise on Laws* with the following division of the types of law comprising the structure: "*Humanum genus duobus regitur, naturali uidelicet iure et moribus.*"[17] Gratian sheds light on this two part division of law in the first *causa* of this first *distinction* when he quotes Isidore as saying:

> *Omnes leges aut diuinae sunt, aut humanae. Diuinae natura, humanae moribus constant, ideoque he discrepant, quoniam aliae aliis gentibus placent. 1. Fas lex diuina est: ius lex humana. Transire per agrum alienum, fas est, ius non est.*

The passage begins with a differently worded two-part division. Whereas the first division was Natural Law and Custom, the second is divine law and human law. The terms divine or human can be reconciled to the earlier division, Natural Law and Custom. The second phraseology refers to their origin where as the first refers to a representative type of each genus produced by divine or human agency. Huguccio in his commentary on Gratian confirms the divine origin of Natural Law and verbally links this opening to the passage

---

[17] Gratian, *Decretum* D. 1 ("The human race is ruled by two things: namely natural law and long standing custom").

by Isidore.[18] He also explains that custom (*mos*) is human law (*jus humanum*) which is invented by Man.[19] Isidore says that Divine Laws stand in or are based on (*constant*) nature whereas human law is based on custom. Hence Natural Law has its origin in God and custom is the creation of human law. The Ordinary Gloss on this opening passage explains "natural" law as "divine" and "custom" as "customary law or written or unwritten human law."[20] Isidore further notes since human laws are rooted in customs of nations they can vary from nation to nation and are therefore not universal. The implication is that that Divine Law, rooted in nature, does not so vary. The Divine Law is immutable as it has its source in nature which is universal.

The text then introduces yet another pair of words to identify each of these two categories. First it calls laws of divine origin (that which stands in the nature of things) "*fas.*" This indeclinable Latin word means that which is right or fitting or proper according to the will or command of God.[21] Huguccio describes *fas* as whatever is

---

[18] Huguccio, Pisanus, *Summa Decretorum* contained in *Monumenta Juris Canonici Series A Corpus Glassatorum* Vol. 6, page 13 (Biblioteca Apostolica Vaticano 2006) (glossing naturali videlicet jure as "id est divino"); see also Huguccio, *Derivationes,* quoted in Stephan Kuttner, *The History of Ideas and Doctrines in the Middle Ages,* V, 99 (Variorum Reprints 1980) (drawing a similar parallel between positive justice and natural justice, which he calls *fas*, Huguccio claims that *iustitia positiva* has been made by Man whereas *iustitia naturalis* is extended from the effects of nature).

[19] Ibid. at 10 ("*Quo nomine committur ius humanu,* Ibid *est ab homine inuentum*").

[20] Ordinary Gloss to *Decretum* D.1 (emphasis added).

[21] See Charlton T. Lewis, Charles Short, *A Latin Dictionary* (defining *fas* as "belonging to the religious language, *the dictates of religion, divine law;* opposed to *jus,* or human law"). The following are examples of the use of the word in the Holy Bible: "*audiebant autem eum usque ad hoc verbum et levaverunt vocem suam dicentes tolle de terra eiusmodi non enim fas est eum vivere*" "And they heard him until this word, and then lifted up their voice, saying: Away with such an one from the earth; for it is not fit that he should live" (Acts 22:22). "*contigit autem et septem fratres cum matre adprehensos conpelli a rege contra fas ad carnes porcinas flagris et taureis cruciatos*" "It came to pass also, that seven brethren, together with their mother, were apprehended, and compelled by the king to eat swine's flesh against the law, for which end they were tormented with whips and scourges" (2 Machabees 7:1). "*hii vero qui intus erant confidentes in stabilitate murorum et adparatu alimoniarum remissius agebant maledictis lacessentes Iudam ac blasphemantes et loquentes quae fas non est*" "But they that were within it, trusting in the strength of the

"permitted," "said to be appropriate and good" and "ought to be said to be pleasing."[22] The text then calls all human laws *"jus."* This is a general Latin term often translated as "law," but as Kenneth Pennington has argued conveys a rich penumbra of meanings beyond mere legal enactments.[23] It encompasses the sense of that which is right or just in light of human judgment.[24] Justinian's *Digest* contains a general definition of *"jus"* as that which is "always equitable and good *(semper aequum ac bonum")*.[25] Cicero in his Letter to Atticus uses the same construction of *fas* and *jus* to refer to all that is right according to divine and human reckoning.[26] Natural law *(jus naturale)* and long standing custom *(mos)* thus stand in the opening lines of the *Decretum* as representatives of these two overarching groupings of everything that is right and good from both the perspective of God *(fas,* rooted in the nature of things or Natural Law) and man *(jus,* rooted in human determinations of what is always right or custom). Both sides of this coin of what is right and good must be examined to determine a rule and measure for conduct. Man is ruled by both Natural Law and Custom, *fas* and *jus.* As the text observes, the human law *(lex humanae)* might prohibit something that could be permissible by divine law *(lex divinae).* Passing through another's field may not be authorized in light of human customs (a country may prohibit it by custom or statute) but may be authorized by Divine Law, *fas.*

---

walls, and the provision of victuals, behaved in a more negligent manner, and provoked Judas with railing and blaspheming, and uttering such words as were not to be spoken" (2 Machabees 12:14).

[22] Huguccio, supra note 18, at 20.

[23] See Kenneth Pennington, "Lex Naturalis and Ius Naturale" 68 *The Jurist* 569, 571-573 (2008).

[24] See *A Latin Dictionary,* supra note 21 ("that which is binding or obligatory; that which is binding by its nature, right, justice, duty").

[25] Justinian, *Dig.*, 1.1.11.

[26] Cicero, *Letter to Atticus,* 1, 16, 6. (Explaining how devastating it is to Rome when corrupt men rendered a wrong verdict he says: *"triginta homines populi Romani levissimos ac nequissimos nummulis acceptis ius ac fas omne delere."* The phrase sums up a complete obliteration of all rightness - "ius ac fac.").

Thus, for a complete understanding of the rule and measure of human action, both groupings of law must be consulted. In this vein, Justinian's *Digest* defines Jurisprudence (the wisdom of law) thus: "*Iuris prudentia est divinarum atque humanarum rerum notitia, iusti atque iniusti scientia*" ("Jurisprudence is the knowledge of divine and human things, and the science of justice and injustice").[27] Natural Law is a component of a dual system. To understand Natural Law, one must know it in this context.

As Gratian comments, this two part division of law is itself subdivided into further species.[28] This first category of Gratian contains the three types of law which Aquinas calls Eternal Law (*Lex Aeterna*), Natural Law (*Lex Naturalis*) and Divine Law (*Lex Divina*). Before considering the details of Natural Law, the species which stands as a ground work within this genus must be surveyed first.

PART III

Eternal Law – The Foundation

A. The Eternal Law as a Real Law

The Eternal Law (*Lex Aeterna*) is the foundation of all other forms of law. Aquinas defines it as "the plan (*ratio*) of Divine Wisdom directing all actions and movements" to their "due end."[29] Eternal Law maintains the entire rational plan (*rationem*) of law. Notice the use of *ratio* by Aquinas. The definition of law requires law to be ordained of reason. The Eternal Law stands in the eternal Reason of God himself. Yet, the Eternal Law is more than pure rationality; it is really a law meeting the definition established by Aquinas. It is a rule as it is "moving all things to their due end."[30]

---

[27] Justinian, *Dig*.1.1.10.2
[28] Gratian, *Decretum* D.1 C2.
[29] *Summa Theologica*, I-II Q. 93 Art. 1.
[30] *Summa Theologica*, I-II, Q. 93, Art. 1.

It serves as the "measure of things."[31] Since the Eternal Law flows from the Divine Reason of God it is connected with the great mystery of the mind of God. It is thus difficult for our human intellect to express with precision its reality. Aquinas needs several words and images, drawn from the discipline of art, to capture the rich nature of this *ratio divinae sapientiae*.

> Just as in every artificer there pre-exists a type of the things that are made by his art, so too in every governor there must pre-exist the type of the order of those things that are to be done by those who are subject to his government. And just as the type of the things yet to be made by an art is called the art or exemplar of the products of that art, so too the type in him who governs the acts of his subjects bears the character of a law, provided the other conditions be present which we have mentioned above (Article 90). Now God, by His wisdom, is the Creator of all things in relation to which He stands as the artificer to the products of his art, as stated in the I, 14, 8. Moreover He governs all the acts and movements that are to be found in each single creature, as was also stated in the I, 103, 5. Wherefore as the type of the Divine Wisdom, inasmuch as by It all things are created, has the character of art, exemplar or idea; so the type of Divine Wisdom, as moving all things to their due end, bears the character of law. Accordingly the eternal law is nothing else than the type of Divine Wisdom, as directing all actions and movements.[32]

Eternal Law has the system (*rationem*) of art (*artis*) or exemplar (*exemplaris*) or eternal prototype (*ideae* with its allusions to the Platonic concept). Significantly, all these terms contain the concept of origin, direction and perfection. Each word contains the idea of defining and directing both the end of, and manner in which, a future act or movement is to be done. The analogy to art is strong in this

---

[31] *Summa Theologica*, I-II, Q. 93 Art.2 Reply to Obj. 3.
[32] *Summa Theologica*, I-II, Q. 93, Art. 1.

passage; Aquinas several times refers to God as an artificer or artist. Before an artist begins to construct his product, he needs an idea (a general nature of what he is to create). The idea identifies what is to be done. The artist than applies an *exemplar*, or style,[33] to guide the nature of the specific representation of the chosen idea. Finally the artist employs a set of skills (art) to execute the idea in the style chosen. It is in this sense that the Eternal Law permeates the universe and all creation. The Eternal Law is the idea of the universe in all its particulars flowing from the mind of God. It contains the end to which all things are directed. It also contains the exemplar or the pattern for the universe, the style each is to use in pursuing that end. Finally it contains the skill or art needed to achieve the particular idea.

It is important to understand in what sense the universe is ruled by the Eternal Law. The Eternal Law, although it is the art, exemplar and eternal prototype of all that exists, provides for the participation of man in causing the particular determinations of each individual act or operation.[34] Again the analogy to art is illuminating. Two artists might have the same idea for a painting (of a Madonna and Child). They might even follow the same style or exemplar (that of the school of Raphael) and both have attained the same level of artistic skill. Yet, the individual paintings of each artist flowing from these common determinants will nonetheless be unique. The product, the painting, is caused both by the idea, exemplar and style which govern the product as well as the individual cooperation of the artist with this style, or we might say, the artist's participation in this style. Thus, the individual elements of the created world will exhibit variety and difference but are united by the *ratio* of the

[33] Although Aquinas does not use the word "style," Pauline Westerman has convincingly argued that it is a suitable English word to capture the essence of Aquinas's comparison to art. See Pauline C. Westerman, *The Disintegration of Natural Law Theory: Aquinas to Finnis,* 26-30 (Brill 1998).

[34] See John Rziha, *Perfecting Human Action St. Thomas Aquinas on Human Participation in Eternal Law,* 66-78 (Catholic University of America Press 2009) (Explaining how Aquinas understands that human acts are determined by the Eternal Law as primary cause but human choice as instrumental cause and showing how the Eternal Law really does determine all things but allows for variety in human action).

Eternal Law which directs their due end. "The *exemplar* God has in mind directs the way the world is *and* should be. In short, the world is created in such a way that it is best fitted to these ends. It is because of the directive power of the *exemplar* that it [Eternal Law] can properly be called "law."[35]

Eternal Law is not just analogically like law; it is truly law. It is a rule and measure of all that is. It prescribes the end of each thing and thereby prescribes that not directed to such end. It contains an ordered system, an *exemplar*, which measures the proportions of all things with respect to their due end. The Eternal Law is ordained of reason, the Divine Wisdom. The Eternal Law is directed to the most common good, the due end of the created universe. It has its origin in He who has care of the community of the universe, God the Creator and Sustainer of all things. Finally, it has been promulgated through the act of creation, that moment when the idea of each thing passed from the *ratio Divinae Sapientiae* where it existed *in potentia* to created reality where it existed *in actualitate*. I believe Aquinas here gives a hint to resolving the apparent paradox that the Eternal Law is really eternal yet has been promulgated through the act of creation. Promulgation, it will be recalled, requires a public utterance of the law.[36] Aquinas explains that through Eternal Law "all things have been created" (*per eam cuncta sunt creata*). This phrase echoes Scripture's reference to the role of the Word (*Verbum*), Christ in creation. St. Paul says "*omnia per ipsum et in ipso creata sunt.*"[37] St. John's Gospel says of the Word "*omnia per ipsum facta sunt*"[38] Thus the Eternal Law is really promulgated through the utterance of the Word, by which all things were made.

---

[35] Westerman, supra note 33, at 29. Westerman, despite being a legal positivist who ultimately rejects the usefulness of natural law, offers one of the best explanations of Aquinas' understanding of the Eternal Law which she calls the "divine style." She argues that later natural law scholars who did not fully incorporate this idea of the eternal law in their theory erected a natural law theory on an edifice without a foundation.
[36] *Summa Theologica* I-II, Q. 90 Art. 4.
[37] Col. 1:16.
[38] John 1:3.

Having made a reference to the way creation occurs through the Word, Aquinas makes explicit that the Eternal Law is promulgated through the Word (*etiam ipsa lex aeterna verbo ipso exprimitur.*)[39] Just as all things created by God are expressed (created through the Word (*Dei opera exprimuntur hoc verbo*), so too the Eternal Law is really promulgated through the Word.[40] Since this Word is a personal name of God (who is eternal), this Word's expression or promulgation of the rational plan of God (Eternal Law) is also eternal. Eternal Law is really a law and is really eternal.

Such an understanding provides an answer to later Natural Law scholars who struggled to understand how the Eternal Law could be a "real" law, *i.e.,* fulfilled the requirement of promulgation in the definition of a law. For example, Suarez concludes that if a law is eternal, it cannot be promulgated[41] since there would be no time before its promulgation. He reasoned that Eternal Law thus could not really be a law. Suarez only sees the later posited Divine Law, which for St. Thomas is a distinct category, as real law; the Eternal Law is not properly speaking a law.[42] If Suarez had understood the promulgation of the Eternal Law as part of the theological understanding of the Word, this may have resolved his difficulty with the Eternal Law. The promulgation of the Eternal Law occurs through the Word in the same way that the Word is eternally begotten.

Those theories of law which fail to fully accept the Eternal Law as law seem to result in a minimization of Natural Law if not its ultimate rejection. Grotius is famous for the impious hypothesis—that Natural Law could exist even if God himself did not exist or did not order the universe.[43] Although Grotius personally may have

---

[39] *Summa Theologica* I-II, q. 93, art. 1, Reply to Objection 2.
[40] Ibid.
[41] Francisco Suarez, "Tractatus de Legibus ac Deo Legislatore," *Selections from Three Works of Francisco Suarez,* II. I., 11 (ed. James Brown Scott and trans. G. L. Williams et. al. Oxford 1944).
[42] See Ibid. at II.IV, 7.
[43] Grotius, *De Jure Belli ac Pacis Libri Tres,* Prolog. 11 (1625) ("What we have been saying

accepted the existence of God, his theory either eliminates any Eternal Law or at most minimizes its importance solely to the desire for self preservation and may limit it only to the realm of human beings and not all of creation.[44] Three centuries later, John Finnis has little place for Eternal Law. He dismisses God's existence as unnecessary to the study of Natural Law early on in his *Natural Law and Natural Rights*.[45] Finnis does include a brief discussion of the Eternal Law, but it is literally an appendage to his theory. Not only is it placed at the very end of the work, but Finnis concludes that if God and Eternal Law exist they are superfluous to Natural Law and his seven incommensurable goods: "[W]hat can be established by argumentation from the existence and general features of this world, concerning the uncaused cause of the world, does not directly assist us in answering those practical questions."[46] Finnis also undermines the status of Eternal Law as a real law by eliminating a personal law giver (one who has care of the community). He does not discuss God as a personal being but rather a "state of affairs" which can be conveniently labeled "D."[47] Without a personal law giver, Eternal Law cannot be a real law. Ultimately, Finnis dismisses any consideration of Eternal Law as irrelevant to understanding the Natural Law: "it [Eternal Law] must not be treated as a theory which could guide investigation and verification of suggested norms in any of the four orders; rather it is a speculation about why those norms whose holding has been appropriately verified or established do hold. . . . [and] the speculation that the norms intelligible to us in any of the four orders are expressions or indications of D's[48] creative

---

[about natural law] would have a degree of validity even if we should concede . . . that there is no God or that the affairs of men are of no concern to him").

[44] Westerman, supra note 33, at 136-139.

[45] John Finnis, *Natural Law and Natural Rights* 49 (Clarendon Press 1980). To be fair, Finnis does not dismiss all consideration of God's existence as irrelevant in itself (*per se*) but as irrelevant to the study and application of Natural Law.

[46] Finnis, supra note 45, at 404.

[47] Finnis, supra note 45, at 387.

[48] Although Finnis occasionally, and I would add with hesitation, uses the word God, "D" is his general term for referring to God.

plan in no way warrants the further speculation that D's creative plan is understood by us."[49]

Unlike Grotius and Finnis, Aquinas places Eternal Law as a real law at the very heart of his explanation of Natural Law. It encompasses the entire ordering of the universe by determining what makes each thing what it is (by measuring all things) and by fixing each thing's end (setting its rule). It is the source of obligation for as we have seen the Eternal Law fixes the end and the style for achieving that end. As will be discussed, *infra*, Natural Law is about discovering those ends and types. The source of their obligatory nature is located in this foundation of Eternal Law. As St. Thomas says: "Accordingly all that is in things created by God, whether it be contingent or necessary, is subject to the eternal law."[50] The source of the obligation to conform to the Eternal Law, a question that plagues those who think about law after David Hume, is contained in this nature of Eternal Law as designating the ends of all things. Men have no choice. Men cannot stop being rational or corporeal. They can choose actions which are disoriented; not oriented to the end incorporated in their nature, but they cannot change the imprint of the Eternal Law on them which defines their due end, their style and their art. Just as a builder can build a house either well or poorly, his action is necessarily directed by the personal law giver which lays down the idea and style of building, the architect.

Yet, Eternal Law involves variety within its uniformity. It acts differently upon different aspects of creation. Eternal Law has imprinted on all of nature the principles of action,[51] but different things in nature are imprinted in different ways, depending on whether they are rational or irrational.[52] To understand this statement, one needs to understand how Eternal Law is imprinted on things. Eternal Law contains direction to the end of each thing in the sense of the idea

---

[49] Finnis, supra note 45, at 390.
[50] *Summa Theologica*, I-II, Q. 93 Art. 4.
[51] *Summa Theologica* I-II, Q. 93 Art. 5.
[52] *Summa Theologica* I-II, Q. 93 Art. 5, Reply to Obj. 2.

of the end, the exemplar guiding the route to that end and the skill to achieve it. Thus, Eternal Law determines the essence of things by determining the end of each thing and the means at its disposal to reach that end. In this sense Aquinas says that although Men can make laws about what Men do, human made laws cannot decide and imprint what makes a Man a Man. "[B]ut what pertains to the nature of man is not subject to human government; for instance, that he should have a soul, hands or feet."[53] The Eternal Law determines the "respective inclinations to their [each creature's] respective proper actions and ends."[54] It fixes what makes a dog a dog and a man a man and by so doing it determines the function and end of each thing. This order is ruled by Eternal Law by imprinting the style on each class of created beings. How is each type of creature imprinted with this style; how does it participate in the Eternal Law? Each will do so differently, depending on its nature. Rational creatures are subject to the Eternal Law in all aspects of their nature, including their rationality. Irrational creatures, by definition lacking rationality, are not imprinted with the Eternal Law in a rational way. Thus, irrational creatures are imprinted with the Eternal Law in that they are moved or propelled by it through instinct. Whereas, human beings are imprinted partly in this way but as they possess an additional attribute, reason, the Eternal Law also imprints through reason or understanding of the Eternal Law. "Consequently, irrational creatures are subject to the eternal law through being moved by Divine Providence; but not as rational creatures are, through understanding the Divine commandment."[55] Thus, the way the Eternal Law works in Men is that it "imprints on their minds a rule which is a principle of action."[56] This "rule" is imprinted in the nature of Man and Man cannot but be subject to it. However, the rule serves as a principle for choosing action and since

---

[53] *Summa Theologica* I-II, Q. 93, Art. 4.
[54] *Summa Theologica* I-II Q. 91 Art. 2.
[55] *Summa Theologica* I-II q. 93, Art. 5.
[56] *Summa Theologica* I-II q. 93, Art. 5.

human action is a product of the Will of Man, actions are a matter of choice. Thus, rational creatures, unlike irrational creatures, can choose actions that either accord with the rule imprinted on the mind or that do not. A builder's product may or may not measure up to the designs just as Man's actions may or may not measure up to the idea and exemplar set by Eternal Law.

B. The Relationship between Eternal Law and Justice

Before examining further the role of these natural inclinations imprinted by Eternal Law, it is necessary to pause for a moment to reflect again on Aquinas' general definition of law. It differs from a common conception of law. When one hears the word law, the image of a list or system of detailed rules likely comes to mind. Aquinas has not defined Eternal Law in the same way. Eternal Law is a system but not a system of detailed precepts (as in Divine Law). It is a system explaining things as they are. As Brian Tierney has demonstrated in his discussion of Villey's theory of Aquinas on Natural Law, St. Thomas maintains a distinction between law as describing things they way they are and ought to be and law as a set of precepts.[57] The second sense of the term law seems to dominate later Natural Law thinkers' understanding of all kinds of law to the exclusion of the first. Suarez focuses on law "as binding precepts promulgated to rational creatures only who are directed to a morally good life."[58] As the centuries have gone by this second concept of law, law as precepts, and not the former, law as that which is and ought to be has come to dominate. The two meanings are related for St. Thomas. Law, in the first sense of the state of affairs that exists and that should exist, produces precepts. The former is necessary to produce the latter. It is in this sense that human laws (as precepts) are derived from the Natural Law principles which in turn are derived from the due ends

---

[57] Brian Tierney, *Natural Law and Natural Rights* 23-24 (William B. Eerdsman's Publishing Company 1997).
[58] Westerman, supra note 33, at 82.

contained in the exemplar, idea and type of all laws, the Eternal Law. In this sense, law can be understood both as an objective reality (it exists) and a subjective reaction to that reality (how, in particular, people respond to it). An examination of St. Thomas' definition of *jus* (which as discussed *supra* is that which is just according to the laws of Man as opposed to *fas*) in the *Summa* will assist in understanding this process more fully. St. Thomas considers in depth the meaning of *jus* where he discusses the virtue of Justice. Interestingly many authors who present interpretations of St. Thomas's Treatise on Laws in the *Summa* fail to connect their reading with this later text. The very term *jus*, as we shall see, inextricably connects the idea of detailed laws and the idea of justice.

In Question 57 of the Second Part of the Second Part of the *Summa*, St. Thomas asks whether *jus* is the object of justice. Early in considering this question he dismisses perceptive law (for which he uses the word *lex* which can have the connotation of specific legal enactments) as the object of justice. He says that "law [*lex*] is the object not of justice but of prudence."[59] *Lex* is thus related to the intellectual virtue of prudence whereas, justice is a virtue of the will. Aquinas highlights the distinction when he concludes that, law is not the same thing as *jus* (*lex non est ipsum ius*).[60] By this distinction we can see that *jus*, although often translated as "law" is something greater than particular legal enactments and related to the volitional virtue of justice. St. Thomas indicates that the term *jus* has several different, but related, meanings. It is "the just thing itself" (*ipsam rem iustam*)[61] or as Isidore says in a passage quoted by Aquinas "'*jus* is so called because it is just [*justum*]."[62] What is meant by the "just thing itself" or that which is by its very nature just? It is that which is right or correct, *rectidudino*.[63] Beyond rightness or correctness,

---

[59] *Summa Theologica* II-II Q. 57 Art. 1, Obj. 2.
[60] *Summa Theologica* II-II Q. 57 Art. 1, Reply to Obj. 2.
[61] *Summa Theologica* II-II Q. 57 Art. 1, Reply to Obj. 1.
[62] Isidore, Etymologies. v, 2 quoted by Aquinas in *Summa Theologica* II-II Q. 57 Art. 1 *Sed Contra*.
[63] *Summa Theologica* II-II Q. 57 Art. 1 ("*Sic igitur iustum dicitur aliqu*Ibid*, quasi habens*

"justice implies equality."[64] Drawing on his definition of justice in the next question, Thomas understands the object of the virtue of justice to be rendering "to each one his right or due (*jus suum*)."[65] As is also pointed out in this next article, justice is always in relation to another. Thus, it is not just the way things ought rightly to be in themselves, but right actions in relation to another. *Jus,* as the object of justice, is that which is correct, due and equitable or as John Finnis summarizes "acts, objects and states of affairs, considered as subject matters of relationships of justice."[66]

Drawing on the *Digest*, Aquinas notes that the original meaning of *jus*, as that which is good and equitable, has expanded to encompass a second sense of *jus* as "the art of goodness and equity."[67] Aquinas qualifies this second meaning given in the *Digest* by recasting it as the "art whereby it is known what is just."[68] Since, that which itself is just (*jus*) is the object of justice,[69] we can see the relationship between this art of knowing what is just itself and the definition of justice as "the habit which makes men capable of doing just actions."[70] And justice itself is defined in the next article as "a habit whereby a man renders to each one his due (*jus suum*) by a constant and perpetual will"[71] The term *jus* bridges, in a sense, the intellectual and volitional elements necessary to the habit of justice. To have the constant and perpetual will to render to one his *jus*, a person must possess the art of knowing what is correct, and equitable.

The third meaning of *jus* given in the *Digest* is with respect to particular instances of the exercise of this habit of knowing and willing that which is correct and equitable. *Jus* "refers to the place

---

rectitudinem iustitiae, ad quod terminatur actio iustitiae" "A thing is said to be just, as having the rightness of justice, when it is the end of an act of justice").

[64] *Summa Theologica* II-II Q. 57 Art. 2 Reply to Obj. 3.
[65] *Summa Theologica* II-II Q. 58 Art. 1.
[66] Finnis, supra note 45, at 206.
[67] Justinian, Dig. 1.1. quoted by Aquinas in *Summa Theologica* II-II Q. 57 Art. 1 Obj. 1.
[68] *Summa Theologica* II-II Q. 57 Art. 2 Reply to Obj. 1.
[69] *Summa Theologica* II-II Q. 57 Art. 1.
[70] *Summa Theologica* II-II Q. 57 Art. 1 *Sed Contra*.
[71] *Summa Theologica* II-II Q. 58 Art. 1.

where justice is administered" and "a man, who has the office of exercising justice, administers the *jus*."[72] This most particular meaning of *jus* highlights the connection between *jus* and *lex*. Particular laws (*leges*), which are related to the knowledge of justice through prudence, are "an expression of right [*jus*]"[73] *Jus* is the good and right which the virtue of justice compels one to will towards others. The term *jus* signifies both the justice that is to be known through particular *leges* as well as the justice which the will should continually and perpetually desire to render to others.

To understand this relationship between that which is *jus*, and its particular expression, in a *lex*, Aquinas draws on the analogy, used so extensively in the discussion of Eternal Law, a craftsman or artist. "Just as there pre-exists in the mind of the craftsman an expression of the things to be made externally by his craft, which expression is called the rule of his craft, so too there pre-exists in the mind an expression of the particular just work which the reason determines, and which is a kind of rule of prudence. If this rule be expressed in writing it is called a 'law.'"[74]

In a very subtle way Aquinas has worked out the relationship among Eternal Law, justice and particular law as well as the connection between knowing and willing good, equitable and right actions. *Jus* is the idea, exemplar and art of Justice, just as the Eternal Law acts in such a way for the other forms of law. The Eternal Law fixes the ends (or good) of all created things. *Jus*, as that which is right and equitable in the actions or states of affairs among people, is the idea or end of justice. The virtue of justice is the habit of choosing that which is *jus*, as a consequence of the *jus* having become known through the expression of the *jus* in *lex*. Justice is the imprint of the style or exemplar of the *jus* in *lex*. This virtue is expressed in particular acts of justice, or we could say, particular acts of law. *Jus* can also be said to contain the style for

---

[72] *Summa Theologica* II-II Q. 57 Art. 1 Reply to Obj. 1.
[73] *Summa Theologica* II-II Q. 57 Art. 1 Reply to Obj. 2.
[74] *Summa Theologica* II-II Q. 57 Art. 2 Reply to Obj. 2.

achieving the object of justice, by defining *jus* as the art of knowing what to do in relationships with other people—that which is correct and equitable and then forming the habit of doing them. All laws that follow the exemplar of *jus* are particular expressions of the idea of *jus,* and thus when rendered in a particular place are said to be given *in jure.*[75] This entire discussion is filled with expressions resonating with the language of the earlier discussion of Eternal Law (which used the metaphor of art and God as artificer).

Thus, as St. Thomas argues in Question 57, *jus* and justice are connected; *jus* is the object of justice. The jurist Bulgarus observed that God is the author of justice (*justitia*) whereas Man is the author of human expressions of justice in law (*jus*).[76] Even though Man is the author of *jus* through law, since *jus* is the object of justice (whose author is God), God is the ultimate authority of *jus.* The *jus* may have its direct authority from Man, but it "has its beginning and continued existence through God."[77] That which is good, right and equitable is patterned on or rests upon the Eternal Law of God. As the Eternal Law determines the natures of all things, God determines through the Eternal Law the nature of justice. Justice determines the nature of the *jus.* Laws (*leges*) made by Man have their beginning and existence through God mediated by their particular exemplar or type, *jus,* the object of justice. *Jus* is the exemplar of laws (*leges*) as Eternal Law is the exemplar of all things. The tiny word *jus* thus summarizes and contains an elaborate system of relationships among existence, authority and objects and among God, the Eternal Law, justice, and human law. Further, *jus* establishes a connection between knowing the just (*justitia*) and doing the just thing in a particular case (*suum jus*). By developing his explanation of Eternal Law, Aquinas is able to add a new explanation to the already rich penumbra of meanings surrounding the legal term *jus.*[78] He

---

[75] *Summa Theologica* II-II Q. 57 Art. 2 Reply to Obj. 2.
[76] Bulgarus, *Materia Institutionum,* quoted in Kuttner, supra note 18, at V, 78 ("[S]icut dixi auctor iusticie Deus est, iuris auctor homo est.").
[77] Huguccio, supra note 18, at 19.
[78] See Pennington, supra note 23.

connects the purpose and meaning of a legal system of precepts to the concepts of justice, equity, goodness, rightness and the Divine plan of order (*ratio Divinae Sapientiae*) in the universe known as Eternal Law. This elusive concept of the *jus* is made clearer by the earlier explanation of Eternal Law serving as idea and exemplar. *Jus* is the particular idea and exemplar for laws which is itself contained within the Eternal Law's idea and exemplar of justice.

Having laid this foundation for law and justice, the analysis can ascend to consider the manner in which what might be called the Eternal *jus* is expressed in particular precepts or rules. This process of particularization of *jus* is the Natural Law (*Jus Naturale*).

PART IV

Natural Law

A. Man's Participation in the Eternal Law

Before turning to the understanding of *jus*, the discussion of Eternal Law ended by establishing that rational and irrational creatures participate in the Eternal Law in different ways and that rational creatures participate by being imprinted with a rule that serves as a principle for choosing action. An examination of the relationship between Eternal Law and Natural Law can build on this consideration. As Aquinas says, Natural Law is nothing other than "the participation (*participatio*) of the eternal law in rational creatures."[79] Participation, meaning to take part in (*partem capere*), indicates a process whereby one receives and makes his own something belonging to another.[80] Thus, by his ability to participate in the Eternal Law, a rational creature is both ruled and governed by

---

[79] *Summa Theologica* I-II Q 91, Art. 2.
[80] See Rziha, supra note 34, at 9 (discussing one of Cornelio Fabro's insights with respect to participation and using the analogy of water participating in heat when tepid water is heated).

the Eternal Law from above but also takes part in the Eternal Law by the use of reason.

The nature of this participation may be understood by use of the story of Plato's Cave.[81] A group of prisoners are chained in a cave. They watch shadows on the cave wall in front of them cast by people carrying objects behind them. They pass their time speculating about the shadows they see on the wall. One person is unchained and turns around to see the source of the shadows—the light of a fire and the sun illuminating the artifacts being carried. Although the prisoners made use of their reason to speculate about the images they saw on the cave wall, they could not see (until one was turned around) the source of those images. Socrates explains that the light which was causing the shadows represents "the idea of the good" and "the cause for all things of all that is right and beautiful, giving birth in the visible world to light, and the author of light and itself in the intelligible world being the authentic source of truth and reason."[82] Even though they are initially unaware of the nature of the source of the light, the prisoners' speculation is directed and guided (ruled) by that source. In this sense they participate in that source. It directs the form of their speculation.

Eternal Law has its source outside of the cave of Man's rational thought but it penetrates into and casts shadows on the cave. Eternal Law rules and measures the use of Man's reason but allows for the participation of that reason in reaching conclusions. If anyone has seen children make shadow figures, one immediately realizes that there is scope for "seeing" different images in the shadow but that scope is not unlimited. Its limits are ruled by the form of the shadow cast.

The use of the power of rationality to consider the shadows cast by the Eternal Law is the participation of Natural Law thought. These shadows illuminate the end of Man which Man is capable of understanding through his reason. Such an insight adds a dimension

---

[81] Plato, *Republic*. VII.514a-517b (contained in *Collected Dialogues of Plato*, Princeton University Press 1961).
[82] Ibid. at VIII 517b-c.

to the statement that Man is the image and likeness of God.[83] As John Finnis rightly points out, Man is not an image of God in the sense of a static photograph[84] but rather in the sense that the original of the image serves as an exemplar or rule or idea of Man. As Aquinas explains a created thing "approaches that likeness of God more perfectly than if it were only good in itself if it is not only good but also is able to act for the good of others."[85] Note, to attain perfection in this rule or measure involves individual action (the ability to do good to others). A few lines later Aquinas comments that although all creation is good singly in its individual nature, "but all creation taken together they are exceedingly (*valde*) good, according to the order of the universe, which is the final and noblest perfection of creation."[86] The Eternal Law, the order of the universe, provides the exemplar of Man, the image of God. This image progresses in perfection towards that likeness through actions (ability to do good to others). Natural Law, then, is the ability of humans, as rational creatures, to understand this order of the universe reflecting on and in them, to have a share in the Eternal Reason that promulgated this Eternal Law, and to understand and thus choose actions in accordance with that order.[87]

Aquinas has defined the Natural Law as the participation of the Eternal Law in Man, the rational creature. The Eternal Law sets and illuminates the end of Man and Natural Law involves Man's participation in achieving this end. The nature of this participation

---

[83] Genesis 1: 26-27; Acts 17:28; Colossians 3: 10; cf. Romans 8: 29.

[84] John Finnis, "Reason, Revelation, Universality and Particularity in Ethics," 53 *Am. Jour. Juris.*, 23, 28 (2008).

[85] Aquinas, *Summa contra gentiles* II, c. 45, n. 4 ("*Perfectius igitur accedit res creata ad Dei similitudinem si non solum bona est sed etiam ad bonitatem aliorum agere potest, quam si solum in se bona esset*").

[86] Aquinas, *Summa contra gentiles* II, c. 45, n. 10 ("*Quia singula quidem sunt in suis naturis bona: simul autem omnia valde bona, propter ordinem universi, quae est ultima et nobilissima perfectio in rebus*").

[87] Huguccio also links Natural Law with the divine plan for rationality, inclination and the order of nature. Huguccio, supra note 18, at 18 (*divine: id est a Deo tradite sine ministro, ut lex naturalis que dicitur ratio et que dicitur instinctus et ordo nature. . . .*").

is by contemplating the inclinations present in the form of Man as a rational animal.[88] Natural law consists in the "natural inclinations to proper [in the sense of obligatory] acts and ends" (*inclinationem ad **debitum** actum et finem*).[89] Gratian likewise locates the origin of Natural Law not in some detailed enactment but in natural inclinations present in all peoples.[90] These inclinations, imprinted in the form of Man through which Man can come to know the Natural Law, have their origin in the Eternal Law.[91]

The way in which Man has an inclination to proper acts and ends differs from the natural instinct of animals. Although not present in Aquinas's writing this discussion will use the term inclination to refer to the operation of the unique faculty in Man (not present in animals) but instinct to the faculty that operates in other animals. Inclination has a connotation of bending towards something but not necessarily doing so by automatic reflex. For example Cicero uses the term to describe the changing attitude of the Republic when he says "a certain inclination towards a better hope has been seen to come about."[92] Earlier in the *Summa* Aquinas distinguished man as rational from irrational animals which are moved only by instinct.[93] Animals do not know and choose their ends or their actions. Man on the other hand possesses both natural inclinations (about which he does not have an unrestricted freedom as they just exist in him) and a free will with respect to the pursuit of those ends determined by natural inclinations. He says:

> We have free-will with respect to what we will not of necessity, nor by natural instinct. For our will to be happy

---

[88] See, *Summa Theologica* I, q. 80, art. 1 (observing that "some inclination follows every form").
[89] *Summa Theologica* I-II, q. 91 art. 2 (emphasis added).
[90] Gratian, *Decretum*, D.1 C.7.
[91] See *Summa Theologica*, I, q. 91, art. 2.
[92] Cicero, *Orationes: Cum Senatui gratias egit, Cum populo gratias egit, De domo sua, De haruspicum responso, Pro Sestio, In Vatinium, De provinciis consularibus, Pro Balbo* (ed. Albert Clark) XXXI, 67. ("*fieri quaedam ad meliorem spem inclinatio visa est*").
[93] *Summa Theologica* I q. 18 art. 3.

does not appertain to free-will, but to natural instinct. Hence other animals, that are moved to act by natural instinct, are not said to be moved by free-will.[94]

Man in his nature possesses an innate inclination to be happy but his acceptance of this end as an object of action and the choice of means to it are not pre-ordained as the ends of animals are. Now Man possesses two faculties that animals do not. These faculties interact with this natural inclination, the power to know and the power to choose. In explaining the distinction between the operation of instinct in animals and inclination in Man, Aquinas says:

> Hence such animals as move themselves in respect to an end they themselves propose [Men] are superior to these [animals]. This can only be done by reason and intellect; *whose province it is to know* the proportion between the end and the means to that end, and duly *coordinate* them.[95]

The operation of the rational nature involves an ability to know what particular actions to undertake and to will (coordinate) those actions. Notice, he does not say Man determines his own ends; these exist by natural inclination. What distinguishes Man from animals is the ability to know that end indicated by natural inclination.

The fact that Man has the ability to know (discern and understand) the natural inclinations implies that he has the ability not to know them. Since he has the mere potentiality to know them, he can fail in actualizing it. The natural inclinations can be confused with other feelings or desires. This is because, in addition to natural inclination, Man also has instincts (in the sense of the sole faculty operative in other animals and inclinations acquired by habit[96]). Irrational animals

---

[94] *Summa Theologica* I q. 19 art. 10.
[95] *Summa Theologica* I q. 18 art. 3. (emphasis added).
[96] See J. Budziszewski, *The Line through the Heart* 61-77 (ISI Books 2009) (discussing how unnatural inclinations can be acquired and become co-natural).

cannot be confused about the instincts they have; rational Man can confuse instinctive feelings with natural inclinations. If Man were like irrational animals in this respect, there would be no work in the participation in the Eternal Law. Man would just know the ends and automatically do what appears to be a means to that end. Beyond instincts, Man can also develop habits of vice (*i.e.*, ways of acting which are contrary to the natural ends of Man) which can corrupt natural inclinations.[97] The rational participation in the Eternal Law involves the discernment (knowledge) of the uncorrupted natural inclinations as opposed to the instincts and corrupted inclinations. The work of Natural Law, and a trap for the poor practitioners of it, is to properly separate instinctive feelings (which the reason and will can redirect and control) from the proper natural inclinations of Man. The statement "natural law involves doing what is natural to Man" is laden with potentially dangerous ambiguity. Natural Law is not about merely following innate instinctive feelings but rather orienting them in light of the natural inclination. J Budziszewski coherently distinguishes these two different senses of what is "natural" with the terminology higher and lower nature. He explains:

> According to what might be called the lower meaning, the natural is the spontaneous, the haphazard, the unimproved: think of our first parents in the jungle, or for that matter think of the jungle itself. From this point of view a human being is at his most natural when he is driven by raw desires [what I called instinct], "doing what comes naturally," as we say. But according to what might be called the higher meaning, the natural is what perfects us, what unfolds the inbuilt purposes of our design, what unlocks our directed potentialities. This time think of our first parents not in the jungle but in the Garden, or for that matter think of the Garden itself. From this point of view, a human being is most genuinely "doing what

---

[97] *Summa Theologica* I-II, q. 85, art. 2 (arguing that the natural inclinations, or the "good of nature," cannot be completely destroyed by vice but can be "diminished").

comes naturally" when he is at his best and bravest and truest—when he fulfills his creational design, "when he comes into his own."[98]

We might even add to the end of his last sentence "even when doing so requires controlling what instinct causes him to desire." Failing to recognize these different senses of "natural" and to recognize that the work of participation in the Natural Law is to distinguish and redirect the lower sense has been a great failing of Natural Law critics and some supporters alike. Budziszewski goes so far as to describe this tension between the natural instincts and the natural inclination as the great "scandal" of Natural Law—a scandal that often frightens people away from the fact of Natural Law. He says:

> The natural law scandalizes us because our actual inclinations are at war with our natural inclinations, because our hearts are riddled with desires that oppose their deepest longings, because we demand to have happiness on terms that make happiness impossible.[99]

St. Paul seems to be alluding to this very tension when he says: "For the flesh lusteth against the spirit: and the spirit against the flesh; for these are contrary one to another: so that you do not the things that you would."[100] This war, this scandal within the process of participating in the Eternal Law (this conflict between the natural inclinations and the actual desires or instincts we may feel) is itself not "natural" but a consequence of the Fall,[101] as St. Thomas explains:

---

[98] Budziszewski, supra note 96, at 62-63.
[99] Budziszewski, supra note 96, at 5.
[100] Gal. 5:17.
[101] The effects of the Fall provide further proof of the Eternal Law's status as law. To be law, punishment must follow failure to follow law. When Man acted contrary to the plan of his nature in Eternal Law, the law of the *fomes* became a law of punishment for him. See *Summa Theologica*, I-II, Q. 91, Art. 6.

> As a result of original justice, the reason had perfect hold over the lower parts of the soul, while reason itself was perfected by God, and was subject to Him. Now this same original justice was forfeited through the sin of our first parent, as already stated (81, 2); so that all the powers of the soul are left, as it were, destitute of their proper order, whereby they are naturally directed to virtue; which destitution is called a wounding of nature.[102]

As a result of this wounding of nature "the inclination to the good of virtue [the natural inclination] is diminished in each individual on account of actual sin."[103] Thus, Men cannot always trust their felt inclinations; are they the natural inclinations, the lower instincts or corrupted inclinations? Men need to use their reason to work to distinguish the natural inclinations placed in them according to the plan of God, the Eternal Law, from other impulses lacking proper orientation. The call of the natural inclination within Man is weaker than it ought to be (it is diminished) as a consequence of actual sin. This conclusion implies that the more one sins the greater the diminishment, which fact accounts for the differing struggles of people in making this critical distinction. This insight answers a challenge to Natural Law. If it exists why do so many people get it wrong; why have Men tolerated evils such as slavery, abortion, genocide if the Natural Law directs otherwise? The answer: Men have been participating in the Eternal Law with a great handicap caused by the effect of sin. There is a shadow obscuring the light cast from the Eternal Law on the mind of Man.

Returning to how Aquinas's understands this process of distinguishing the natural inclinations from mere instincts, he argues that it involves two faculties. First, there is the act of the intellect; we "discern what is good and what is evil" by "the light of natural

---

[102] *Summa Theologica* I-II, Q. 85, Art. 3.
[103] Ibid.

reason . . . which is the function of the natural law"[104] Later when Aquinas announces the first precept of the Natural Law, he explains the relation between this knowledge of what is to be done and the second faculty, action: "whatever the practical reason naturally apprehends as man's good (or evil) belongs to the precepts of the natural law as something to be done or avoided."[105] We now see the connection between the Eternal and Natural Law; the Eternal Law or order of the Universe fixes Man's end and illuminates that end through the natural inclinations; the function of the Natural Law is to enable Man to know this end and once known to obligate him to choose actions in accordance with it.

How does Aquinas make the leap from the ability to know what is good to being obligated to do it? The obligation arises from the definition of the "good" spoken of by this first principle of the Natural Law as an end. The "good" is none other than the end of Man, fixed by Eternal Law. Aquinas considers "end" and "good" to be related: "every agent acts on account of an end, and to be an end carries the meaning of to be good."[106] Good and end are also related to a third concept, being. The end of Man is the correspondence of Man to what he is designed to be by the Eternal Law. Aquinas explains: "the good and evil of an action, as of other things, depends on its fullness of being or its lack of its fullness."[107] To make the logic explicit, the end of something is defined as the "good" of that thing and something is judged as good to the extent it achieves the fullness of being. Thus, by substitution, the end of something is to achieve the fullness of being which is "good."[108]

But how is this end (this fullness of being, the good) known? Aquinas says: "Consequently the first principle of the practical reason is one founded on the notion of good, viz. that good is that

---

[104] *Summa Theologica* I-II q. 91 art. 2.
[105] *Summa Theologica* I-II q. 94 art. 2.
[106] *Summa Theologica* I-II Q. 94 Art. 2.
[107] *Summa Theologica* I-II Q. 18 Art. 2.
[108] See Rziha, supra note 34, at 36 ("Thomas argues that although humans make a distinction between goodness and being in their knowledge, they are the same in reality").

which all things seek after."[109] All things by virtue of the imprint of the Eternal Law seek after their natural type, exemplar or idea. The definition of what Man is contains the definition of Man's end. As Professor Maria T. Carl states:

> St. Thomas holds that good and being are really the same, although they differ in their concept of notion (*secundum rationem*) or in thought in that that they are not predicated of a thing in the same way. Being signifies that something is, either absolutely (*per se*) as a substance is, or relatively (*per aliud*) as an accident is. Goodness expresses actuality and perfection, and ultimately goodness expresses the complete actuality of a being.[110]

Man is obligated to do good in the sense that Man is obligated to be himself. Goodness is the perfection (fullness) of Man's very existence. Recently, Pope Benedict XVI echoed this connection between Natural Law and "being" when he defined Natural Law as "the ethical message contained in being."[111] Hence, the relationship between the properly discerned natural inclinations and goodness lies in the fact that Man is inclined to be what he is. Men thus desire, or are inclined towards, the good, the complete or perfect actualization of their being (which is not equivalent to their instincts). In this sense, Man cannot help but be obligated to do good because he cannot help but be what he is. How he knows this fact about himself, is another matter, but the sense of obligation has been located in existence as established by Eternal Law.

---

[109] *Summa Theologica* I-II q. 94 art. 2.
[110] Maria T. Carl, *The First Principles of Natural Law A Study of the Moral Theories of Aristotle and Saint Thomas Aquinas,* 149-150 (Doctoral Dissertation Marquette University December 1989), available at http://epublications.marquette.edu/dissertations/AAI9014051/.
[111] Pope Benedict XVI, *Address to the International Congress on Natural Moral Law*, February 12, 2007, available at http://www.vatican.va/holy_father/benedict_xvi/speeches/2007/february/documents/hf_ben_xvi_spe_20070212_pul_en.html.

Aquinas has defined the object of this natural inclination of Man as "the will to be happy."[112] Professor Carl explains:

> St. Thomas distinguishes two senses of happiness, perfect or supernatural and imperfect or natural. His notion of imperfect happiness, the happiness which can be attained in this life, is a complex concept which explicitly accords with Thomas' understanding of Aristotle's definition of happiness. . . . Final and perfect happiness consists in the direct and immediate contemplation of God, which is attainable only through grace in the afterlife. . . . .St. Thomas is clear that the natural law is ordered to man's natural end and is thus inadequate to direct man to his supernatural end. . . .[113]

Although Professor Carl is correct that the Natural Law is directly operative in relation to the imperfect or natural end of Man, her conclusion may fail to recognize a connection between these two ends. Although the Natural Law is inadequate to attain the supernatural end of Man, it is still necessary to attain that end. One might say the Natural Law is directly oriented to the imperfect happiness but proximately oriented to the perfect. Although the relationship between the Natural and Divine Law requires further elaboration, for now it is sufficient to note that there is a relationship between the natural and the supernatural. The two ends of Man are not disjointed ends of separate roads; the supernatural end subsumes the natural end and thus the Natural end is related, as a part to the whole, to the supernatural end. Similarly, Gratian when defining Human Law explains that it consists in laws established by men "for divine or human reasons."[114] Likewise, Gratian explains that human-made laws "will be all that reason [which term we have seen is an aspect of the Natural Law] has already confirmed – all at

---

[112] *Summa Theologica* I q. 19 art. 10.
[113] Carl, supra note 110, at 153-155.
[114] Gratian, *Decretum*, D.1 C.8.

least that is congruent with religion, consistent with discipline and helpful to salvation."[115] Thus, the natural end of Man, recognized even by Aristotle, is not disconnected from the supernatural end but is a necessary component of it. Although Natural Law is directly related to the natural aspect of the end of Man it is indirectly related to the supernatural.

Aquinas' understanding of this first principle of the Natural Law, good ought to be done, can be restated as what is consistent with what Man is on a natural and then supernatural level ought to be done. This understanding is consistent with the way both Gratian and earlier Roman Law scholars understood the basic precept of Natural Law. In the opening of the *Decretum*, Gratian sums up Natural Law as the Golden Rule: Do to others what you want done to yourself and do not do to others what you do not want done to yourself.[116] Since what everyone wants (in the sense of is naturally inclined to) is the good, the perfection of his nature, the Golden rule commands "do" what the Natural Law says we ought want to be done, the good; avoid the opposite. What Man wants done to him, is associated with what Man is. This connotation is stressed by the common gloss on the text which says "interpret wants as ought to want."[117] This gloss emphasizes the objective nature of inclinations and hence the Golden Rule. It is not do unto others what one subjectively may feel he wants done but what he ought to want done which is *jus suum*. The Digest contains a text from Ulpian stating this same first principle of the Natural Law when he defines the basic principles of *jus* as "to live honestly, to not injure other people, and to render everyone their due (*jus*)".[118] Again, the ideas all tie to back to doing good, consistent with the exemplar of human nature as established by Eternal Law. The *Digest* includes in the notion of *jus* that which is always "good and equitable" which is

---

[115] Gratian, *Decretum,* D. 1 C. 5.
[116] Gratian, *Decretum*, D.1
[117] Ordinary Gloss to *Decretum* D.1.
[118] Justinian, *Dig.*, 1.1.10.1

thus *jus naturale*.[119] Aquinas, Gratian and the Digest's definitions of Natural Law thus accord with one another in their substance.

Since the obligation to do good and avoid evil (Thomas's first precept of the Natural Law) is obligatory because it is a function of being, the next level of precepts necessarily must serve as a definition of "good" based on the being of Man. As Ana Maria Gonzales has said "the reference to good, at the principle level, involves a reference to a not yet specified content."[120] Since the "good" is a function of the nature of things; it is what all things seek after or are inclined towards by their nature, the content can be specified by considering what all things seek after. Put another way, the content summarized by "good" can be found by considering the essence or being of Man as Man, in all his hierarchy of capacities. The good must be broken down into more precise statements relating to the various aspects of Man's existence. Gratian and St. Thomas contain two very similar lists of the next level of detail of the Natural Law (beyond do good and avoid evil.) Gratian includes the following list composed by Isidore:

> The union of men and women, the succession and rearing of children, the common possession of all things, the identical liberty of all, or the acquisition of things that are taken from the heavens, earth or sea, as well as the return of a thing deposited or of money entrusted to one, and the repelling of violence by force.[121]

This list of things according to Isidore are held to be "natural and equitable (*naturale equumque*")*.[122] This last phrase has resonances of one of the definition of the term *jus* from the *Digest*. Its substitution of the word "natural" for "good" is consistent with St. Thomas's

---

[119] Justinian, *Dig.*, 1.1.11
[120] Ana Maria Gonzales, "Natural Law as a Limiting Concept: A Reading of Thomas Aquinas," *Contemporary Perspectives on Natural Law* 24 (Ashgate 2008).
[121] Gratian, *Decretum*, D.1 C.7.
[122] Ibid.

relation of natural being to the good. That which exists by nature (*naturle*) is what is good (*bonum*).

Aquinas' list of the second tier of general principles of the Natural Law although substantially similar, contains some important differences:

> Wherefore according to the order of natural inclinations, is the order of the precepts of the natural law. Because in man there is first of all an inclination to good in accordance with the nature which he has in common with all substances: inasmuch as every substance seeks the preservation of its own being, according to its nature: and by reason of this inclination, whatever is a means of preserving human life, and of warding off its obstacles, belongs to the natural law. Secondly, there is in man an inclination to things that pertain to him more specially, according to that nature which he has in common with other animals: and in virtue of this inclination, those things are said to belong to the natural law, "which nature has taught to all animals" [Pandect. Just. I, tit. i], such as sexual intercourse, education of offspring and so forth. Thirdly, there is in man an inclination to good, according to the nature of his reason, which nauture is proper to him: thus man has a natural inclination to know the truth about God, and to live in society: and in this respect, whatever pertains to this inclination belongs to the natural law; for instance, to shun ignorance, to avoid offending those among whom one has to live, and other such things regarding the above inclination."[123]

Many of the specific precepts included by Aquinas are identical to those in Isidore. St. Thomas, however, adds two important aspects. First, St. Thomas gives an indication of how these principles are proven to be part of the Natural Law. Second he introduces an ordering or hierarchy.

---

[123] *Summa Theologica* I-II Q. 94. Art. 2.

St. Thomas explains that Man is actually a composite of different natural aspects. The good can be defined as a composite construction of the various principles derived from these individual aspects. The inclinations to which each aspect gives rise can be identified. First, St. Thomas identifies that Man, like all other living substances is alive and is inclined to remain alive. Thus the first principle of this second tier of Natural Law is: do "whatever is a means of preserving human life" and avoid "its obstacles." In addition to being a living substance, Man is an animal. All animals are inclined to undertake acts which lead to the pro-creation of more like themselves and to the extent consistent with their particular form care for their young. As man is a rational animal, capable of being educated, this inclination includes for man the "education" of children. Next, Man is distinguished from animals by the presence of a rational soul, one that can know and choose. This dual aspect of Man's soul leads to two more objects of good, knowledge of truth and willed action consistent with man's social nature. The attribute of an intellect makes man capable of, and therefore suited to, knowledge of the truth. Secondly, Man's ability to think about and then choose actions makes Man, in the words of Aristotle "a social and political animal."[124] Irrational animals can live in groups but there interaction is governed by instinct, irrational desire. Man is capable of, and therefore suited to, comprehending the implications of his interactions and capable of choosing among a range of possible interactions. This aspect of Man's nature, unique among animals, makes man both social (coming from *societas*, a chosen association or community of people) and political (again an association which is willed). Finally, Aquinas adds to these natural aspects of Man's nature, the supernatural ability to know not only the truth about the material world but to "know the truth about God."

This last aspect of this definition of the "good" serves as the bridge between the natural and supernatural ends of Man.[125] Much

---

[124] Aristotle *Politics* I.
[125] Budziszewski uses the image of the mezzanine level of a house to describe this

has been discussed over the centuries about Aquinas' conception of the relationship between and separation of the natural and supernatural spheres. I do not intend to engage in that question directly but only wish to note that at least with respect to Natural Law Aquinas clearly sees a relation between Man's natural end and his supernatural end, *beatitudino,* knowledge of God. Thus, although Aquinas understands that complete knowledge of God requires supernatural virtues and grace (which are beyond the reach of Natural Law), some knowledge of God is suitable to human nature. Thus, he presents five proofs for the existence of God in the *Summa* which are based completely on the use of natural reason (not on any supernatural revelation). Although many aspects of the nature of God are unknowable by unaided human reason (i.e. the Trinitarian nature of God), God's existence, his role as uncaused cause of the material world, etc. are accessible by the use of natural reason and obligatory under the precepts of Natural Law. In fact, Man has an inclination to know about these ultimate questions of origin. The connection between natural knowledge of God and supernatural knowledge is analogous to the relationship between Eternal and Natural Law. Man does not know the Eternal Law directly in its entirety. As we have seen, the Eternal Law is the Divine Reason itself, thus beyond Man's natural reason. But Natural Law has been defined as the "participation" of Man in the Eternal Law. Thus, Natural Law, as its very name suggests, functions on the level of the natural world (in Man's natural rational capabilities) but it touches the supernatural in that it is a participation in the Eternal Law.

The second addition by St. Thomas to the list of precepts is an imbedded notion that they exist in a hierarchy. The list is not a random list of elements of the aspects constituting the good. It is an ordered hierarchical structure of definitions. Unfortunately, John Finnis feels compelled to depart from Aquinas's understanding of the good as corresponding to the hierarchical nature of Man's essence. For Finnis, the definitions of the good (which he calls

---

relationship. See Budziszewski, supra note 96, at 195-197.

the basic goods) are comprised of unrelated elements as they are incommensurable.[126] Although Finnis cannot deny that Aquinas lists the elements of the good in a threefold hierarchy, as with Eternal Law, he dismisses the ordering as irrelevant, a "questionable example" which "plays no part in his [Aquinas's] practical (ethical) elaboration of the significance and consequences of the primary precept of natural law."[127]

Possibly, Finnis' hostility to the hierarchical definition of the elements defining the "good" results from a particular visualization of hierarchy. The image of hierarchy Finnis may have in mind might be a product of the Positivist notion of legal hierarchy, such as the Supremacy Clause of the U.S. Constitution. Hierarchy, from this perspective, is a method for determining whose will wins. The top of the hierarchy gets to obliterate or supersede the will of the lower level. "The will of the Prince has the force of law" and it nullifies the will of a lower level. In the American system, a federal statute is supreme over that of a state or municipality. Hierarchy in this sense implies power and victory of the higher level over the lower.

An alternative understanding of hierarchy, which St. Thomas likely had in mind, is necessary to understand the way Aquinas speaks of the hierarchy of the precepts of the Natural Law. Hierarchy can involve not the victory of one thing over another but the enlargement of the lower levels within the higher. Each higher level does not take priority over the lower but rather contains the lower levels within itself plus something additional. Architecturally, one may picture a hierarchy as a pyramid which implies a narrowing as the hierarchy is ascended. Alternatively, the image of an inverted pyramid more accurately portrays this second type of hierarchy. Thus the narrowing and enlarging notions of hierarchy can be constructed thus:

---

[126] See Finnis, supra note 45, at 92-95.
[127] Finnis, supra note 45, at 94.

Hierarchy as Narrowing

Hierarchy as Incorporating Lower Levels

An understanding of the nature of Man as Aquinas sees it clarifies the relationship among the elements of the hierarchy of the good required to be done by the Natural Law. For Aquinas, Man is on a higher level of being than other animals (occupies a higher position in the hierarchy). Yet, Man is not in opposition to animal but rather animal is contained within the definition of Man.[128] Man is a *rational animal*. The higher order, Man, in addition to his unique rationality, contains the lower attributes of irrational animals, which include inclinations to pro-creation and care of offspring. For Finnis, admitting a hierarchy of elements of the good may necessitate choices among them.[129] It would entail a moral system where one resolved conflicts by choosing between conflicting goods, choosing knowledge in opposition to preserving life. Although Finnis concedes that people can and should subjectively order their commitment to one or more of the basic

---

[128] *Summa Theologica* I-II, Q. 94, Art. 2 and I, Q. 2, Art. 1.
[129] See Finnis, supra note 45, at 92-95.

goods,[130] he maintains that "there is no objective hierarchy amongst them;"[131] they are incommensurable.[132] He may be concerned that a hierarchy necessitates moral rules which choose one element in opposition to the other or where one element can become merely instrumental to the higher ranked element.[133] Such a moral system would result in choosing to pursue knowledge and destroy life since knowledge is higher than life in the hierarchy. This may be what Finnis means when he suggests that a hierarchical commensuration of the elements of the good results in fanaticism.[134]

Yet, hierarchy understood as the inverted pyramid where each higher level contains the lower, can never involve an imperative to do something furthering an aspect of the good which necessitates the destruction of another lower element of the hierarchy since the higher good contains within its very own definition the lower. Remembering that for Aquinas "end" and "good" are self referential, he explains this relation among the hierarchical ends of man in his commentary on Aristotle's *Ethics* thus:

> There are also, it seems, many degrees of ends. Some of these we choose purely for the sale of something else, riches, for instance, which are sought for their utility in human living. . . . All such instruments are ends sought merely because of their usefulness. It is obvious that such ends are imperfect [incomplete]. The best end namely the ultimate end, must be perfect [complete]. Therefore if there is only one such end, it must be the ultimate end we are looking for. If, however there are many perfect ends, the most perfect [complete] of these should be the best and the ultimate.[135]

---

[130] See, Ibid. at 93.
[131] See, Ibid. at 92.
[132] Ibid. at 93.
[133] See Ibid.
[134] See Ibid. at 110.
[135] Aquinas, *Commentary on the Nichomachean Ethics*, I Lecture IX, 110 (Dumb Ox Books 1964). I have placed the word "complete" after perfect as a reminder that for Aquinas

Thus a command to do the highest ranked good must be a complete end which contains within it the incomplete ends. Aristotle expresses the concept thus: "we reach the conclusion that the good of man is an activity of the soul in conformity with excellence or virtue, and if there are several virtues, in conformity with the best and *most complete*."[136] The best end necessarily contains within itself all of the other elements of the hierarchy of the definition of that end since to be the best it must be the most complete. In this way one could never say that the injunction to do the good identified as procreation could require one to choose to kill (violate the good of the lower good of preservation of life) because contained within pro-creation is the element of life preservation which is a lower order (less complete good). For example, complying with the highest element of the hierarchy to know the truth about God can never involve a requirement to violate the precept to preserve life. Thus, if one concluded that one will know the truth about God only after this life and thus concluded he should commit suicide so as to further this inclination, this conclusion would be checked by the fact that the element of the good called knowledge of the truth about God contains within it the preservation of human life thus it would be a violation of the very element of knowing the truth about God to take one's life (since not taking life is part of the element of knowing the Truth about God).

This proper understanding of the hierarchy of the second tier specifications of the good not only conveys the idea that each higher level contains the lower orders but also indicates a directional movement, or rule. Recall that Aquinas has defined the "good" commanded by the first principle of the Natural Law both as the "end" of Man (his fullness of being) as well as "that which all things seek after." The cognitive and volitional elements have been combined. The good involves knowing the end and seeking after it or moving towards it. Aquinas combined these two elements in a passage in *De Veritate* when he said:

---

perfection means completeness or fullness of being.
[136] Aristotle, *Nicomachean Ethics* I, 1098a7-18 (emphasis added).

> Since the essence of good consists in this, that something perfects another as an end, whatever is found to have the character of an end also has that of good. [The first element of good is that we know it by that which equates to its perfection or its end.] Now two things are essential to an end: it must be sought or desired by things which have not attained the end and it must be loved by things which share the end, and be as it were enjoyable to them. [the inclination shared by Men or that which all things seek after.][137]

As Aquinas argued in the *Commentary on the Nichomachean Ethics* quoted supra,[138] when faced with a hierarchy of ends we should be ruled by the most complete of those ends, the end which contains all the lower order of ends. Thus, the inclination of Man directs him ultimately upward in the fullness of being towards a higher end. A higher good is to be chosen over a lower good not in the sense of in opposition to but in that by so choosing the higher we choose both the higher and the lower. Thus, the first principle of the Natural Law also contains a rule of direction in decision making oriented towards higher and eventually the ultimate and complete good.[139]

Some conclusions about the content of the principles of the Natural Law can be drawn from this hierarchy of goods or ends. The first principle of the Natural Law contains the precept to "do good." Good is defined as an end directing action. Based on these premises, Aquinas concludes that the Natural Law commands all virtuous acts, acts that are directed towards the hierarchic ends of Man. As he says:

> Thus all virtuous acts belong to the natural law. For it has been stated that to the natural law belongs everything to

---

[137] St. Thomas Aquinas, *De Veritate* 21, 2 (Rome 1970).
[138] See text accompanying note 135, supra.
[139] For a good discussion of this understanding, see Westerman, supra note 33, at 47.

> which man is inclined according to his nature. Now each thing is inclined naturally to an operation that is suitable to it according to its form: thus fire is inclined to give heat. Wherefore, since the rational soul is the proper form of man, there is in every man a natural inclination to act according to reason and thus is to act according to virtue. Consequently considered thus, all acts of virtue are prescribed by the natural law: since each one's reason naturally dictates to him to act virtuously.

Again the interconnection of being (form), inclination to an end and reason are evident. Since Natural Law obligates Man to act always in accordance with his end or that which is good in light of his nature, all acts of virtue are prescribed by the obligation to do good.

The other half of the first precept is the mirror image of the first—"avoid evil." Thus the command to do always what is good contains the opposite command to avoid that which is contrary to the hierarchy of the ends of Man. Thus both Aquinas' and Gratian's primary definition of the Natural Law contains a command and prohibition—Do good and avoid evil[140] and do unto others as you would have done to yourself and avoid doing to others what you would not want done to yourself.[141] Gratian's use of the Golden Rule form of this precept emphasizes its connection to nature and natural inclination. Man is inclined as Aquinas would say to what is good for Man, in accordance with his form and proper ends. Thus what Man is properly inclined toward is what he ought to want done unto himself and what he ought to do to others.

---

[140] *Summa Theologica* I-II Q. 94 Art. 2
[141] Gratian, *Decretum* D.1.

PART V

Conclusions

Stepping back from the specifications of the edifice of laws, what can be said about the relationship between the foundation, Eternal Law, and the frame built on it, Natural Law? First, Eternal Law and Natural Law really are law; they are not, as John Finnis claims, "only analogically law."[142] It is not in the form of Title 3, Chapter 12 sub paragraph 4 etc. But the form of verbosely written laws with which moderns have become all too familiar is not essential to the definition of law. Positivism has limited the nature of law to sets of arbitrary, detailed precepts promulgated by one with power to do so. For classical Natural Law thinkers like St. Thomas, law (in the sense of *jus*) is a much richer, broader concept. Beyond precepts it includes the idea or the exemplar of that which is always good, right and equitable. The idea of law is the exemplar of the just thing itself. It is in this way that law is understood as a rule and measure. The Eternal Law, in which rational creatures participate through the Natural Law, is a real law. It is "the act of God's practical reason commanding all creation to act for its divinely appointed end."[143]

With this understanding of *jus* in mind, *jus naturale* is really a rule and measure of willed action determined by the Eternal Law. It is a rule because its principles are the exemplar of the proper end of action. It acts as a directing rule because its principles identify and elucidate the hierarchy of ends of Man's nature flowing out of the Eternal Law. In light of these ends Men can measure to what extent

---

[142] Finnis, supra note 45, at 280. In this quotation Finnis is only speaking of Natural Law, not Eternal Law. Given his dismissal of Eternal Law at the end of the book I doubt he would disagree with applying this phrase to it as well. Also, in certain contexts, Finnis might consider some principles of Natural Law as real law but I believe in the context of the discussion where he uses this phrase (the relationship between Natural Law and positive law) he clearly does not consider Natural Law to function as a real law in conjunction with positive law.

[143] Rziha, supra note 33, at 34.

proposed courses of action are oriented towards or in opposition to one or more of those ends. As a rule a principle such as preserve human life, exists to guide decision making by providing a goal or end. It serves to measure the advisability of a proposed course of action in light of the good embodied in it. Thus, if it is proposed that elderly people should be euthanized to save money for the healthcare system, this does not measure up to the end of preservation of life as a rule.

Eternal and Natural Law have also been promulgated by one having care for the common good of the community. As a universal law the community affected is all of Mankind. He who promulgated the Eternal and the Natural Law participation in it is the One with ultimate care for this community, its Creator. Natural Law is concerned with the common good of that community as its principles address the common ends (or good) of all members of that community, Men. The Natural Law has really been promulgated by God through the Eternal Law which itself has been promulgated through the mystery of the Word. Natural Law participates in the recognition of the imprinted natural inclinations by the rational faculty of Man. The Eternal Law which fixes the ends (or good) of Mankind is made temporal and concrete in the rational mind of Man to the extend it participates in this order by recognizing the imprint of Eternal Law.

This participation is not without difficulty. Due to the Fall, Man labors under the difficulty of seeing natural inclinations through the shadows of other instincts and affections. This discernment resides in the intellect, for it is here that the Eternal Law has made its imprint. This intellectual act of discerning the natural inclinations and their resulting hierarchy of ends gives rise to an act of the will, the choice of action.

Understanding the relation between intellect and will in this theory of Natural Law returns an important balance to the process of thinking about the making of human laws. After centuries of Legal Positivism, law making is generally associated with an act of the will. A law is a law because it has been willed by the applicable legislator. The alternative vision places a striking emphasis on the intellectual capacity of the soul. The participation of Natural Law requires the intellectual act of discerning amidst the shadows of inclinations the natural inclinations, identifying the ends to which they tend, and drawing correct conclusions from them. Clearly Natural Law involves volition; its first precept is that "good must be done." Yet, complying with "do good" presupposes an intellectual activity of discerning what is good or what is an end. Natural inclinations do not point to any end but "towards a proper act and end" (*ad debitum actum et finem*).[144] The process is analogous to the act of building a house, which presupposes knowledge about what properly constitutes a house. Loss of attention to the intellectual prerequisite to the process of law making has resulted in a philosophy and a legal system rooted in power manipulation and coalition forming. Modern law is all about exercising power. A law can be shown to be rational because it is internally consistent; it is actually directed to whatever end the will of the legislator, or the will of those he represents, has chosen. Natural Law involves demonstrating not only internal consistency but also that the end of the law is inclined to a due end contained in the idea and exemplar of the blueprints of the Eternal Law.

Yet constructing Natural Law on this foundation of the Eternal Law raises a fundamental question. Natural Law theory embodied in Gratian and St. Thomas is an entire metaphysical system of law. It is a grand design of law. Natural Law rests on the foundation of the Eternal Law. The natural inclinations towards the good (or ends of Men) bind Men to rule and measure decisions in light of them because those natural inclinations have been fixed and promulgated through the Eternal Law. The obligatory nature of Natural Law is connected to the process of the rational participation in the Eternal Law, the attempt to conform the order of Man's mind to the order of its reality. Men cannot help but participate in the Eternal Law

[144] *Summa Theologica* I-II, q. 91 art. 2.

as it is imprinted in their very being. Men can participate well or poorly but their rational nature makes Men inextricably bounded by the Natural Law which itself is ruled by the style of the Eternal Law. This great question therefore can be phrased: "Is the Natural Law of any practical relevance to one who does not acknowledge God's existence?" Put more parochially, can an atheist talk about and accept Natural Law? Are arguments of Natural Lawyers of no use in an atheistic age?

The answer to this question is qualified. In one sense the answer is no. The Natural Law is utterly dependent upon the entire grand design of an edifice of law of which it is a part.[145] One cannot ultimately explain the obligatory nature of Natural Law without eventually some reference to the foundation on which it rests. "If they [laws] be just, they have the power of binding in conscience from the eternal law, whence they are derived."[146] Thus, the obligatory nature of all law is rooted in the foundation of the Eternal Law. To the extent a law is derived correctly through the process of participation in the Eternal Law, it is obligatory. If the Eternal Law is struck out from the system, Natural Law is a loose frame, floating in space. The foundation of its obligation has been severed. When thinkers like John Finnis dismiss God's Will (expressed through the Eternal Law) as the ultimate source of obligation,[147] all that remains is a justification of obligation which bears an air of utilitarianism. Law is obligatory because we need it to be. The ultimate source of obligation for Finnis lies in the following principles: "that the common good is to be advanced, that authoritative determination of co-ordination problems is for the common good, and that legal regulation is (presumptively) *a good method of authoritative determination.*"[148] Law is obligatory because it is a good (useful)

---

[145] *Summa Theologica*, I-II, q. 19, art. 4 ("It is from Eternal Law . . . that human reason [*i.e.*, Natural Law] is the rule of the human will").
[146] *Summa Theologica* I-II, Q. 96, Art. 4.
[147] John Finnis, supra note 45, at 342-343 (dismissing the notion of obligation in God's Will as "conceptually misdirected").
[148] Ibid., at 335 (emphasis added).

method for solving co-ordination problems.[149] Even Finnis acknowledges that this need based justification for law's obligatory force leaves questions unanswered.[150] When Natural Law theory is rooted in the Eternal Law, principles of Natural Law are recognized by the use of reason but are obligatory because they are contained within the Eternal Law.

Yet, the understanding of legal obligation rooted in the foundation of Eternal Law does not lead to legal obligation becoming mere "mechanics"[151] as it may in extreme voluntarist theories of legal obligations. As this Article has shown, the Will of God expressed in the Eternal Law is "the plan of Divine *Wisdom*."[152] Thus, a theory of Natural Law rooted in the Eternal Law is inextricably connected to both reason (Eternal Law is the plan of the Divine Wisdom) and an act of the will (in the promulgation of the Eternal Law).[153] Natural Law is obligatory because it is the participation in a higher law, a law of reason promulgated by the command of an ultimate lawgiver. Severed from Eternal Law, explanations of the obligatory aspect of Natural Law ultimately end at an unsatisfactory and incomplete utilitarian argument of some sort. Thus, it would seem that it is impossible to discuss Natural Law without reference to at least some understanding of the rational Divine lawgiver.

---

[149] Certainly Finnis' understanding of the common good is much more nuanced and encompassing than utilitarian notions of utility and preference. Finnis' argument is not therefore strictly speaking utilitarian; yet its source of ultimate justification bears similarity to utilitarian logic. Law is obligatory because it works, not because it conforms to the way the Divine artificer intended it.

[150] Ibid., at 343.

[151] Ibid., at 342.

[152] *Summa Theologica*, I-II, Q. 90, Art. 3 (emphasis added).

[153] For Aquinas, the act of commanding (promulgating a law) is an act of reason; yet this act of reason itself involves an act of the will. See *Summa Theologica* I-II, Q. 17, Art. 1. ("Command is an act of the reason presupposing, however, an act of the will."). When considering whether law is an act of the reason or the will, St. Thomas concludes it is an act of the reason yet references this earlier discussion as a reminder that this act of the reason in commanding presupposes an act of the will as well. See Ibid. at I-II, Q. 90, Art. 1., Reply to Obj. 3.

Yet, the rational nature of Man means that he cannot, in a certain sense, help but participate in the Eternal Law (by being rational). Whether he is aware of it or not, the "natural guide of reason impels towards that which is contained in the law of God."[154] Thus, even one not acknowledging God (and hence the Eternal Law) if following the natural guide of reason[155] is participating in the Eternal Law. The denial of God's existence may affect one's ability to observe and consider the natural inclinations, but it does not obliterate them. Even if he does not turn around and see the source of the shadows cast by the Eternal Law in the cave of rationality, a Man is still able to consider what the shadows, as shadows, mean. He may not know the source of light causing them; yet he sees them nonetheless. As St. Thomas says:

> [S]ince all things ... are ruled and measured by the eternal law ... it is evident that all things partake somewhat of the eternal law, in so far as, namely, from its being imprinted on them, they derive their respective inclinations to their proper acts and ends.[156]

By making use of reason to discern the ends illuminated by the natural inclinations one is participating in the Eternal Law. As the example of Aristotle shows, even without revelation or a clear articulated understanding of Eternal Law, human rationality can arrive at certain principles and conclusions of the Natural Law. As Scripture affirms the Natural Law is available to all (even those who have not heard the specific revelation of the Artificer of the Eternal Law. "For when the Gentiles, who have not the law, do by nature those things that are of the law; these having not the law are a law to themselves: Who shew the work of the law written in their

---

[154] Huguccio, supra note 18, at 19 ("*quia ad ea que in divino iure continentur natrualis ductus rationis ... impellit*").
[155] "*Naturalis ductus rationis*" is a phrase used by Huguccio to describe the natural law. See *e.g.*, Huguccio, supra note 18, at 19.
[156] *Summa Theologica* I-II, Q. 91, Art. 2.

hearts, their conscience bearing witness to them. . . ."[157] The law written on the heart, the natural inclinations, is the starting point of all reasoning. This is because all rationality begins with what is known naturally. As St. Thomas explains early in his *Treatise on Laws*:

> Every act of reason and will in us is based on that which is according to nature . . . for every act of reason is based on principles that are known naturally. . . . Accordingly the first direction of our acts to their end must needs be in virtue of the natural law.[158]

Men begin reasoning by examining what is known naturally. They hence begin to participate in the Eternal Law without realizing they are doing so.[159] When they do so, they are making use of the Eternal and Natural Law even if not calling it such. In a sense, one can engage all Men in discussion of the Natural Law particularly at the level of its most basic principles which are directly derived from the natural inclinations. Yet, as St. Thomas emphasizes, this step is only the "first direction" on which the use of reason is "based." Ultimately contemplating the framework of what is known naturally will lead to questions of origin. Some knowledge of God is accessible to the mind even without the supernatural aid of grace (as demonstrated by St. Thomas' proofs for God's existence). Participating in a reasonable inquiry based on what is known naturally will, naturally, lead to the Eternal Law since it is none other than a participation in it. Thus, discussions of Natural Law may commence without explicit incorporation of Truths about God and the Eternal Law, but it is unnatural to think the entire exercise can proceed without

---

[157] Rom. 2: 14-15.
[158] *Summa Theologica*, I-II, Q. 91, Art. 2, Reply to Obj. 2.
[159] See Clifford Kossel, "Natural Law and Human Law," *Ethics of Aquinas*, 171-93 (Georgetown University Press 2002) (explaining that although in the order of causation the Eternal Law precedes the Natural Law yet in the order of knowledge, we come to know the Natural Law first and then come to know its cause, the Eternal Law).

reaching eventually that in which one is participating. The time for integration of the framework with the foundation may vary but the Eternal Law is not as Finnis suggests irrelevant for Natural Law just as the foundation of a house is not irrelevant to the frame, even though one may not initially see the foundation covered over by the frame.

Not seeing the foundation at first is one thing; removing the frame from it is quite another. Such an exercise is doomed to ultimate failure. Doing so leaves the Natural Law drifting without a mooring where it cannot stand. Natural Law itself will eventually crumble leaving only human positive law subject to no other rule or measure than that which it makes for itself. Natural Law without God although capable of stumbling upon individual successes along the way ultimately is building a house on bear ground. As J. Budzieszewski remarks:

> That was the Enlightenment's project. Little by little, natural law thinkers scrubbed from their little cups of theory whatever grime of influence might have remained from the centuries of faith, whatever benefit they might have gained from the teacher's help. . . . In the end they found that they had scoured away the ground that they were standing on.[160]

To avoid such a collapse Natural Law theory needs to be firmly rooted within the context of the entire edifice of which it is a part. This does not mean that every argument regarding a particular contingent matter needs to explicitly reference the Eternal Law. Yet, to avoid ultimate collapse at the theoretical level, defense and exposition of Natural Law must rest explicitly on an understanding of the foundational role of Eternal Law. Since the very concept of justice itself is caught up in the idea of Eternal Law even justice itself cannot stand without the foundation.

---

[160] Budziszewski, supra note 96, at 59.

In 1993, John Paul II clearly rejected building Natural Law on pure rationality not rooted in a recognition of the Eternal Law:

> Some people, ... disregarding the dependence of human reason on Divine Wisdom and the need, given the present state of fallen nature, for Divine Revelation as an effective means for knowing moral truths, even those of the natural order, have actually posited a "complete sovereignty of reason" in the domain of moral norms regarding the right orderings of life in this world. ... In no way could God be considered the Author of this law . . . . These trends of thought have led to a denial, in opposition to Sacred Scripture (Mt. 15:3-6) and the Church's constant teaching, of the fact that the natural moral law has God as its author, and that man, by the use of reason, participates in the eternal law, which it is not for him to establish. . . .[161]

Ultimately, a complete understanding of Natural Law avoids the error of natural lawyers merely trying to beat the positivists at their own game and thus in practice becoming positivists themselves. If one merely seizes the will of the prince and changes the law by force of conquering the system (by relying on disembodied rational argument) a natural lawyer will have won a battle but lost the war. What needs to change even more desperately than individual unjust human laws (of which there is a plethora today) is the entire philosophical and jurisprudential foundation of the system. For when the system rests on the will of the prince or the will of the Supreme Court or the will of the people, it is easily changed with a change of power or judge or public opinion. The war will only be won when the entire understanding of the system of law is changed.

Positivism has swelled the greatness of Human Law by exalting it as the only law, casting aside the Eternal and with it the Natural Law. It has thus cast aside the heart of Natural Law, the unique role of Man as rational. Law has become its own justification severed

---

[161] John Paul II, *Veritatis Splendor* No. 36.

from the rational participation of a rational creature Man in the Eternal plan of the universe. By denying the fact that making law involves this rational participation of Man in the Eternal Law we have become "an empire of laws, and *not of men.*"[162] Only men can attain rational participation in the Eternal Law for only men (and not laws) have rational faculties. A government not of men is therefore not one of rational participation in the exemplar or idea of the way things ought to be. Such an empire of laws and not of Men is therefore an empire with no foundation, nor rules and nor measures. Its laws are therefore not rational. Since law must stand with reason, ironically a government merely of laws is lawless. By cutting away the foundation, positive law is all that remains, making it supreme. The result is exactly what Cicero predicted, the greater the law, the greater the injuries. The world has seen inflicted more injuries than Cicero could have imagined under, through and in the name of the rule of laws. It is time that Natural Law put human law back where it belongs within the architectural structure of law. It is time to construct a government of Men and not of mere laws built on the foundation of the Eternal Law and framed by the principles derived from natural inclinations discerned by the use of reason.

---

[162] John Adams, *Thoughts on Government,* Ch. 4, Document 5, Papers 4:86-93 (April 1776) (emphasis added).

LAW WITHOUT DISGUST: A FETID FREEDOM
Matthew Jordan Cochran

INTRODUCTION

Having forgotten to pay the water bill, and parched by noontime summer heat, a young man seizes the only source of refreshment to be found in his refrigerator: an old carton of milk. Opening the carton unleashes an unpleasant odor. Fighting the cue to retch, he notes the milk's expiration date was weeks ago. He nevertheless concludes any risk of drinking it is outweighed by the urgency of his thirst. With steely resolve, the bachelor furrows his brow and lifts the flimsy box to his lips, draining its viscous contents in an heroic quaff. After an eerie (but brief) gastrointestinal calm, he begins to vomit uncontrollably. Later that day, he is hospitalized.

Meanwhile, a nursing home patient living in a persistent, near-vegetative mental state has been raped. The defendant has refused a plea bargain, and his criminal trial will soon be underway. The following colloquy took place during voir dire between the prosecutor and Juror Five:

> PROSECUTOR: Is there any reason you cannot sit as an impartial juror in this case, in which the defendant is charged with first degree rape?
> JUROR: No.
> PROSECUTOR: Do you understand that the State must show beyond a reasonable doubt that the defendant is guilty as charged?
> JUROR: Yes.
> PROSECUTOR: Do you approve of people who have intercourse with animals?
> JUROR: No.
> PROSECUTOR: How about sex with human corpses? Anything wrong with that?
> JUROR: Well, that's different. Animals cannot consent to

the act, and that's what makes it wrong. But a dead body is just a pile of molecules, so sex with a corpse doesn't hurt anybody.

Hearing this, the prosecutor sighed with disgust, and notified the trial judge that he would be exercising a peremptory challenge, striking Juror Five.

If Juror Five is a minority, an appellate judge may be faced with the task of reviewing the peremptory challenge as racially discriminatory and the prosecutor's line of questioning as a mere pretext for a race-neutral reason to strike the juror. She might ultimately consider whether the forces influencing the prosecutor's response to Juror Five are the same forces at work in the bachelor's mind and senses, and whether they should have been allowed to affect the legal outcome. Likewise, scholars have asked whether these forces may properly inform the law of a society committed to a liberal respect for pluralism. While such "forces" arguably are more complex than any single label can convey, I shall call them *disgust*. May disgust, then, function on some level as a normative influence operating to shield persons from what is revolting, and even delimiting a perimeter beyond which otherwise harmless, self-regarding conduct becomes legally regulable?

Professor Martha Craven Nussbaum answers these questions in the negative. In *Hiding from Humanity* and subsequent pronouncements on the topic, she has offered a meandering commentary against the legal relevance of disgust, her arguments hung loosely upon a psychoanalytical and empirical claim that disgust fuels hierarchical stigma and discrimination in the law and thereby dehumanizes us.[1] Writing prior to Nussbaum, Dr. Leon

---

[1] See, e.g., Martha Craven Nussbaum, *Hiding from Humanity* (2004); Martha Craven Nussbaum, "Danger to Human Dignity: the Revival of Disgust and Shame in the Law," *Chronicle Rev.*, Aug. 6, 2004, at B6, available at http://chronicle.com/free/v50/i48/48b00601.htm; see also Paul Corcoran, "The Rhetoric of Shame in the Lachrymose Country," *Australian Rev. Pub. Affairs*, Nov. 8, 2004, http://www.australianreview.net/digest/2004/11/corcoran.html (complaining that *Hiding from Humanity* "has a tendency to

Kass defended something akin to disgust, maintaining that our "repugnance" response is undergirded by a wisdom that cautions against even incremental encroachments on our unique dignity as humans.² Kass's disapproval of inroads on our "*given* human nature" have earned him broad criticism.³

In Part I of this Article, I probe both Nussbaum's and Kass's positions regarding the nature of disgust, observing how these arguments fit with their authors' respective notions of respect for persons. I delve more critically into Nussbaum's arguments in Part II, identifying key inconsistencies and suggesting that much of her "original" analysis is dangerously irrelevant, distracting us from its real-world implications. Having accounted for these analyses, I suggest in Part III that if law cannot be based on disgust, society may find itself with no way to combat practices which have dehumanizing effects.

In essence, I argue that respect for human dignity may be honored in our system of laws by reference to the lesson learned

---

ramble and wander, revisiting problems again and again that might have been dealt with once and for all").

² See Leon R. Kass, "The Wisdom of Repugnance," *New Republic*, June 2, 1997, available at http://www.catholiceducation.org/articles/medical_ethics/me0006.html.

³ Ibid. (emphasis added); see, e.g., Posting of Damon Linker to New Republic Blog, http://blogs.tnr.com/tnr/blogs/linker/archive/2009/04/02/x.aspx (April 2, 2009, 22:18 EST) ("[A]s any number of people have argued against Kass, the 'yuck' response is an extremely weak basis on which to build an argument about [human] nature because the things that disgust human beings change so much over time, and because such responses are so often wrapped up with ignorance and prejudice."). Nussbaum herself paints Kass's argument as "nothing more than superficial rationalization" and a "startling and novel theological position" that is unlikely "to persuade someone who does not accept that particular religious teleology." Nussbaum, supra note 1, at 81, 82. Given this anti-Kassian current, my contentions in this Article are directed at Nussbaum's account, which—in spite of what I shall identify as its inconsistencies and dubious relevance—has been received rather warmly. See, e.g., Stefanie A. Lindquist, Book Review, 14 *Law & Politics Book Rev.* 708, 710 (2004) (hailing "Nussbaum's exceptionally thorough evaluation of shame, disgust and the law" as "a remarkably wide ranging and nuanced treatise"); John Wilson, "You Stink, Therefore I Am: Philosophers Ponder the Meaning of Disgust," *Boston Globe*, May 2, 2004, http://www.boston.com/news/globe/ideas/articles/2004/05/02/you_stink_therefore_i_am (describing the anti-disgust arguments advanced by Nussbaum as "characteristically lucid").

from the bachelor's nausea and similar reactions of disgust or repugnance.[4] The political result envisioned by Nussbaum would actually frustrate her own stated objectives, precipitating human *in*dignity and (inevitably) promoting mutual avoidance. Rather than mandating a state of sordid separatism and nominal equality, a Kassian appreciation for disgust would provide us with extrapolitical *reasons* to cherish human dignity as well as *incentives* to cultivate mutual respect and constructive social compassion.[5]

I. A PRIMITIVE SHRINKING—OR WISDOM?

I now address the Nussbaumian and Kassian presentations of disgust. My objective is not to peel the entire phenomenological onion surrounding this emotion.[6] Rather, I will identify and then

---

[4] Compare William O. Krohn & Samuel J. Crumbine, *Graded Lessons in Physiology and Hygiene* 42 (1919) (warning, even some fifty years after the advent of pasteurization, that "[i]t is unsafe to drink milk which is the least bit sour"), with Marlene Zuk, *Riddled with Life: Friendly Worms, Ladybug Sex, and the Parasites that Make Us Who We Are* 229 (2007) (reporting an increase in women's perception of what is disgusting during pregnancy, measuring their disgust-based responses to "potentially disgusting situations, like being about to drink spoiled milk").

[5] Cf. Nussbaum, supra note 1, at 105.

[6] For some of that discussion, see William Ian Miller, *The Anatomy of Disgust* (1997), upon whom Nussbaum has relied heavily in making her psychological and social-stigma arguments, though she finds fault with some of his conclusions. Cf. Michael Hauskeller, "Moral Disgust," 13 *Ethical Perspectives* 571 (2006) (investigating our responses to various outrages, and arguing that there is such a thing as "moral" disgust distinct from the nausea-type disgust, and that the former can be relied upon); Robert Weisberg, "Norms and Criminal Law, and the Norms of Criminal Law Scholarship," 93 J. *Crim. L. & Criminology* 467, 575–87 (2003) (outlining responses to Miller's book made by Dan M. Kahan in "The Anatomy of Disgust in Criminal Law," 96 *Mich. L. Rev.* 1621 (1998), in which he argues that even the liberal cause advances by utilizing "good" disgust against those who promote illiberal values—an argument distinct from my own); Kathryn Abrams, Colloquium, "'Fighting Fire with Fire': Rethinking the role of Disgust in Hate Crimes," 90 *Cal. L. Rev.* 1423 (2002) (criticizing Kahan's arguments in terms eerily similar to those used by Nussbaum—without reference—roughly two years later). But it is beyond the purposes of this Article to regurgitate the vast body of scholarship on disgust. What is important here is to understand the portrayal of disgust in the competing (yet in some senses compatible) accounts of Kass and Nussbaum, and then to see (more particularly) that Nussbaum's respect for equal dignity is not well-served by her arguments.

work from Nussbaum's description of disgust as an "emotion."[7] And because both Nussbaum and Kass have hung their hats (in different ways) on notions of human dignity, this discussion will identify their competing conceptions of what such dignity actually *is*, and of what it means to be human.

Nussbaum, claiming the auspices of political liberalism, describes mankind as simply a human animal, whose dignity stems from his capacities and whose disgust is a panicked response to reminders of his own animality, leading him to oppress others.[8] Kass appears to recognize that simply *being* human is hierarchic, and that disgust plays a part in conforming man to the image of God.[9] So against what is essentially Nussbaum's obeisance to *animality* as chief among "psychological foundations of liberalism,"[10] I will describe elements of Kass's discourse on the wisdom of repugnance and on his conception of human nature.

---

[7] See Nussbaum, supra note 1, at 36, 70. Again, I decline here to rehash the multitude of observations on disgust offered by the "cognitive sciences" not because it is inconvenient to do so, but because those observations are not relevant. For is not some faulty conclusion regarding the "cognitive content" of disgust (as Nussbaum describes it) that fuels my objections to her argument *qua* argument, but rather, the pockmarked nature of her attack on this universal emotion's role in law and liberty—an attack hostile to Nussbaum's own goals, as I will argue in Part III.

[8] See Julian Sanchez, "Discussing Disgust: On the Folly of Gross-Out Public Policy (An Interview with Martha Nussbaum)," *Reason*, July 15, 2004, http://www.reason.com/news/show/33316.html (describing disgust as "inherently hierarchical" and "set[ting] up ranks and orders of human beings").

[9] See *Charlie Rose: A Conversation About Bioethics with Leon R. Kass* (PBS television broadcast July 1, 2003), available at http://www.charlierose.com/view/interview/1904 ("There's nothing that I know as a scientist that requires me not to follow and somehow trust [the Genesis] account for what that account has to show us; [and] the most important thing in that is that 'being' is somehow hierarchic; that man is higher than the son; that man is somehow the most Godlike of beings—because he somehow participates in freedom and reason and concern and judgment, like the story says the Creator does.").

[10] Nussbaum, supra note 1, at 16.

A. Nussbaum: Disgust as a Stigmatizing and Irrational Shrinking from Contamination

Martha Nussbaum devotes much of her discussion in *Hiding from Humanity* to "evaluat[ing] people's emotions and judg[ing] that some are based on a more reasonable appraisal of important goods than others."[11] One key facet of her case against disgust is an argument that the "evaluative beliefs" underlying it are "irrational or unreasonable," and that therefore it should be rejected as a basis for law because it is "groundless, based on . . . bad thinking."[12] So Nussbaum first attempts to establish that disgust is "problematic in *principal*."[13] In the process, she argues that disgust is problematic in *practice*.[14]

In developing her account of the evaluative beliefs inherent in disgust, Nussbaum observes that "appeals to emotion are prominent in the law" (presumably, American law).[15] Some of these appeals have been held essential to justice, like those made to the compassion of jurors during the penalty phase in a capital case.[16] Sometimes even the emotional response of the criminal defendant himself—such as his anger upon learning of the gross molestation of his child—may reduce his act of murder to manslaughter.[17] These emotions are recognized as having been "reasonable" under the circumstances,

---

[11] Ibid. at 56; see also ibid. at 34 ("[A]ppraisals of evaluative beliefs are central to the roles played by emotion in the law.").
[12] Ibid. at 33 (internal quotation marks omitted).
[13] Ibid. at 107 (emphasis added).
[14] E.g., ibid. at 122; See also Wilson, supra note 3 (observing that "[Nussbaum] wants to draw attention to the way in which disgust has often gone hand-in-hand with prejudice," and stating that "[i]n this connection her argument has an immediate practical application to the law"). Ultimately, however, the relationship between Nussbaum's principle and practical emphases is not so simple as this bifurcated description would suggest.
[15] Nussbaum, supra note 1, at 21.
[16] See ibid. at 69. North Carolina's former death penalty statute, for example, was held unconstitutional because it did not allow defendants to "appeal to the compassion of the jury" by presenting their life story during sentencing. Ibid. (discussing Woodson v. North Carolina 428 U.S. 280, 303 (1976)).
[17] See ibid. at 102.

though not necessarily "rational."[18] Nussbaum points out that, generally speaking, giving emotions a place in law is in keeping with her view of political liberalism,[19] which resembles that of John Rawls.[20] Anger, for instance, can be explained without reference to any particular religious or ontological view that falls outside the overlapping social consensus.[21] She has since explained, "If my child has been murdered and I am angry at that, I can persuade you that you should *share* those reasons; if you do, you will come to *share* my outrage."[22]

On the other hand, Nussbaum posits that "certain emotions are especially likely to be repositories of . . . unreasonableness."[23] Such emotions reflect views that are in conflict with the social consensus because they are not "based upon reasons that can be publicly shared."[24] Surely in certain cases, even anger might not have been a reasonable response, and in those cases it would not justify mitigation.[25] But Nussbaum maintains that there are certain whole categories of emotions—not just instances of the response they produce—that may *never* be reasonable, regardless of the facts or beliefs by which they are triggered.[26] Because of this, she is skeptical of legal practices that are "too deferential to prevailing norms in emotion."[27] She asks, "What norms of reasonableness in emotion are the right ones to build into the law, both expressing and nourishing appropriate emotions in its citizens?"[28] By "appropriate," of course, she means accordant with political liberal values.[29]

---

[18] See ibid. at 33, 68

[19] See ibid. at 57 (confronting the "imagined liberal objection" to her view of "the role of emotions in the law").

[20] See ibid. at 153.

[21] See ibid. at 61 (agreeing with Rawls' conception of core liberal values).

[22] Sanchez, supra note 8 (emphasis added).

[23] *Hiding from Humanity*, supra note 1, at 36 (emphasis added).

[24] Ibid. at 75 (distinguishing "indignation" as based on reasons that are publicly shared).

[25] Ibid. at 69–70.

[26] Ibid. at 69.

[27] Ibid. at 36–37.

[28] Ibid. at 16 (emphasis added).

[29] Cf. Sanchez, supra note 8 ("[A]nyone who cherishes the key democratic values of

Her answer here involves an evaluation of the cognitions these emotions embody and a determination of "how *reliable* they are likely to be given their specific subject matter and their typical process of formation."[30] "[T]he specific cognitive content of disgust," she argues, "makes it of dubious reliability . . . , especially in the life of the law."[31]

Rejecting the idea of emotions being "unthinking forces,"[32] Nussbaum looks to psychological research in unearthing these cognitions.[33] According to psychoanalytic psychologists, the primary objects of our disgust include feces, decaying corpses, rotting foods, and the like.[34] Nussbaum has characterized our disgust for these nauseating substances as a useful heuristic that "very likely played a valuable role in our evolutionary heritage," steering us away from real danger.[35] (Recall our example of the spoiled milk.) On these

---

equality and liberty should be deeply suspicious of the appeal to [certain] emotions in the context of law and public policy.").

[30] Ibid. at 74 (emphasis added).

[31] Ibid. But as we will see, the *purpose* for which law might errantly "rely" on an emotion is not entirely clear. One reviewer explained that "[b]ecause disgust may often be linked to . . . 'group-based thinking' through the emotion's social construction, Nussbaum finds it particularly unreliable as a guide for the legal regulation of human action." Lindquist, supra note 3, at 709. Yet as I shall point out *infra*, simply calling disgust an unreliable guide for regulating behavior does not explain anything, without more. At the heart of Nussbaum's "unreliability attack" is her poorly vetted conviction that disgust makes for laws which run afoul of Mill's harm principle. If she is justifying her psychologically informed conclusion about disgust's unreliability based on appeal to the harm principle, of what freestanding value is *her* argument?

[32] Nussbaum, supra note 1, at 24–28; See also ibid. at 37 ("[E]motions are not mindless surges of affect, but, instead, intelligent responses that are attuned both to events in the world and to the person's important values and goals.").

[33] See ibid. at 87–89.

[34] See ibid. at 83, 97.

[35] See ibid. at 121; Sanchez, supra note 8 ("Even today, when we have many [other] ways of finding out about danger, the sense of disgust is a useful heuristic."); "On Point: Disgust, Shame and the Law" (NPR broadcast May 11, 2004) [hereinafter NPR Interview], available at http://www.onpointradio.org/shows/2004/05/disgust-shame-and-the-law (interviewing Martha Craven Nussbaum and clarifying *Hiding from Humanity*'s account of disgust). Accord Alexandra W. Logue, *The Psychology of Eating and Drinking* 47 (3d ed. 2004) (stating that "[o]ur bodies have evolved in such a way that any substance must pass several tests before we judge it acceptable and ingest it" and that "[t]he senses of taste and smell

grounds, Nussbaum approves certain nuisance laws as properly cognizant of a disgust reaction to such primary objects as noxious factory pollutants and hog-farm odors.[36]

But even the heuristic form of disgust appears suspect, says Nussbaum, because we continue to be repulsed by gross-seeming things even if we know with certainty that they are not harmful.[37] Indeed, Nussbaum's preferred mantra is that disgust expresses our "refusal to be too much mixed up with something that of course really is a part of us—our animality and decay."[38] She concludes that "disgust embodies a shrinking from contamination that is associated with the human desire to be *non*animal."[39] This shrinking from contamination, says Nussbaum, is a "projection-reaction" in which we project our disgust for the primary objects onto *other* objects when they likewise remind us of our animal propensity to become a corpse.[40]

The problem with these projective disgust reactions to Nussbaum is that they "are *irrational* . . . both because they embody an aspiration to be a kind of being that one is not, and because, in the process of pursuing that aspiration, [disgusted persons] target others for gross harms."[41] In support of this, Nussbaum cites as examples various practices which she claims are motivated by "our interest in policing the boundary between ourselves and nonhuman animals"—presumably, projection-reactions to "our own

---

are both part of this testing process, with smell being an earlier line of defense and taste being a later line of defense").

[36] See Nussbaum, supra note 1, at 158–60.

[37] See ibid. at 88.

[38] NPR Interview, supra note 35.

[39] Nussbaum, supra note 1, at 74 (emphasis added); see also Sanchez, supra note 8 (explaining that the projective—as opposed to heuristic—form of disgust is that "in which we deem certain groups of people disgusting and assimilate them to feces, corpses, and disgusting animals").

[40] Nussbaum, supra note 1, at 75; see also NPR Interview, supra note 35.

[41] Nussbaum, supra note 1, at 74 (emphasis added). Note also that Nussbaum is quite careful to explain that she draws this conclusion—namely, that disgust is irrational—only after having developed her account of the cognitions the emotion embodies. See ibid. Emotions can only be evaluated based on the "appraisals" they contain. Ibid. at 33–34, 37.

animality."[42] These include instances of discrimination against the mentally and physically handicapped,[43] persecution of Jews,[44] and "American discrimination against homosexuals."[45]

With respect to the latter, Nussbaum gleefully reports that "campaign literature on behalf of Colorado's Amendment Two (the law that denied local communities the right to make non-discrimination laws for sexual orientation, overturned in *Romer v. Evans*) said that gay men eat feces and drink raw blood."[46] With respect to the Jews' plight, Nussbaum cites anti-Semitic propaganda in Europe and its portrayal of Jews as "disgustingly soft and porous" and "sticky, womanlike in [their] oozy sliminess."[47] Finally, she also characterizes discrimination against the mentally and physically handicapped as a projection-reaction, suggesting that encountering someone with mental infirmity, or seeing "a person with a stump instead of a limb," reminds us of our vulnerable, mortal character.[48]

Common in these examples is a result Nussbaum does not like: the treatment of groups or people as unequal, which runs contrary to the liberal ideals of "human dignity and the equal worth of persons."[49] For "[b]y classifying a person as a cripple, a mongoloid idiot, [or] a homosexual, we deny both the humanity we share with the person and the person's individuality."[50] Accordingly, Nussbaum declares that disgust can be "antithetical to the values of a liberal society" because it manifests in "the subordination of both individuals and groups based on features of their way of life."[51] For Nussbaum, "the desired condition is one of interdependence, rather than control

---

[42] See ibid. at 89.
[43] See ibid. at 160–61 (discussing Cleburne v. Cleburne Living Center, 473 U.S. 432 [1985]); Lindquist, supra note 3, at 709.
[44] See Nussbaum, supra note 1, at 81–82.
[45] Sanchez, supra note 8.
[46] Ibid.; see also Nussbaum, supra note 1, at 151, 256, 264–66.
[47] Ibid. at 108.
[48] Ibid. at 93.
[49] See ibid. at 338.
[50] Ibid. at 221 (internal quotation marks omitted).
[51] Ibid. at 321.

and self-sufficiency,"[52] and projective disgust is fundamentally an attempt to control what comes near us.[53]

And so, attributing these "gross evils" to the social implementation of disgust (the interwoven "practical" component of her argument to which I alluded earlier[54]), Nussbaum concludes that this problematic emotion should be made *irrelevant*, legally speaking, regardless of the context.[55] Whether mitigating or aggravating a crime, informing the contours of pornography and obscenity laws, or making a practice illegal, "disgust is an utter red herring, . . . occluding the salient issues of harm;" and we should distrust it "as a device we employ to deny our own capacities for evil."[56] Nussbaum has even rejected what she calls the "moralized" form of disgust (where society *can* share the reasons for calling certain conduct disgusting), saying that "it is frequently a screen for the more primitive kind of disgust" and, even when it is not, it is "ultimately an unproductive social attitude."[57] She distinguishes moral disgust, of course, from indignation.[58] And in difficult cases such as bestiality and necrophilia (as well as others that I shall address), Nussbaum maintains that disgust is not necessary or useful as a guide in regulating the questionable conduct, because that conduct is better judged on the basis of the harm it causes.[59] According to her,

> [w]here law is concerned, it is especially important that a pluralistic democratic society protect itself against [disgust-based] projection-reactions, which have been

[52] Nussbaum, "Danger to Human Dignity," supra note 1.
[53] See NPR Interview, supra note 35.
[54] Recall text accompanying supra note 14.
[55] See Nussbaum, supra note 1, at 75.
[56] Ibid. at 75
[57] Sanchez, supra note 8; see also Nussbaum, supra note 1, at 103–06.
[58] See ibid.
[59] See Lindquist, supra note 3, at 709 (reading Nussbaum as arguing that even "where disgust may certainly arise over . . . father-daughter incest, eating human flesh, or having sex with animals, Mill's principle against causing harm to others already exists to justify the legal prohibition of such acts").

> at the root of gross evils throughout history, prominently including misogyny, anti-Semitism, and loathing of homosexuals. Thus while the law may rightly admit the relevance of indignation as a moral response appropriate to good citizens and based upon reasons that can be publicly shared, it will do well to cast disgust onto the garbage heap where it would like to cast so many of us.[60]

But what is not clear is whether disgust would cast *humanity* onto this "garbage heap," or whether it would simply dispose of certain aspects and accoutrements of human existence which rightfully *belong* in the wastebasket. Indeed, I argue—along with Kass, in a sense—that disgust may serve a role in cleansing humanity of trash that can reasonably be discarded, even in a pluralistic society. Stripping the law of its ability to recognize disgust allows societal garbage to pile up to such an extent that human dignity itself is unrecognizably besmirched, and the human experience waylaid, by the ever-worsening stench of commonality issuing from the exhaust pipe of individual liberty. But I am getting ahead of myself.

Before moving on, it is important to understand the basics of Nussbaum's thoughts on the nature of human beings and the meaning of human dignity. As one reviewer correctly observed, "Nussbaum's argument is not simply about the law, but about a whole conception of human society and what it means to be human."[61] *Hiding from Humanity* makes unceasing reference to "human dignity," yet it gives the term no definition. One writer has described Nussbaum's view of dignity as a sort of relativism "focus[ing] on developed quality-of-life capabilities without an acknowledgment of . . . the *unique* dignity of the human being."[62] This characterization, I believe, is quite accurate.

---

[60] Nussbaum, supra note 1, at 75.
[61] Wilson, supra note 3.
[62] Diana Schaub, "Commentary on Nussbaum, Shell, and Kass," in *Human Dignity and Bioethics: Essays Commissioned by the President's Council on Bioethics* 381, 381 (March 2008), http://www.bioethics.gov/reports/human_dignity/human_dignity_and_bioethics.pdf [hereinafter *Dignity Essays*] (emphasis added).

"[F]ull and equal human dignity," says Nussbaum in an essay commissioned by the President's Council on Bioethics, "is possessed by [anyone] who has . . . basic capabilities for major human life-activities."[63] In her view, the word "human" throughout that sentence is interchangeable with any other species, because dignity amounts to an animal's capacity to engage in its characteristic behaviors.[64] Dignity is simply grounded "in a varied set of capacities that are all elements in the life of a type of animal being."[65] This conception, she freely admits, "would not accord equal human dignity to a person in a persistent vegetative state, or an anencephalic child, since it would appear that there is no striving there, no reaching out for functioning."[66] Nussbaum thus defines any species—human or otherwise—according to its developed capabilities, presenting the dignity of a human (for example) as an acquired quality, not an inherited one.[67]

In Nussbaum's view, respect for human dignity simply means "creating conditions favorable for development and choice."[68] For this reason, it is not a violation of human dignity to pull the plug on a vegetative human being—one who cannot choose or develop his capabilities. Yet she believes her conception of dignity will nevertheless militate against social hierarchies which "inhibit the characteristic functioning of the dignified human being."[69] We will see that, in contrast, Kass would seem to recognize "being" itself as innately hierarchic.[70]

Nussbaum purports "to recognize that the world contains many distinct varieties of dignity, some human and some belonging to other

---

[63] Martha Craven Nussbaum, "Human Dignity and Political Entitlements," in *Dignity Essays*, supra note 62, at 351, 363.
[64] See ibid. at 357–59.
[65] Ibid. at 365.
[66] Ibid. at 363.
[67] See Schaub, supra note 62, at 385.
[68] Nussbaum 2008, supra note 63, at 359.
[69] Ibid.
[70] See language quoted supra note 9.

species."[71] But her discussion of emotions in *Hiding from Humanity* suggests that she views human beings as just another species:

> [M]ost contemporary researchers, and many in the ancient world, . . . hold that some *nonhuman animals* have emotions, at least some types. . . . Many animals probably have [fear, anger, grief, and compassion]. . . . There is compelling evidence that the ascription of a wide range of emotions is essential to explaining animal behavior.[72]

When it comes to disgust, Nussbaum does *not* see the emotion as a uniquely "human" response at all. She allows for no metaphysical understanding of the human being, or of human dignity (citing the demands of pluralism).[73] Thus, my dignity as a human is merely something possessed by any animal: an existence characterized by the pursuits and capabilities of my species. Aside from creating laws which give me a variety of political entitlements, respecting my dignity means simply letting me do my thing—however disgusting that may be—and maintaining a perceived pluralistic equilibrium.

B. Kass: Disgust as a Defender of Human Dignity

Against Nussbaum's picture of disgust, and of humanity and its dignity, we now compare (more briefly) the account of these matters given by bioethicist and University of Chicago professor Dr. Leon Kass. Some seven years before Nussbaum wrote *Hiding from Humanity*, Kass wrote an essay called *The Wisdom of Repugnance*, which focused on the ethics of human cloning.[74] Yet his comments in this brief work have been read and applied in a more general sense, and are among several "pro-disgust" positions Nussbaum attempts to discredit.[75]

---

[71] Nussbaum 2008, supra note 63, at 365.
[72] Nussbaum, supra note 1, at 25 (emphasis added).
[73] Nussbaum 2008, supra note 63, at 352.
[74] Kass, supra note 2.
[75] See, e.g., Nussbaum, supra note 1, at 79–82.

While he does not use the term "disgust" in his paper, Kass uses similar words to convey emotions involving some of the same "cognitions" Nussbaum attributes to disgust. These words include: repulsion, repugnance, revulsion, and even horror.[76] Besides human cloning, the hypotheticals Kass lists as capable of evoking such emotions include: "father-daughter incest (even with consent), or having sex with animals, or mutilating a corpse, or eating human flesh, or . . . raping or murdering another human being . . . ."[77] Kass thinks it rather impossible to "give an *argument* fully adequate to the horror [of these things]."[78] He explains:

> Revulsion is not an argument; and some of yesterday's repugnances are today calmly accepted—though, one must add, not always for the better. In crucial cases, however, repugnance is *the emotional expression of deep wisdom*, beyond reason's power fully to articulate it.[79]

A given disgust response, then, is largely inarticulate—"one of those instances about which the heart has its reasons that reason cannot entirely know."[80] But Kass does not see this as weakening his case—for "[w]ould anybody's failure to give full rational justification for his or her revulsion at these [vile] practices make that revulsion ethically suspect? Not at all."[81] It is as it should be that "we intuit and feel, immediately and without argument, the violation of things that we rightfully hold dear."[82]

Like Nussbaum, Kass would consider disgust "emotional" in nature; yet unlike her, he would distinguish it from any

---

[76] Kass, supra note 2.
[77] Ibid.
[78] Ibid. (emphasis added). Note that Nussbaum thinks an adequate argument *is* possible, as she tries to demonstrate why these behaviors cause harm to a nonconsenting other and can thus be dealt and regulated with under Mill's harm principal (making disgust unnecessary). See Nussbaum, supra note 1, at 80–81. But she is clearly wrong, as I will point out later.
[79] Kass, supra note 2.
[80] Ibid.
[81] Ibid.
[82] Ibid.

psychoanalytically deduced series of cognitions. Moreover, disgust according to Kass can—and should—be "moralized" in a way Nussbaum is unwilling to recognize as valid.[83] To him, repugnance it is not fueled by a subconscious fear of becoming *more* human than we wish to be. Instead, the inverse is true, and the deep wisdom in our disgust warns that we stand to become *less* human if we do not heed it. Kass's own words make the point quite well:

> Repugnance . . . revolts against the excesses of human willfulness, warning us not to transgress what is unspeakably profound. Indeed, in this age in which everything is held to be permissible so long as it is freely done, in which our given human nature no longer commands respect, in which our bodies are regarded as mere instruments of our autonomous rational wills, *repugnance may be the only voice left that speaks up to defend the central core of our humanity.*[84]

As it becomes more and more unwise for us to trust human dignity to the vagaries of culture, our repugnance (or disgust) with the world around us may continue to provide a check that brings us unpleasantly to full attention, making us mindful that the exercise of a reckless and glorified autonomy threatens the integrity of our human nature.[85] For a culture—even (or perhaps especially) one proclaiming the political liberal ideas that are sacrosanct to Nussbaum—may increasingly aim to achieve "major alteration, indeed, a major violation, of our *given nature.*"[86]

We might already stop and say that with a stroke of genius, Kass's very brief discussion in *The Wisdom of Repugnance* illuminates one of the key weaknesses in Nussbaum's attack on disgust in light

---

[83] See sources cited supra note 57.
[84] Kass, supra note 2 (emphasis added).
[85] See ibid.; cf. Nussbaum, supra note 1, at 82 ("[I]n Kass's view the culture itself is corrupt, and we turn to disgust precisely because we cannot trust the culture.").
[86] Kass, supra note 2 (emphasis added) (explaining that cloning of humans would work such an alteration).

of her capabilities-based view of human dignity: if a society can somehow convince itself that a particular group of people does not manifest a "reaching out for functioning" in the way or to the extent society prefers,[87] a political liberalism which hangs its hat on "equal respect for *persons*" may comfortably treat that group as something less than a "person."[88] But we need not stop there, as Kass seems to respond directly to Nussbaumian notions of human dignity in a later essay to the President's Council on Bioethics (of which he was formerly Chairman):

> For partisans of the "equal dignity of human being,"... the ground of our dignity lies in the humanly specific potentialities of the human species, but this basic dignity is not *dignity in full*, [and] is not the *realized* dignity of fine human *activity*. Questions again arise regarding the dignity of those members of our species who have lost or who have never attained these capacities, as well as those who use them badly or wickedly. The horizontal ground of the egalitarian dignity of human being appears to be shifting in the direction of the vertical scale of being (more and less) actually and actively human.[89]

Here and elsewhere in his essay, Kass rejects what is essentially Nussbaum's view of the person as "human animal" and as being deserving of equal dignity. Fundamentally, he would distinguish "between the basic dignity of *having* freedom and the greater dignity of *using it well*."[90] It would seem his concern is not so much that her view varies with his in a metaphysical sense (which it does), but that it is insufficient to safeguard *full* human dignity and true equality.[91]

[87] Nussbaum 2008, supra note 63, at 359.
[88] Nussbaum, supra note 1, at 338 (emphasis added) (stating with undue confidence that "[w]e have found fault with disgust . . . simply by thinking about human dignity and the equal worth of persons").
[89] Leon R. Kass, "Defending Human Dignity," in Dignity Essays, supra note 62, at 297, 320–21.
[90] Ibid. at 312.
[91] See ibid.; ibid. at 329 ("The fullest dignity of the god-like animal is realized in its

To Kass, "equality can be grounded only in the equal *humanity* of each human being," not in vague and unsubstantiated proclamations about an unconditional equality of dignity.[92] And this dignity of being *human* is "the dignity of human flourishing, the dignity of living well."[93]

Because of this view of dignity as flourishing, Kass can candidly observe that "our taboos against incest, bestiality, and cannibalism, as well as our condemnations of prostitution, drug addiction, and self-mutilation—having little to do with defending liberty and equality—all seek to defend human dignity against (voluntary) acts of *self*-degradation."[94] Nussbaum no doubt views this conception as illiberal and paternalistic.[95] To her, "respecting human dignity requires ... permitting adults to make a full range of choices, including *unhealthy* ones."[96] (Thus, for example, she favors decriminalizing drug use—except in competitive sports, bizarrely enough.[97]) But a respect for *only* this basic sort of dignity does not support the notion of the "inviolability" of human life which is so central to a political conception aimed to furnish society with important goods.[98]

In an earlier writing, Kass confessed that "[a]lthough the term 'human dignity' has a lofty ring, its content is quite difficult to define. . . . Yet all are struggling to reveal that elusive core of our

---

acknowledgement and celebration of the divine.").

[92] Kass 2008, supra note 89, at 323.

[93] Ibid. at 306.

[94] Ibid. at 298.

[95] See Nussbaum, supra note 1, at 343.

[96] Nussbaum 2008, supra note 63, at 372 (emphasis added). I cannot resist quipping here that a Scriptural perspective on Nussbaum's theses might challenge her "hands-off" brand of respect for persons, assuming paternalism is, in her view, no more suitable for animals than for men: we use "[a] whip for the horse, [and] a bridle for the ass," so why not use "a rod for the fool's back"? *Proverbs* 26:3. Indeed, "[h]e that spareth his rod *hateth* his son: but he that *loveth* him chasteneth him betimes." *Proverbs* 13:24 (emphasis added). Thus we might say that if Nussbaum *really* had compassion or love for the prospective members of her political liberal world, she might cease to mistake abandonment of persons for respect for persons.

[97] Nussbaum 2008, supra note 63, at 371.

[98] See ibid. at 355.

humanity, *those special qualities that make us more than beasts yet less than gods.*"⁹⁹ Human life, after all, "is *more* to be respected than animal life," because "man is said to be god-like."¹⁰⁰ Kass draws heavily from the Book of Genesis in describing his philosophy of the person in terms of his having been made "in the image of God;" and he finds it important that the Divine "is concerned with the *goodness* or *perfection* of things."¹⁰¹ But humanity did not know what was "good" until it tasted of the tree of the knowledge of good and evil.¹⁰² And tasting of the tree was a decision prompted by this line: "ye shall be as gods."¹⁰³ Adam and Eve instead found themselves naked—but they quickly sought to transcend this state as well, sewing fig leaves. The metaphor could continue in more detail, but it suffices to note that, as Kass so methodically observes, it appears that from the very beginning, human beings were defined by "the search for wisdom, and a reaching for the eternal and divine."¹⁰⁴ Kass thus concludes that at the "elusive core of our humanity" may lie the very thing Nussbaum deems an irrational disgust-cognition: *aspiration*.¹⁰⁵ This transcendental aspiration is "the mother of all aspects of the dignity of being human."¹⁰⁶

"In sum," says Kass, "the human being has *special* dignity because he shares in the godlike powers of reason, freedom, judgment, and moral concern, and, as a result, lives a life freighted with moral self-consciousness—a life above and beyond what other animals are capable of."¹⁰⁷ Finally, then, we may make this most crucial observation: for Kass, while disgust is *not* a primitive hiding from one's humanity, it is easily (to paraphrase Nussbaum)

---

⁹⁹ Leon R. Kass, "Reflections on Public Bioethics: A View from the Trenches," 15 Kennedy Inst. Ethics J. 221, 240 (2005) (emphasis added).
¹⁰⁰ Kass 2008, supra note 89, at 323–24 (emphasis added).
¹⁰¹ Ibid. at 324 (emphasis added).
¹⁰² Ibid. at 328.
¹⁰³ *Genesis* 3:1–5.
¹⁰⁴ Kass 2008, supra note 89, at 328.
¹⁰⁵ Compare text accompanying supra note 41, with Kass 2008, supra note 89, at 328.
¹⁰⁶ Ibid. at 328.
¹⁰⁷ Ibid. at 325.

an embodiment of our aspiration to be something greater or more excellent than what we currently are; a striving to attain God-likeness that, while sometimes resembling a hiding (viz., our fig leaves), is absolutely and undeniably part of our human nature. And because of this, "it is *beneath our human dignity* to be indifferent" to those things by which we are disgusted.[108]

II. ADDRESSING ERROR AND IRRELEVANCE

Ultimately, what Nussbaum says about disgust is true of her own position: it is problematic both in principle and in practice. In this part of the discussion, I shall show that the Nussbaumian assault on disgust is defective *in its arguments*—that is, it is defective in principle—because these arguments either defeat themselves, or they cannot be justified except by reference to Mill's utilitarian harm principle (which Nussbaum reads as holding that "a necessary condition of the legal restriction of conduct is that it be harmful to nonconsenting others").[109]

As we have seen, Nussbaum provides essentially two objections to the role of disgust in the law: (1) it is "irrational," and (2) it has a tendency to construct social hierarchies. The first of these objections is both flawed and inconsistent with Nussbaum's own analysis, and is made largely irrelevant, in any event, by its dependence on

---

[108] Ibid. at 298 (warning that "[a]s we become more and more immersed in a world of biotechnology, we increasingly sense that we neglect human dignity at our peril, especially in light of gathering powers to intervene in human bodies and minds in ways that will affect our very humanity, likely threatening things that everyone, whatever their view of human dignity, holds dear").

[109] Nussbaum, supra note 1, at 64; see also John Stuart Mill, *On Liberty* 168 (Longmans & Co. 1869) ("[T]he individual is not accountable to society for his actions, in so far as these concern the interests of no person but himself."); ibid. at 175 ("[P]urely self-regarding misconduct cannot properly be meddled with in the way of prevention or punishment."). In Part III, *infra*, I shall argue that Nussbaum's position is bad "in practice" too, because (among other things) it does not further the social goals she announces; for when put into play, her arguments serve to frustrate the only justification for liberty that might distinguish her argument from Mill's harm principle and make it relevant: the importance of human dignity and mutual respect.

the *second* objection—which, sure enough, Nussbaum attempts to strengthen by reference to the *first*. The second objection is also suspect, argumentatively speaking, and in any event cannot be distinguished meaningfully from the "harm principle" pioneered by John Stuart Mill.

A. The Irrationality Attack

Nussbaum has attacked both the physiological-response (or heuristic) form of disgust and the projective form of disgust as being irrational and unreasonable. But she spends far more time blasting the latter form. Recall that her argument in this respect revolves around the substance of her psychoanalytic findings, which lead her to make the claim that disgust is "an aspiration to be a kind of being that one is not" (and of course, that this aspiration is irrational).[110] Disgust to Nussbaum is "an inherently self-deceptive emotion, whose function . . . is above all to conceal from us, on a daily basis, facts about ourselves that are difficult to face."[111] Kass, meanwhile, sees this sort of aspiration as a key human pursuit—one upon which the dignity of being human depends.[112] "Human aspiration depends absolutely on our being creatures of need and finitude, and hence of longings and attachments. Pure reason and pure mind have no aspiration; the rational animal aspires in large part because he is an animal."[113]

Deciphering these claims requires recalling what "kind of being" Nussbaum thinks we are, as well as what these "facts about ourselves" are. As I have pointed out, Nussbaum's view on human beings is hard to distinguish from her view on animals. Particularly, she extends to animals the same form of *dignity* she advocates for humans.[114] The "kind of being" I am is simply mortal, and animal.

---

[110] Ibid. at 74.
[111] Ibid. at 206.
[112] See Kass 2008, supra note 89, at 321.
[113] Ibid. at 326.
[114] See sources cited supra notes 60–110.

I share with "nonhuman animals" the production of waste products, bodily fluids, vomit, and other filth, as well as the propensity to become a corpse.[115] There is no such thing as the human nature—there is only the human species.

But even viewing the human being in this way, it is far from clear that his desire to avoid or suppress certain facts, or even his aspiration to transcend these surly dictates of humanity,[116] should be deemed "irrational" in the strict sense—or especially (as Nussbaum says) "in the normative sense."[117] And even if it *is* irrational, such an observation hardly proves relevant to Nussbaum's goal of removing disgust from the law. Her "irrationality attack" is therefore suspect for at least three reasons: (1) it is logically flawed; (2) even if logically sound, it is inconsistent with other of Nussbaum's conclusions about the role of emotions in law; and (3) whether logical or not, it proves itself irrelevant to the question of disgust's appropriateness for law in liberal society.

1. Disputing Rationality

In arguing that even the sometimes-useful *heuristic* disgust is nevertheless irrational, Nussbaum cites with amusement how we are disgusted by the thought of ingesting certain objects even when told that they cannot harm us or even make contact with our bodies. She reports, for example, that (according to researchers) people will refuse to swallow a cockroach that is completely sealed

---

[115] See Nussbaum, supra note 1, at 87–90; NPR Interview, supra note 35.
[116] The phrase "dictates of humanity" (which I have used pejoratively) was used in the positive sense by Reverend Jonathan Ward in a speech calling for the abolition of slavery. See Jonathan Ward, *American Slavery, and the Means of its Abolition* 7 (Perkins & Marvin 1840). It was also used in the prosecution of Nazis for war crimes. See *Judgment of the International Military Tribunal for the Trial of German Major War Criminals* 45 (His Majesty's Stationery Office, London 1951) ("Prisoners of war were ill-treated and tortured and murdered, not only in defiance of the well-established rules of international law, but in complete disregard of the elementary dictates of humanity.").
[117] Nussbaum, supra note 1, at 74.

in an indigestible capsule.[118] Similarly, test subjects refuse to drink a beverage which has been stirred with an old flyswatter, despite the fact that it is completely sterilized.[119]

But is it really *irrational* to react to these sorts of things with disgust even where the "utility" of the heuristic has been disproved in that particular circumstance? Nussbaum seems to think so. She seems to argue that *reason* tells us there is no point in being afraid of something that cannot harm us, despite its resembling things which do pose some danger. But assuming this is true, *experience* suggests that even where something is deemed non-dangerous by scientists (or by logicians for the purposes of obscure hypotheticals), it may nevertheless present some risk of contamination and therefore a reason to be disgusted.

What if the encapsulated cockroach comes "un-sealed" somewhere between my throat and my colon? What if the flyswatter was not cleansed of a microbe that (unbeknownst to science) is immune to the usual sterilization process? And, to use a more banal example, what if the condom breaks? Finally, suppose our bachelor, after being released from hospitalization, later opens a brand new container of milk which he knows is not expired and which has been properly processed and stored.[120] Can we call him irrational if (when he begins to taste it) a subtle odor reminds him of his earlier experience with the spoiled milk, and he refuses to drink another drop?

It seems clear that even if our fear of contamination in these situations is based on a very, very small probability of an undesired event occurring, our disgust response cannot be described as "irrational." Instead, it seems guided by prudence.[121] Now the

---

[118] See ibid. at 88; NPR Interview, supra note 35.
[119] See ibid.
[120] The bachelor vignette appears in the introduction to this Article.
[121] For Aristotle, this prudence—practical wisdom—is deeply concerned with things about which it is possible to deliberate. See Aristotle, *Nicomachean Ethics* 161 (Robert Williams trans., Longmans & Co. 1st ed. 1891) (bk. 6). Indeed, it is one of the parts of the rational soul. Ibid. at 169. The man of practical wisdom, "by the use of his reason, hits upon that

question is, does this prudence cease when disgust becomes *projective*, as opposed to merely a physiological revulsion to an immediate stimulus? Nussbaum's position is that our projection-reactions are irrational attempts to hide from our vulnerability by controlling or stigmatizing those people who somehow remind us of our own disgusting qualities. But leaving aside the question of whether this violates the dignity of the stigmatized, are attempts to regulate their self-regarding conduct always projection-reactions or unreasonable physiological shrinkings?

Consider the example of eating human flesh.[122] Suppose I know that my next door neighbors routinely purchase unclaimed and unidentified bodies from the local morgue, which they then take home and roast outside in their barbecue pit—a feast for the entire family. If the odors that come floating over the backyard fence smell exactly like those of a routine hamburger cookout, is it irrational for me to wish that my neighbors would discontinue that practice? "Why, nuisance law would cover this!" Nussbaum might say. Yet does nuisance law prevent one from grilling a burger on the back porch? What is there to differentiate between the pleasantness of the good old fashioned American grilling experience and the horrors of the more sinister practice other than my knowledge of what is going on next door—and the disgust it creates? I might reasonably feel it necessary, then, to petition my government to outlaw such cannibalism.

Certainly Nussbaum would be correct to conclude that I am trying to police the boundary between myself and gruesome confrontations with the mortality of humanity.[123] But is it irrational for me to want

---

which is for man the best attainable result." Ibid. at 161. And yet he *combines* scientific knowledge with intuitive reason (if he is fortunate enough to have the latter), and does not simply dispose the universal when presented with a scientifically described particular. See ibid. at 161–63. "[W]here men have experience, and age, or in a word are prudent, *we must pay no less regard to their unproved assertions and opinions* than we should to a moral demonstration. For experience has trained their eye to correct vision." Ibid. at 169.

[122] See Kass, supra note 2.
[123] Nussbaum, supra note 1, at 89.

to do so? Nussbaum's analysis is that disgust, regardless of the form in which it manifests, represents an irrational "loathing of our animality."[124] Kass, on the other hand, might respond that our repugnance *need not* be rational in order to be recognized as sound, and that we should even be "suspicious of those who think that they can rationalize away our horror."[125] Thus, the proper course for an advocate of disgust may be to *concede* that the disgust response is not something for which we can give "full rational justification."[126] I therefore do so, and now move on to the next point.

2. Internal Inconsistencies

Let us assume that it is irrational to feel disgust in any case. Does irrationality alone make disgust—or *any* emotion—an unsuitable candidate for legal relevance? A useful example in illustrating the inconsistency of Nussbaum's claim here is that of the appeal to *compassion* in the law; namely, the compassion of jurors weighing the death penalty in a sentencing context.[127] Jurors' compassions cannot be said to be based on rational beliefs, and Nussbaum does not attempt to suggest otherwise. For once the defendant's guilt is established, why should "reason" compel a merciful outcome instead of the death penalty? It does not. A sentencing jury may be swayed in its decision by, for example, its understanding of the harshness of a murderer's treatment by his own parents, developing a feeling of compassion for an offender who has had a "horrible life."[128]

---

[124] Ibid. at 89.
[125] Kass, supra note 2.
[126] Ibid.
[127] See Nussbaum, supra note 1, at 69.
[128] "He's Had a Horrible, Horrible Life," *Sydney Morning Herald*, Oct. 21, 2008, http://www.smh.com.au/news/world/guilty-verdict-in-murder-of-couple-tied-to-anchor/2008/10/21/1224351229053.html (describing the defendant's vicious murders and explaining that his attorney planned to appeal to jury sympathies by relating stories, for example, of the defendant's abuse by his father); see also "Killer of 2 Women Sentenced to Life Instead of Execution," *N.Y. Times,* July 24, 1998, at B9, available at http://www.nytimes.com/1998/07/24/nyregion/killer-of-2-women-sentenced-to-life-

But the horrors of the murderer's life story do not serve as a *reason* to suppose that he will not continue to act homicidally if given a short sentence instead of a long one, or a life sentence instead of death. Nussbaum blasts disgust as an effort to deceive ourselves about the truth of our frailty. The compassion emotion may in many cases be "self-deceptive," as jurors allow themselves to ignore facts about humanity "that are difficult to face" (such as mankind's ability to commit brutal and sadistic murders), thus deceiving themselves into downplaying the culpability of the convicted defendant.[129] Our compassion in the death sentence context may very well embody a desire to transcend our animal propensity for vengeful behavior,[130] or an aspiration to ignore our animal cowardice.[131] Yet Nussbaum speaks approvingly of appeals to compassion.[132] She suggests that good liberals are entitled to make value judgments about emotions in law, notwithstanding the fact that those emotions may lack rational bases.[133] Because she has evaluated compassion without bothering to appraise the beliefs on which that "legally relevant" emotion are based, her focus on the irrationality of disgust is confusingly inconsistent and (as we will next discuss) ultimately irrelevant.

---

instead-of-execution.html (telling how the jury was influenced by testimony of the defendant's siblings, who "described sadistic beatings [the defendant] received from their mother almost from the day he was born").

[129] Nussbaum, supra note 1, at 206; see also text accompanying supra note 111.

[130] See 10 James Hastings et al., *Encyclopaedia of Religion and Ethics* 750 (1919) ("The feeling of settled resentment and consequent . . . lust . . . for revenge . . . is found to some extent in some of the higher animals, which have been known to devise and execute apparently carefully thought out plans of revenge."); Robert R. Britt & Jeanna Bryner, "Animal Instincts: Main Street Seeks Revenge on Wall Street," *LiveScience.com* (Oct. 2, 2008), http://www.livescience.com/culture/081002-bailout-package.html (citing studies showing that chimps and other primates "are known to seek revenge against relatives of an attacker," and describing similar behaviors in other species).

[131] See, e.g., Charles J. Chaput, *Justice, Mercy and Capital Punishment*, http://www.usccb.org/prolife/programs/rlp/Chaput05web.pdf (last visited April 13, 2009) (stating that "[d]ecent people understandably fear the violence in society," but arguing that, in the context of deciding whether to give a convicted murderer the death penalty, "mercy is never the work of a coward," and that "[i]t is always the mark of the strong").

[132] See, e.g., Nussbaum, supra note 1, at 69, 349.

[133] See ibid. at 58.

3. Irrelevancy

Even though we have conceded the rationality argument for purposes of discussion, we saw how it was inconsistent for Nussbaum to attempt to evaluate the rationality of disgust, particularly when, in explaining her book, Nussbaum has stated that the "main reason" for her rejection of disgust is its tendency to construct social hierarchies.[134] For what benefit is there in developing a lengthy account of the allegedly irrational underpinnings of disgust if, in the end, she is going to anchor her book to the perceived relationship between disgust and social hierarchies? Here we see that Nussbaum is as much an activist as she is a self-promoter.[135] It is not cynical to assume that *Hiding from Humanity*—complete with its scatological assault on the disgust emotion's rationality—will be useful for those who wish to make a convenient (albeit specious) argument, viz., that *people are irrational* if they have disgust for a popularized alternative lifestyle or other sort of conduct that happens to be the darling of political liberalism. And while one might generally hesitate to ascribe to an author such a sinister intent, Nussbaum's reputation for unscrupulous activism makes it hard to give her the benefit of a doubt.[136]

In any event, it seems the irrationality component of Nussbaum's argument—standing alone—can have no relevance for the question of whether disgust is a suitable emotion upon which law may be based in a political liberal society. Nussbaum's analysis of the cognitive content of disgust is, without more, merely a psychoanalytic characterization of a given emotion as irrational. If her book rested

---

[134] See NPR Interview, supra note 35.
[135] See Corcoran, supra note 1 ("[Nussbaum's] hasty treatment of many arguments is boldly self-referential. Indeed, its hundreds (no exaggeration) of peremptory references to her own work make *Hiding from Humanity* seem like a collection of hyperlinks to her other books.").
[136] See generally Gerard V. Bradley, "In the Case of Martha Nussbaum," *First Things*, June–July 1994, available at http://www.firstthings.com/article.php3?id_article=4462&var_recherche=nussbaum (describing how Nussbaum's zeal for gay rights led her to perjure herself before the court during the *Romer v. Evans* proceedings).

on this argument, it would amount to a claim that law should not be informed by *any* unreasonable or irrational emotions—and Nussbaum herself has rejected such a position, appearing to concede that an emotion need not be based upon rational beliefs to make for good public policy or to be legally relevant. (Recall her esteem for appeals to jury compassion during sentencing.) We must proceed, therefore, to examine the other prong of Nussbaum's attack on disgust: its role in creating discriminatory and oppressive social hierarchies.

B. The Problem of Oppressive Projections

Recall that Nussbaum seems to attempt to bolster her irrationality attack by describing several groups as the victims of disgust-based projection-reactions: homosexuals, persons with mental or physical disabilities, and Jews. Disgust for these people, she says, represents a projection of our disgust for the *primary* objects ("gross" things, like feces, bodily fluids, corpses, rotting meat, et cetera) onto *other* objects that (presumably) do not share the qualities of the primary objects. But in her undifferentiated description of these discriminatory treatments as embodying the projective form of disgust, Nussbaum applies her own analysis poorly.

Her conception of projective disgust would seem to require that, before characterizing one's disgust in a given case as a response to a primary object or some other object, we first carefully identify what the given object itself actually is. For if I am indeed reacting to gross things, I am disgusted with *primary* objects, and seeking to avoid contamination from them is "irrational" only to the extent those objects actually cannot contaminate me.[137] And as Nussbaum

---

[137] Post hoc criticisms of this type can have little usefulness, and are particularly feeble where there is even the slightest possibility that the primary object *could* contaminate me. And if it is even irrational for me to avoid those things which *could* contaminate me, nothing can be rational. This would be an untenable claim. (Imagine suggesting to someone that they were being irrational for refusing to consume rotted, feces-smeared, maggot-infested meat!) Thus Nussbaum must tolerate the heuristic form of disgust even

observes, even if I am reacting to *other* objects, I am nevertheless doing so, subjectively or subconsciously, "in an effort to insulate [my]self yet further from contamination by the *primary* objects."[138]

Notice how Nussbaum applies (or fails to apply) these definitions to her examples. Popular opposition to homosexuality inevitably involves a disgust reaction—but of what *type*, and to *what* objects? Nussbaum concludes that supporters of Amendment 2 in Colorado saw homosexuals as a source of contamination and shrank from the thought of it.[139] But does she rightfully describe this as the *projective* form of disgust? Only if it is a response to other, and not primary objects. So what *are* the objects of such disgust? The answer is not just "homosexual people," as Nussbaum claims. For instance, Amendment 2 supporters were likely cognizant of the gay male practice of anal intercourse, with its attendant imagery of feces, blood, and semen. The interplay between these primary objects is bound up in very definition of homosexuality.[140] It is to those objects which Amendment 2 supporters reacted with vivid disgust—not to the homosexual person. Thus, this disgust looks more like heuristic disgust than its projective form, and should therefore be presumed rational until it is proven that its objects are *not* sources of contamination—something Nussbaum does not even attempt to argue.

Nussbaum describes anti-Semitism in the same way she describes anti-homosexuality (and cheapens the Jewish struggle in the process,

---

where it may not track "genuine danger," as I have discussed above. See text accompanying supra notes 118–126.

[138] Nussbaum, supra note 1, at 97 (emphasis added). Projective disgust therefore is not a shrinking from *people*, who represent the other objects, but is a continuation of a presumptively rational disgust for *primary* objects to which a person has reason to believe those people will expose him. Like heuristic disgust, projective disgust is only irrational to the extent the *primary* objects cannot contaminate us. To insist, then, that projective disgust is an "irrational" emotion is to argue that the primary objects themselves cannot contaminate us.

[139] See ibid.

[140] If this were not the case, homosexuality would not be a sexual orientation, but an ideology.

I believe). But Jewishness, unlike male homosexuality, does not share any definitional relation to feces or bodily fluids. Jews cannot be described as "disgusting" in the fact-specific, primary-object sense of the word simply because they are Jews. As Nussbaum acknowledges, anti-Semitic movements have projected foul images onto Jews "because there was a need to associate [them] with stereotypes of the animal, thus distancing them from the dominant group."[141] But this is altogether different from the impulse to avoid contamination by primary objects by denouncement of other objects. To argue contrarily is to say that there *is* something about Jews which can contaminate people, biologically speaking.[142] The persecution

---

[141] Ibid. at 111. Note carefully how Nussbaum attempts to misuse the Jewish situation as an example of harmful projection-reactions—even when (as the quoted text indicates) they were not targeted *because* of their contact with gross things, but were instead victimized for other reasons—largely religious and political—and subsequently "talked about in such a way that they *came to be found* disgusting." See ibid. (emphasis added). The opposite is true of gay males, who by definition *do* have a direct and rather intimate relationship with the primary objects of our disgust. So while it is certain that Jews have been (and perhaps still are) horribly caricatured and viciously mistreated, Nussbaum conveniently neglects to reference any sources which actually substantiate her claim that Jews were described with reference to "fluid, stench, and muck." Ibid. Nothing she cites paints Jews as having *first* been found disgusting in a yucky, primary-objects sense of the word, prior to becoming oppressed—and such support is necessary if her projection-reaction argument is to hold. Nussbaum at one point attempts to support her suggestion—even though she later abandons it—by quoting Otto Weininger's analogizing of Jews to women, in which he states that "Judaism is saturated with femininity" and that women and Jews "resent . . . any attempt to require from [them] that [their] thoughts should be logical," are "readily disposed to communism" and appear "at the opposite pole from aristocrats." Otto Weininger, *Sex & Character* 149, 306, 307, 311 (G.P. Putnam's Sons 1907), available at http://books.google.com/books?id=pVbqiVGl6tsC. Perhaps at least two of these things may be said of Nussbaum (who touts herself, ironically enough, as a convert to Judaism). In any event, Weininger, who was himself a Jew, attacked his race not on the basis of its physiognomy, but largely on perceived political and moral defectiveness. See ibid.; Nussbaum, supra note 1, at 108.

[142] To understand how errant Nussbaum's comparison is, suppose two toddlers, A and B, are deposited on a desert island by shipwreck, and somehow manage to survive the elements alone for some twenty years before being rescued. Once these young men are on brought onto the ship, their rescuers (who were sent by the boys' families) reveal to them that A is "Jewish." Neither man has reason to be disgusted at this; for what does "Jewish" even mean to persons who know neither language nor history? Nothing. But suppose, during their return voyage, that B begins having homosexual intercourse with the ship's cabin-boy.

and disparagement of Jews has been a deliberate racial and political attack that—incidentally—has made use of "disgusting" imagery. Anti-Semitism is not rightfully described as an *emotional* byproduct in the first place. Disgust is not what *gave rise* to anti-Semitism; it is merely a tool used by anti-Semites. This, of course, is an insufficient reason to blame disgust for the problem.

In contrast to these examples, consider discrimination against the mentally retarded as well as physically disabled and deformed people. Perhaps at last we have an example deserving of being described as a projection-reaction as Nussbaum defines the term. This is because the subject of the projection in such cases is not a primary object, but human beings—*other* objects. For example, absent some showing that being an amputee or a mentally challenged person bears a *definitional* relation to contamination, my desire to condemn or avoid such people may be said to embody a projection of my disgust for rotting corpses onto others in hopes of avoiding my mortality. Of course, amputees and mentally retarded people are no more definitionally related to mortality than they are statistically more likely to die in the first place.[143]

We can see, then, that Nussbaum is not playing by her own rules when she rushes to describe opponents of homosexuality as

---

If *A* (who has become enamored of the young women aboard) happens to catch *B* in the midst of such behavior, he might react with disgust. *A* understands, at a minimum, that unpleasant, smelly substances issue from the rear. Perhaps his adolescent experiments with self-gratification have taught to him what issues from the front. He has probably learned, at least, to protect his manhood against injury. Thus, the behavior of *B*—in which feces, urine, semen, and blood are mixed with phallus and rectum in an irreverent flogging of the hind parts as with a mortar and pestle—might strike *A* as sickening. "Jew," in contrast, is merely a new sound to him.

[143] In my own experience, it seems the more common reaction to many disabled persons is one of awkwardness or discomfort, not disgust and avoidance. It may be that we are not sure how to engage these folks without appearing patronizing or insincere. Indeed, instead of feeling uneasy because these people "disgust" us, we may feel uncomfortable precisely because of our feelings of compassion and empathy; feelings which we do not know how to express without coming across as just "feeling sorry" for the person. Whatever our response to the presence of persons with amputated limbs or mental retardation, it certainly must be distinguished from an impulse to accuse them of being drinkers of blood and eaters of feces.

disgusted by *other* objects instead of *primary* ones; that is, labeling as gross things which are not. But even that argument assumes that the homosexual lifestyle is *not* gross, and that it is one which is completely disassociated from primary objects. And assuming Nussbaum thus fails in convincing us that to be disgusted by homosexuality is "irrational," what is wrong with incorporating that disgust into our laws?

Her answer is nothing more than an invocation of John Stuart Mill's harm principle—and not a version supplemented or improved upon by Nussbaum, but the harm principle itself.[144] We should repeal laws against sodomy, in other words, not necessarily because such laws are irrational, but because sodomy does not harm anyone.[145] Mill is thus Nussbaum's backup. And if the harm principle is Nussbaum's backup, it is also her downfall; for where conduct does not cause harm to a nonconsenting party, Mill would not regulate it. This is damaging for Nussbaum, because it leaves her with no argument against the legal regulation of conduct that cuts against notions of dignity but which does not cause harm. Presented with difficult cases, Nussbaum must "punt" by saying the conduct to be regulated "has a clear potential for harm."[146]

And yet, while leaning so heavily on Mill, Nussbaum weakly tries to distinguish her arguments from his by proclaiming that her psychological arguments "make a stronger case than Mill himself made for a political principal similar to his harm principle."[147] I have already explained how her psychological argument, which

---

[144] See, e.g., Mill, supra note 109, at 22 ("[T]he only purpose for which power can be exercised over any member of a civilized community, against his will, is to prevent harm to others.").

[145] Thus Nussbaum approvingly comments on the Supreme Court's decision to strike down anti-sodomy laws. See Nussbaum, supra note 1, at 303 (discussing Lawrence v. Texas, 539 U.S. 558 (2003)). But because the type of judicial scrutiny relied upon by the Court in that case is debatable (and is debated) as a matter of constitutional law, a description of the *Lawrence* opinion as holding there is no "rational basis" for laws forbidding sodomy would be a mischaracterization.

[146] Ibid.

[147] Ibid. at 336.

is principally aimed at painting those who are disgusted by self-regarding conduct as "irrational," fails to hold water. But it is also important to understand how Nussbaum tries to distinguish her argument from Mill's.

Nussbaum's distinguishing points are few, and are lame. One is a merely a brief, hair-splitting type of discussion comparing Mill's "person-based" justification for liberty and her own similar arguments (not contained in *Hiding from Humanity*) about respect for human capabilities.[148] As this is an inconsequential distinction, I will focus on her additional claim that Mill's "truth-based" justification for liberty and the harm principle tends to "treat . . . individual citizens as *means* to the general well being."[149]

Mill's truth-based justification says, for example, that even controversial and wild forms of free speech ought not be regulated if the speech does not harm someone else, because it is important that we continue to reevaluate our thinking.[150] But Nussbaum states that "[i]f one starts from the idea that each human being has dignity and deserves respect, and that politics must be grounded in respect for the dignity of all citizens as equals, one will find that Mill has put things just the wrong way around."[151] The problem with a truth-seeking emphasis, she explains, is that it results in "disrespect for the idea of reasonable pluralism, and [ventures] onto a terrain where one is at high risk of showing disrespect to one's fellow citizens."[152] She therefore purports to agree with Rawls, who suggested that the type of mutual respect required in a pluralistic society "requires . . . not showing up the metaphysical claims of religion as damaging, and not adopting a public conception of truth and objectivity according to which such claims are false."[153]

---

[148] See ibid. at 332.
[149] Ibid. at 327 (emphasis added).
[150] See ibid. at 325.
[151] Ibid. at 327–28.
[152] Ibid. at 329.
[153] Ibid. at 330.

We quickly see the hypocrisy of this last statement. For in criticizing Kass's portrayal of the wisdom of repugnance, Nussbaum engages in precisely the sort of "showing up" of supernatural claims she describes as an offense to mutual respect. She attempts to show that the image-of-God metaphysic—which justifies disgust and abhorrence of the corruption of the flesh—is premised on the belief that we are more than animals; a belief she explicitly scorns.[154] And in arguing that the law should dismiss the wisdom of repugnance, Nussbaum is quite certainly doing what she accuses Mill of doing: espousing the adoption of "a public conception of truth and objectivity" that necessarily represses such beliefs, confident that they are false.[155]

Thus, the only point of difference that would seem to make Nussbaum's argument distinguishable from Mill's involves a principle for which she has shown no respect. Yet she attempts to claim that her disgust arguments "avoid the difficulties" of Mill's justifications.[156] She states boldly: "We have found fault with disgust . . . as a basis for law simply by thinking about human dignity and the equal worth of persons."[157] But I do not think "we" have done any such thing.

In the course of unraveling what Nussbaum is saying about how we are to determine right and wrong as political liberals, we should recognize that her preferred methodology is philosophically at odds with itself. In pitting neo-Freudian notions against disgust, Nussbaum treads rather selfishly and intermittently—but never simultaneously—upon reason and experience. She first advances on the shoulders of empiricism (to a point) in unearthing the "thought content" of disgust; but this having done, she leaps to the shoals of reason with a rather Kantian declaration that disgust has no place in the law because it treats people as means to a political end.

---

[154] See ibid. at 74.
[155] Ibid. at 330.
[156] Ibid. at 338.
[157] Ibid.

Moreover, in trumpeting this conclusion, she ignores key factual inquiries which, properly considered by Aristotle's man of practical wisdom, would undermine it. (For example, if homosexuality were responsible for the spread of AIDS in the United States, would it be "irrational" to regulate the practice?)

Absent this incoherent chimera of psychoanalytical second-guessing and name-calling, Nussbaum's attack on disgust is little more than a tortured application of the harm principle so prominent in John Stuart Mill's own discussions, from which she tries desperately to distinguish her own. Ultimately, she must justify the disgust-ridden society she imagines by reference to the harm principle, though she attempts to supplement this by vague pronouncements on the values of liberal society. Thus, her several-hundred page argument about the thought content of disgust and its irrationality is little more than an irrelevant and irresponsible[158] foray into the obsolete catacombs of legal realism. To invalidate disgust, she struggles to identify some sort of harm or lack of consent, even where neither condition is true of the conduct in question. I next illustrate how the harm principle is simply inadequate as a filter against illiberally undignified practices, and that legal recognition of disgust is required if we are to fill the gaps.

III. SLOUCHING TOWARDS INDIGNITY[159]

Some of even the vilest deeds cannot be regulated under Mill's harm principle, and these provide examples of how disgust is essential for protecting the dignity of being human. While many acts are suitable examples, I will discuss bestiality; an act pointed out by Kass against which there is no describable argument save that of our own revulsion to it.[160]

---

[158] See text accompanying supra notes 135–136.
[159] Cf. William Butler Yeats, *The Second Coming* (1919) ("And what rough beast, its hour come round at last, / Slouches towards Bethlehem to be born?").
[160] See Kass, supra note 2.

Arguably, no person is "harmed" when someone decides to have sex with an animal, so the harm principle would not allow regulation of the act. Yet Nussbaum provides a rather flimsy objection to bestiality. She does not dare suggest that the practice might spread disease, because this argument is made by opponents of homosexuality, which she cherishes. Rather, she claims that the practice "inflicts tremendous pain and indignity on animals" and thus *is* covered by the harm principle, making disgust in the law unnecessary.[161] Her reasoning, of course, shows just how much she thinks *we* are animals. But it also shows how blind she is to relevant factual possibilities; for there are glaring holes in her argument.

Suppose a man preparing to have intercourse with his pet goat first *kills* the goat (perhaps in order to avoid inflicting "tremendous pain and indignity") and *then* has intercourse with it? In such a case, there is no harm to a nonconsenting person. We are disgusted not by his killing the goat, but by his sexual involvement with its corpse. Here, the likely response of Nussbaum is that the goat should never have been killed at all. This, of course, shows the tendency of her argument against disgust to result in the *dehumanizing* of human beings: for to make the harm principle work in this instance, she would need to replace the Millian term "nonconsenting other" with just "animal." This result is corroborated by Nussbaum's claims that animals and humans share the same sort of dignity (that is, the capacity to do what one wishes).

But what if the sex with animals is passive on the human's part? For example, what "tremendous pain" does a male dog feel when he mounts a drugged-up prostitute as part of some bizarre bestiality pornography carnival? How does Nussbaum *know* what sort of pain that animal experiences? More importantly, under her definition of "dignity," how can such an act inhibit the animal's capability for development? It does not. It is simply an act in which the animal participates, after which he enjoys the rest of the day chasing tennis balls and chewing on shoes. Thus we may conclude that Nussbaum

[161] Nussbaum, supra note 1, at 80.

is willing to treat animals to a more *paternalistic* articulation of dignity; one to which she objects in her defense of the equal dignity of human beings.

In any case, it does not appear Nussbaum can identify a harm in bestiality that is at all relevant in a society in which the majority of people practically worship their house pets, and yet eat their bacon with no qualms about the "indignity" suffered by the pig when a farmer killed it with electric shock. Society's widespread willingness to give animal interests lower priority is also exemplified by its reactions to the recent "swine flu," which have involved the wanton killing of hogs across the globe.[162] Because bestiality presents no harm to a nonconsenting other, the harm principle will not suffice as a grounds its legal regulation, and Nussbaum's rejection of disgust would therefore leave us with no way to limit the act by law.

Why is Nussbaum willing to use the law to protect animals (perhaps even against their will) from acts she deems violative of their dignity, while at the same time arguing that no such protection can be tolerated when it comes to the conduct of human beings? The answer escapes me, but surely must lie in understanding her political and ideological objectives. Despite her assertions to the contrary, at the heart of her philosophy *cannot* be a humanitarian desire for "a condition . . . of interdependence, rather than control and self-sufficiency."[163] Or at least this is what we must conclude about her unless she is willing to admit that her position on disgust

---

[162] See, e.g., Jessica Gusman, "SWINE FLU: Egypt Slaughters All Pigs to Prevent Outbreak," Huffington Post, Apr. 29, 2009, http://www.huffingtonpost.com/2009/04/29/swine-flu-egypt-slaughter_n_192741.html.

[163] Nussbaum, *Danger to Human Dignity*, supra note 1. Indeed, were I to engage in a psychoanalysis of my own, I might argue that her position is a product of her own drastic responses to the efforts of others in her lives to control *her*. For instance, she has related with pride how her father forbade her to bring any black children into the home, how confused and bothered she was by this, and how it caused her to reject his authority and pursue causes of equality. See, e.g., Robert Boynton, "Who Needs Philosophy?: A Profile of Martha Nussbaum," *N.Y. Times*, Nov. 21, 1999, available at http://www.robertboynton.com/articleDisplay.php?article_id=55. But were her motives in doing so genuine, or were they self-serving?

is incompatible with her political goals and liberal ideals. I will explain.

The Nussbaumian result (a law without disgust) leaves our hypothetical man free to engage in sexual intercourse with a farm animal. This will have the effect of isolating him from fellow humans. For emboldened in his desires by the absence of any legal regulation, he may begin to feel that his exploits are meritorious. Indeed, what is to stop him from taking up the claim used so effectively by homosexuals, viz., that people ought not criticize him, lest they disrespect his sexual autonomy? Regardless of whether he prevails in such arguments, the practical result is that he becomes an outcast: for in the estimation of most of the people in his community, he will be seen as a weird, gross, filthy, and lewd person.

And even if the voting majority of the populace is eventually persuaded that his sexual autonomy should be respected (perhaps by allowing him to marry his goat, dead or alive), it will likely keep its distance from him. Thus, by removing disgust from the law, we cultivate not "interdependence," but isolationism and "clannish solidarity"—the very type of "control and self-sufficiency" upon which Nussbaum frowns.[164] And if society does *not* choose to keep its distance, choosing instead to encourage and promote his type of behavior, it is well on its way to achieving status not as a *human* civilization, but a veritable "society of pigs" (or goats, as the case may be).[165] Conspicuously absent from that society is any genuine human compassion and love, since what matters most has come to be individual desire. Such self-centeredness, Nussbaum should realize, is incompatible with mutual respect.

The key to promoting equal dignity is not to sanction aberrant sexual preferences to the dismay of the moral majority, but to allow the wisdom inherent in the disgust of the morally neutral supermajority to carve out common ground across a variety of hard cases where "harm" is not an issue. Conceivably, even those who

---

[164] Nussbaum, supra note 1, at 102.
[165] Mill spoke of such a society in his discussion of the utilitarian pleasure conception.

practice bestiality may be disgusted by father-daughter incest, even though they cannot explain why. Would they not rather their own desires go unblessed by the law than have the spectacle of incest trotted before them? For a failure to achieve mutual respect happens not because the *law* criticizes certain people's choices, but because *people* frown on them.

Kass's conception of human nature informs (and confirms, I believe) the comments I have just made. For Kass, the harm in bestiality has less to do with a nonconsenting other, and more to do with the thinning of the precious membrane that protects dignity as a human being from the reckless abuses of free moral agency. One virtue of this position in the context of our example is that, even *outside* of any "paternalistic" responses to the practice of bestiality, the act is still disgusting. Thus, without needing to tell people that something they choose may "harm" them, a law against bestiality recognizing the wisdom of repugnance could prevent that affront to human dignity while at the same time protecting animals from the offenses Nussbaum is worried about.

Ultimately it is Kass's position on human nature, not Nussbaum's, which seems more likely to cultivate and encourage mutual respect. For other than saying it is "illiberal" to do otherwise, Nussbaum has given me no *reason* to bear *actual* respect for people who involve themselves in arguably disgusting practices. Kass's arguments *do* provide me with reasons to respect all men as equals, and they draw not upon tortured philosophical ideals which demand a strange result, but on propositions that I can understand as a human being who thinks himself valuable in part because he thinks he has something unique to offer the world. Nussbaum merely tells me, "If you are disgusted by people's strange choices, you are just hiding from your own animal nature." This amounts to a command to defend only *animality*. On the other hand, Kass admonishes me to become a zealous defender of *humanity* because of the deeper (nonanimal) significance of human nature.[166] This

---

[166] This latter approach resonates more meaningfully with me. My own parents, for

serves the cause of liberals even more effectively than political liberalism itself.

This is not the rational self-interest of Rawls, but a genuine call to respect the human being out of an appreciation for *what he is*, not for what his capabilities are. In contrast, the secular humanist-political liberal standard of mutual respect touted by Nussbaum is a very weak guarantor of dignity, for it is one that leaves mankind to wallow in the mire of an altogether fetid freedom.[167] A more compelling standard to adopt, and yet one that is compatible with the operation of disgust in the law, might indeed be something akin to love.[168] Perhaps Nussbaum would decry the rather dubious cognitive content of that emotion, too.

CONCLUSION

Nussbaum's vision of a political liberalism without disgust, like Mill's utilitarian justifications for the protection of personal liberty (which she attempts to distinguish), casts the human being as a means to a political end. But rather than render mankind the tool of truth and progress in the process as would Mill, Nussbaum is willing—in the name of equality and mutual respect—to foist upon persons an *animal* dignity they may not wish to share, and thus unwittingly to promote atomism and isolationism instead of the "genuine and constructive social sympathy" she extols.[169] In contrast, Kass's account is informed by an uncompromised zeal for our uniquely human nature. Rather than striving to invent a society in bondage to

---

example, encouraged me to treat homeless persons with compassion not because those persons are equal in the eyes of "the law," but because they are equal *as people*, having been created in the image of God (though they may have fallen tragically short of the full human dignity described by Kass).

[167] This very well-suited term is borrowed from the musings of an online poet. See Daniel Benisty, Untitled Poem (June 9, 2007), http://blogs.myspace.com/index.cfm?fuseaction= blog.view&friendId=84696060&blogId=274363605 (speaking of "a dark surprise / that love, in all its uncertainty, will cleanse you of your fetid freedom").

[168] See ibid.

[169] Nussbaum, supra note 1, at 105.

"the dignity of all citizens *as equals*,"[170] Kass is concerned with their dignity *as humans*. Rather than cruelly raising before mankind the spectacle of its mortality, Kass would favor a political conception equipped to defend "what is estimable and worthy and excellent about *being* human."[171] While Nussbaum's "respect" for persons would leave them gaping as chimps at the threshold of human excellence, Kass would see them flourish.

---

[170] Ibid. at 327 (emphasis added).
[171] Kass 2008, supra note 89, at 303 (emphasis added).

QUESTIONING AUTHORITY: JUST WAR THEORY, SOVEREIGN AUTHORITY, AND THE UNITED NATIONS
Michael P. Boulette

In the shadow of the second Iraq war, prominent Catholic commentator George Weigel and the Archbishop of Canterbury, Rowan Williams, engaged in a significant, if scholarly, debate on the revival and application of traditional just war theory in the context of contemporary international relations.[1] Notably, of the several topics addressed in the Williams-Weigel debate, the most interesting question may be the one with which traditional just war scholarship has traditionally been least concerned: who has the right to wage war.[2]

Just war theory, as detailed by Thomas Aquinas, typically lists three conditions for waging a just war: sovereign authority, just cause, and right intention.[3] While, contemporary just war theory has tended to treat sovereign authority as either a matter of form or else secondary to the requirement of just cause,[4] the Archbishop advocated for a more substantive understanding of sovereign authority. In his response to Weigel, the Archbishop argued that, for the requirement of sovereign authority to be met, a state must act with "due and visible attention to agreed international processes."[5] Or, perhaps more in the spirit of the Archbishop's argument, a war

---

[1] Rowan Williams, "Just War Revisited," (October 12, 2003), available at http://www.archbishopofcanterbury.org/1214?q=revisited (last accessed October 6, 2009). George Weigel, "Moral Clarity in a Time of War," *First Things*, January 2003, available at http://www.firstthings.com/article/2008/01/001-moral-clarity-in-a-time-of-war-30. Rowan Williams and George Weigel, "War & Statecraft: An Exchange," *First Things*, March 2004, available at http://www.firstthings.com/article/2007/01/war-amp-statecraft-9.
[2] Ibid.
[3] Thomas Aquinas, II-II *Summa Theologica* Q. 40 art. 1 501 (Fathers of the English Dominican Province trans., R&T Washourne, Ltd., 1917).
[4] James Turner Johnson, "Thinking Morally About War in the Middle Ages and Today," *Ethics Nationalist and Just War: Medieval and Contemporary Perspectives* 4 (Henrik Syse and Gregory M. Reichberg eds.) (2007).
[5] Williams, note 1 supra.

waged without the consent of the United Nations Security Council would be unjust insofar as it would be fought without sovereign authority.

This article will address itself directly to the soundness of the Archbishop's argument. Specifically, this article will ask whether, under Aquinas' theory of just war, it is the United Nations, rather than the various member states, that possesses the sole sovereign authority to wage war. In short, has the United Nations supplanted traditional states as the central unit of concern for just war theory?

With this question in mind, section one will briefly examine the meaning and importance of the sovereign authority requirement in Aquinas' just war theory drawing specifically on the scholarship of James Turner Johnson. Section two will then discuss the Archbishop's argument as I understand it, while suggesting that the Archbishop may be hinting at a far stronger argument than the one he openly advocates and outlining the potential form and conclusions of that argument. Lastly, I will argue, in section three, that the validity of the Archbishop's argument ultimately rests on the soundness of his analogy between individuals in civil society and states in the current international order. Drawing on the critiques of George Weigel, I will suggest that the analogy that is central to the Archbishop's argument can be legitimately and forcefully defended. As such, we have good reason to accept the United Nations as the new sovereign authority in contemporary just war analysis.

Before continuing it may be useful to call attention to two additional points. In the first place, it is important to note the relative narrowness of the question being addressed. This article concerns itself solely with the Archbishop's "internationalist" understanding of sovereign authority. That is to say, this paper seeks to understand whether the United Nations has supplanted its various member states as the only body competent to fight a just war. As such, it will not address questions of whom or what constitutes the sovereign authority within a particular state (e.g. "whether a war unconstitutionally waged might be considered 'unjust' in that it possibly violated the condition of legitimate authority").[6] Likewise, questions as to whether terrorist groups, revolutionary organizations, or other non-state organizations can properly be considered sovereign authorities will not be addressed.[7]

Secondly, this essay presupposes that the question of whom or what constitutes a sovereign authority for the purposes of just war doctrine cannot be answered solely by way of the United Nations Charter.[8] In so doing, this essay accepts the possibility of a disconnect between a just war as defined by Aquinas and a legal war as defined by the Charter. By way of example, were Country A, without the authorization of the United Nations Security Council, to declare war on Country B for any reason other than self-defense, Country A would be presumably be in violation of international law.[9] However, if County A met all the other conditions of just war (discussed below), I am suggesting that the question of the justice of Country A's war remains an open question. Indeed it is precisely the question this paper seeks to answer. In short, I do not believe that the ability of the United Nations to determine the legality of a particular war in any way provides a complete answer to the question of whether or not that war is just.

With these points in mind, the following section will briefly outline the concept of sovereign authority in Aquinas' just war doctrine, before proceeding to the Archbishop's argument and my response to it.

---

[6] Roda Mushkatt, "Who May Wage War? An Examination of an Old/New Question," 2 *Am. U. J. Int'l L. & Pol'y* 97, 106 (1987).
[7] Ibid.
[8] Cf. Gregory Reichberg, "Legitimate Authority, Just Cause, and the Decision to Invade Iraq," in *Ethics*, 1 *Law &Society* 1 243, 244 (Jennifer Gunning and Søren Holm eds., 2005) (arguing that international law has placed the authority (both legally and for the purposes of the just war doctrine) to wage offensive war solely in the hands of the United Nations Security Council).
[9] U.N. Charter art. 2, para. 4.

I. AQUINAS' SOVEREIGN AUTHORITY

Of the three just war criteria discussed by Aquinas in the *Summa Theologica* (sovereign authority, just cause, and right intention), sovereign authority seldom garners the same attention or debate as just cause.[10] Sovereign authority has alternately been rejected as irrelevant,[11] treated as a formalistic requirement akin to *competence de guerre*,[12] or as largely subsumed into the requirement of just cause.[13]

However, James Turner Johnson convincingly argues that the requirement of sovereign authority was and is central to understanding Aquinas's theory of just war.[14] Aquinas begins his account of just war with the requirement of sovereign authority,[15] and it is sovereign authority—and not just cause or right intention—that differentiates war (*bellum*) as a legitimate use of force from illegitimate private feuds (*duellum*).[16] Johnson encapsulates this point well: "There is a fundamental moral difference between the use of the sword by one in sovereign authority or on his behalf and use of the sword by a private individual. The former may wage *bellum*, which is the use of the sword on behalf of the common good; the latter may not."[17] Thus, the question of who may wage war matters a great deal, acting as the starting point for all further inquiry.

The brevity and significance of Aquinas' argument makes it worth excerpting in its entirety:

[10] James Turner Johnson, "Aquinas and Luther on War and Peace: Sovereign Authority and the Use of Armed Force." 31 *Journal of Religious Ethics* 3, 7 (2003).
[11] See Cécile Fabne, "Cosmopolitanism, Just War Theory, and Legitimate Authority," 84 *International Affairs* 963 (2008) (arguing that the criteria of legitimate authority should be discarded on the basis of a broader cosmopolitan tradition that envisages individuals, rather than groups or states, as "fundamental units of moral concern").
[12] John F. Coverdale, "An Introduction to the Just War Tradition," 16 *Pace Int'l L. Rev.* 221, 248 (2004).
[13] Johnson, note 4 supra at 4.
[14] Johnson, note 4 supra at 5, and note 10 supra at 7.
[15] Aquinas, note 3 supra at 501.
[16] Johnson, note 10 supra at 15. Mushkat, note 4 supra at 99.
[17] Johnson, note 10 supra at 10.

> In order for a war to be just, three things are necessary. First, the authority of the sovereign by whose command the war is to be waged. For it is not the business of a private individual to declare war, because he can seek redress for his rights form the tribunal of his superior. Moreover it is not the business of a private individual to summon together the people, which has to be done in wartime. And as the care of the common weal is committed to those who are in authority, it is their business to watch over the common weal of the city, kingdom or province subject to them. And just as it is lawful for them to have recourse to the sword in defending that common weal against internal disturbances, when the punish evil-doers...so too, it is their business to have recourse to the sword of war in defending the common weal against external enemies.[18]

In addition, Aquinas directly cites Romans 13:4: "for [rulers] are a servant of God for your good. But if you do evil, be afraid, for [rulers] do not bear the sword without purpose; it is the servant of God to inflict wrath on the evildoer,"[19] as the biblical foundation for his argument.[20]

For Aquinas, the sovereign authority is understood to be the ultimate guardian of the common good, and it is precisely this responsibility that justifies the sovereign authority's monopoly on the use of force.[21] Conversely, recourse to the sword is unavailable to private parties at least in part because they have recourse to a higher authority meant to protect the common good.[22] Under either formulation, Aquinas directly links the legitimate use of force to a responsibility for common good. Protection of common good justifies the sovereign authority's monopoly on legitimate force.

---

[18] Aquinas, note 3 supra at 501.
[19] Romans 13:4 (*New American Bible*, 2d).
[20] Aquinas, note 3 supra at 501.
[21] Johnson, note 10 supra at 9.
[22] Ibid.

Understood in this way, in the presence of a sovereign authority the individual never has a legitimate claim to resort to force even in service of the common good. Although we may accept that injustice occurs even within the sovereign state, Aquinas denies individual citizens even a limited right of vigilantism.[23] Service of the common good through violence is simply beyond the purview of the private individual.

It is also worth observing, as Johnson does, that the requirement of sovereign authority is, in part, aimed at limiting the contexts within which force may be legitimately used.[24] In Aquinas' world of dueling knights, marauding bandits, and bellicose feudal lords, the concentration of power in the hands of a single sovereign authority placed strict limitations on the use of violence in what was otherwise an extraordinarily violent world.[25] Thus, the requirement of sovereign authority should be read not just as legitimating the use of violence by certain actors, but as purposely delegitimizing the use of violence by others. Sovereign authority, while acting as a grant of force, should be understood more fundamentally as a limitation on force by a wider number of groups who might conceivably wield it.[26]

It is also important to understand, at least superficially, Aquinas' understanding of the common good and the overriding importance of order its central element.[27] Aquinas and his contemporaries understood that while order may lack either justice or peace, both

---

[23] While Aquinas does permit individuals to defend themselves when attacked, the use of violence in any other context (even in the service of justice) is denied to them. See Aquinas, II-II *Summa Theologica* Q. 41 art. 1 511 ("but in him who defends himself, it may be without sin, or it may sometimes involve a venial sin, or sometimes a mortal sin; and this depends on his intention and on his manner of defending himself. For if his sole intention be to withstand the injury done to him, and he defend himself with due moderation, it is no sin, and one cannot say properly that there is strife on his part").

[24] Johnson, note 4 supra at 5

[25] Ibid.

[26] Ibid.

[27] Johnson, note 10 supra at 11.

justice and peace are founded on order.²⁸ The centrality of order to the political system has been memorably made by Thomas Hobbes who observed "that during the time men live without a common power to keep them all in awe, they are in the condition which is called warre; and such a warre, as is of every man against every man."²⁹ Thus, the sovereign authority is primarily responsible for ensuring order, not to the exclusion of justice and peace, but as a necessary precondition for them.³⁰

Order as the central (though not exclusive) element of the common weal also closely mirrors the historic Christian understanding that feared chaos far more than the concentration of power in the hands of the state.³¹ As noted above, feudal lords, gangs of bandits, and violent itinerant knights (many of whom viewed violence as a right of their station) constantly posed a threat to the peace.³² To guarantee justice and peace, the sovereign authority first had to establish order, and reign in these more violent elements of society. Although later generations would grow distrustful of excessive state power (critiques of Hobbes are instructive), the ability of a powerful sovereign, alone possessed of the legitimate use of force, promised a peace unknown in the medieval world.³³

Taking this section as a whole, it is clear that the sovereign authority's exclusive claim to legitimate force is founded on its unique responsibility to foster and protect the common good. In addition, the requirement that only the sovereign authority may wage war should be fundamentally understood as a limitation rather than an expansion of the legitimate use of violence. Lastly, the sovereign

---

²⁸ Ibid.
²⁹ Thomas Hobbes, *Leviathan* 88 (Richard Tuck ed., Cambridge University Press 1996). Thomas Nagel offers a particularly clear formulation of the connection between sovereignty and justice in his essay "The Problem of Global Justice," 33 *Philosophy & Public Affairs* 114, 114-115 (2005).
³⁰ Johnson, note 10 supra at 11-12.
³¹ Ibid.
³² Ibid. Here Johnson specifically references the Peace of God movement in the late tenth century.
³³ Ibid.

authority's duty to protect the common good consists, first and foremost, in the maintenance of order as the necessary precondition for peace and justice. Thus, in seeking to indentify the proper sovereign authority for the purposes of just war theory (either as the state or the United Nations), the relevant question may be: who is appropriately charged with the protection of the common good, how to limit (rather than expand) the legitimate use of force, and how to best maintain *order* at the international level. The following section will seek to understand the Archbishop's argument in light of the foregoing discussion, paying particularly close attention to the Archbishop's analogy of the modern state to Aquinas' individual and the United Nations to the sovereign authority.

II. THE ARCHBISHOP'S ARGUMENT FOR INTERNATIONALISM

As has been previously stated, the thrust of the Archbishop's argument hinges on analogizing Aquinas' private individual to the United Nations' member states, "if a state or administration acts without due and visible attention to international process, it acts in a way analogous to the private individual."[34] What may strike us as odd, however, is the Archbishop's insistence that member states failure—in acting outside the international legal process—is a result of the state acting as the judge of its own interest.[35] As noted above, Aquinas' argument stresses that private individuals may not legitimately use force because it is the sovereign authority, not the individual, who is charged with the protection of the common good. Thus, the private individual's acts are *duellum* rather than *bellum* not necessarily because they are acting as the judge of their own interests, but because they have usurped the power of the sovereign authority to defend (and to some extent determine) the common good.

However, despite his unusual characterization of the problem,

---
[34] Williams, note 1 supra.
[35] Ibid.

the Archbishop's argument may be sound more generally. Earlier in his lecture, the Archbishop notes that the sovereign authority's exclusive right to use force to protect the public good is directly connected to the fact that "those charged with preserving the public good are competent and legitimate judges of the public good."[36] Consequently, although the private individual may perceive the extent to which her own interests have been damaged, she is not equipped to address the broader damage done to the common good.[37] In this sense, her offense may be less that she is acting as the judge of her own interests (as the Archbishop states later), but that she has substituted her understanding of the common good for the sovereign authority's—the body directly charged with the protection of the common good.

While there may be some persuasive value in the Archbishop's argument that nations ought not be the judge in their own case, I would suggest that his argument would be strengthened by focusing more straightforwardly on the sovereign authority's duty to protect the common good and primarily the sovereign authority's duty to foster and preserve order. An argument along these lines would set aside the more process based concerns of who is the proper judge and focus on the fundamental nature of international law and international relations. Accordingly, this argument would stress the analogical parallels between Aquinas' private individual and member states and Aquinas' sovereign authority and the United Nations. Although this is not how the Archbishop formulates his argument, I would suggest that the general structure of his reasoning demands—or at least hints at—this stronger argument making further inquiry both desirable and necessary.

To better reach the heart of the Archbishop's argument, I would reformulate it as follows. In the first place, the United Nations, as constituted, is essentially analogous to Aquinas' sovereign authority. Like the sovereign authority, the United Nations is charged with the

[36] Ibid.
[37] Ibid.

protection of the common good primarily understood as the creation of order and the preservation of peace.[38] Indeed, the very existence of the United Nations can, and should, be understood—like the Aquinas' sovereign authority—as limiting the legitimate use of force by granting the right to use such force to a higher authority. Just as Aquinas' original just war doctrine relegated the warlike actions of lesser nobles and knights to the category of *duellum*, by vesting the right of *bellum* in a higher sovereign authority the United Nations has similarly limited the category of *bellum* to actions taken by the Security Council.[39]

Second, just as the private individual may not properly resort to force because she may seek redress from a superior authority charged with the protection of a common good, a member state may appeal to the Security Council and the International Court of Justice for the peaceful resolution of disputes or, failing that, the Security Council may take additional action in furtherance of international peace.[40] Insofar as member states have recourse to a superior authority bound to protect the international common good (understood as order), those states are barred from using force even to achieve otherwise just ends. Read together, these propositions create the foundation for the basic analogy upon which the Archbishop's argument is based: the first analogizing the United Nations to a sovereign authority, and the second equating the member states role, at least at the international level, with Aquinas' private individuals

Moreover, and to anticipate an initial objection, just as Aquinas' just war doctrine does not divest the individual of her inherent

---

[38] U.N. Charter Preamble and Art. 1 par. 1 (characterizing the primary purpose of the United Nations as "maintain[ing] international peace and security, and to that end: to take effective collective measures for the prevention and removal of threats to the peace, and for the suppression of acts of aggression or other breaches of the peace, and to bring about by peaceful means, and in conformity with the principles of justice and international law, adjustment or settlement of international disputes or situations which might lead to a breach of the peace").

[39] U.N. Charter Art. 42.

[40] U.N. Charter Art. 33-38 and 39-42

right to self-defense;[41] neither does the Charter prevent member states from protecting themselves in the event of an armed attack.[42] Notably, just as this limited right to self-defense does not undermine the sovereign authority's monopoly on legitimate force, neither does it disprove that only the United Nations may properly authorize a just war.[43] Both Aquinas' theory of strife and the United Nations' Charter reserve the right to self-defense to the private individual and the member states respectively. Understood in this way, the right to self-defense enshrined in the charter does not—strictly speaking—vest member states with a limited right to wage just war.[44] Instead, the state continues to function in its capacity as a private individual exercising a fundamentally distinct right (the right to self defense) from the right to wage *bellum*.

This point is particularly worthy of attention because it is one of the grounds upon which Weigel has challenged the analogy central to the present argument. Under the analogy I am proposing, in which member states function essentially as private individuals on the international stage, violence between nations is properly understood as *duellum*, strife, addressed in Question 41 of the *Summa Theologica*.[45] Aquinas' explains strife as "a kind of private ware... tak[ing] place between private persons, being declared not by the public authority, but rather by an inordinate will."[46] However, even accepting the sinfulness of strife (*duellum*), an individual acting in self-defense need only show that "his sole intention be to withstand the injury done to him, and [that] he defend[ed] himself with due moderation."[47]

---

[41] Aquinas, note 3 supra, at 511.
[42] U.N. Charter Art. 51.
[43] Weigel appears to disagree arguing that because the Charter recognizes an inherent right of self-defense, the Security Council cannot be said to have the same monopoly on force as Aquinas' sovereign authority. Williams & Weigel, note 1 supra.
[44] U.N. Charter Art. 51.
[45] Aquinas, note 3 supra, at 511.
[46] Ibid.
[47] Ibid.

The parallels between Aquinas' account of strife and self-defense and the inherent right of self-defense enshrined in the United Nations Charter are striking. Like Aquinas' limited right of self-defense, Article 51 of the United Nations Charter recognizes and enshrines the "inherent right of individual or collective self-defense" until the "Security Council has taken measures necessary to maintain international peace and security."[48] Moreover, and to repeat the point made in the previous paragraph, the right to self-defense does not carve out a limited exception for when a state may engage in *bellum*. Self-defense is understood purely as private—albeit justified—violence, not as the ability of the individual to requisition the power of the sovereign authority for their own purposes:

> In order for a war to be just it must be declared by authority of the governing power, as stated above (Q. XL., A. I); whereas strife proceeds from a private feeling of anger or hatred. For if the servants of a sovereign or judge, in virtue of their public authority, attack certain men and these defend themselves, it is not the former who are said to be guilty of strife, but those who resist the public authority. Hence it is not the assailants in this case who are guilty of strife and commit sin, but those who defend themselves inordinately.[49]

Aquinas' emphasis on proportionality further mirrors the limited right of self-defense in international law. Just as the right of self-defense is—at least arguably—superseded by the action of the Security Council[50] ("until the Security Council has taken measures necessary to maintain international peace and security"), the individual acting in self-defense may do no more than "withstand the injury done to him," within the bounds of "due moderation."[51]

[48] U.N. Charter 51
[49] Aquinas, note 3 supra, at 512.
[50] Cf. Eugene V. Rostow, "Until What? Enforcement Action or Collective Self-Defense?" 85 *Am. J. Int'l L* 506 (1991).
[51] Aquinas, note 3 supra, at 511

Similarly, the requirements of proportionality have been enshrined in international law in the various Hague Conventions, limiting the means by which wars (even defensive wars) may be fought.[52] Thus, far from undermining the similarities between member states and the private individual, the right to self-defense offers additional support to the analogy presented above.

Lastly, Aquinas' recognition of order as the prerequisite to peace and justice (as interpreted by Johnson)[53] only further strengthens the analogy. Although the United Nations may not, in all instances, be able to ensure perfect justice, it is essentially an organization aimed at the orderly and peaceable resolution of disputes.[54] To the extent that we must ensure order if we ever hope to achieve justice, the United Nations may well be the international sovereign authority capable of providing it. While my position might be disputed on an empirical level, the centrality of order an peace to the purpose of the United Nations should be relatively uncontroversial.[55] Thus, even if the United Nations falls short of its ultimate goal, it is the effectiveness of the United Nations as a sovereign authority—rather than its status as a sovereign authority—that are called into question. While I do not mean to suggest that the efficacy of the United Nations is unimportant, I believe it is an analytically distinct question from whether the *status* of United Nations falls under Aquinas' just war theory. Just as a sovereign authority may fail to protect its subjects or may lack the ability to maintain order, these shortcomings do not necessarily imply that the individual or institution serving as the sovereign authority no longer holds a monopoly on the protection of the public good and the legitimate use of force.

Taken together, analogizing United Nations member states with Aquinas' individual and the United Nations with Aquinas' sovereign authority strongly supports the conclusion that no just war may be

---

[52] Hauge IV laws and customs of land war Art. 22-28.
[53] Johnson, note 4 supra at 5.
[54] See note 38 supra.
[55] UN Charter Preamble

waged without the authorization of the United Nations Security Council. Yet, if member states are genuinely in the same position as Aquinas' private individuals, why does the Archbishop settle for the weaker conclusion that just war requires only that states act with "due and visible attention to agreed international process?"[56] Aquinas' just war doctrine does not permit private individuals to resort to violence after "due and visible attention," to the legal structures in place. The use of force by private individuals may not be justified solely on the grounds that they turned to the sovereign authority first. Likewise, a member state acting outside the United Nations simply acts beyond the pale regardless of how much attention it may have paid to the international legal process. Assuming I have not misread the analogy between member states and the individual, upon what basis does the Archbishop settle for such a weak conclusion?

Without resolving the apparent shortcomings in the Archbishop's argument, the final section of this paper will suggest that the Archbishop need not accept this weaker conclusion. Rather, I will maintain that the stronger conclusion I have presented above can be more than adequately defended. I will argue that the critiques of the Archbishop's argument— perhaps most persuasively presented by George Weigel — overstate the failings of the Archbishop's analogy. As such, the final section will be dedicated to enunciating and responding to Weigel's critiques, arguing that the analogy presented by the Archbishop, and the strong internationalist implications it yields, are capable of withstanding close and careful scrutiny.

III. DEFENDING THE ARCHBISHOP

In response to the Archbishop, Weigel—quite moderately— accepted that "just war tradition demands a form of internationalism," while denying that the United Nations satisfied this requirement.[57] Central to Weigel's objection is the perceived failure of the analogy

---

[56] Williams, note 1 supra.
[57] Williams & Weigel, note 1 supra.

discussed above. Weigel argues that "today's UN is entirely the tool of states, many of the most important of which…are not making their policy calculations on genuinely internationalist grounds, or on grounds of moral reasons rightly understood." [58] The analogy also falls short, Weigel argues, because it ignores the fact that member states remain responsible to promote the common good in a way which the individual in civil society does not.[59] As sovereign authorities in their own right, individual nations cannot legitimately discharge their right to wage just wars without betraying their fundamental obligation to protect their citizens and the common good.[60] In short, Weigel attacks the analogy from both sides, arguing that the United Nations cannot be a sovereign authority insofar as it has and continues to be unresponsive the needs of the international system, remaining, instead, a tool of the member states (particularly those with a permanent seat on the Security Council). Second, the member states cannot be properly analogized to the private individual because, unlike the individual, they retain a responsibility as sovereign authorizes to protect the common good of their citizens. Thus, the analogy fails on both counts and must be rejected.

A. Member States as Private Individuals

Weigel's argument rightly focuses on the potential failure of the Archbishop's analogy between individuals and states. While individuals in civil society do not possess a duty to protect the common good, states in the current international order still must safeguard their citizens against external threats.[61] That is to say, insofar as states are morally obligated to protect their citizens and preserve order, they are fundamentally unlike individuals who have no such obligation. Thus, a state cannot surrender its monopoly on

---

[58] Ibid.
[59] Weigel, note 1 supra.
[60] Williams & Weigel, note 1 supra.
[61] Williams & Weigel, note 1 supra.

legitimate force without also surrendering its duty to protect the common good. To the extent that the very purpose of the state is to protect the common good, it could be argued that a state that has surrendered its duty to protect the common good to the United Nations Security Council or any other authority has ceased to be a (legitimate) state.

In contrast, an individual does not cease to be an individual because she fails to protect the common good; indeed Aquinas specifically prohibits her from assuming this role. Individuals in civil society are expressly forbidden from acting as min-sovereigns, protecting the common good as they see fit (in no small part because doing so expands the legitimate use of violence and correspondingly undermines the order that is essential to justice and peace). Were individuals, rather than the sovereign authority, appropriate protectors of the common good, violence would inevitably usurp order and the ability of a sovereign to promote a unified ideal of order, justice, and peace would be severely limited if not destroyed. Thus, it is the basic duties of the member states as sovereign authorities in their own right that renders them fundamentally distinct from individuals and undermines the analogy being argued for.

Admittedly, Weigel's argument has persuasive value, particularly for those frustrated with the perceived inefficiency of the United Nations and its failure to respond to severe human rights abuses and "rogue states." However, Weigel's critique fundamentally misunderstands the Archbishop's analogy. Rather than analogizing the member state to the private individual in *all circumstances*, the analogy should be limited to states acting internationally. Understood in this way, the state is not divested of its domestic responsibility to protect the common good. Instead, the analogy essentially works to sever the sovereign authority to defend against internal disturbances from the sovereign authority to wage war, rendering the state a sovereign authority on the domestic stage and a private individual internationally.

In Aquinas' account of sovereign authority, he analogizes the sovereign authority's right to defend against internal disturbances with the right to "defend the common weal against external enemies."[62] By analogizing the member state to the private individual *on the international stage*, the argument essentially denies the similarity between the domestic and international uses of force in the presence of a larger body charged with maintaining international peace and security (i.e., the United Nations). The member state has not surrendered its sovereign authority in every respect, rather—in ratifying the Charter—it has opted to act as a sovereign authority internally and a private individual internationally.

In response, Weigel might argue that this argument proves too much and overly simplifies his objection. Admittedly I have purposely misunderstood the nuance of Weigel's point to demonstrate more clearly the primary premise of my argument. Taking Weigel's argument more seriously, he would maintain that the analogy I am defending assumes that sovereign authority can, in fact, be separated into domestic and international components, and that defense of the common good on the international level is fully—or at least largely—severable from defense of the common good on the domestic level. To the extent September 11 and oppressive leaders like Saddam Hussein, the Taliban, and Mahmoud Ahmadinejad have taught us anything, Weigel would respond, they have proved that our international common good is inextricably intertwined with our domestic common good.[63]

Moreover, Weigel would argue, our domestic common good is more than preventing or responding to an armed attack but "the irreducible core of the 'national interest'...composed of those basic security concerns to which any responsible democratic statesman must attend."[64]

---

[62] Aquinas, note 23 supra at 501.
[63] Weigel, note 1 supra.
[64] Ibid.

Member states—as guardians of the common good—must act with "a larger sense of national purpose and international responsibility," that consists, *inter alia*, of:

> the obligation to contribute, as best we can, to the long, hard, never-to-be-finally-accomplished "domestication" of international public life: to quest for ordered liberty in the evolving structure of international public life capable of advancing the classic goals of politics—justice, freedom, order, the general welfare, and peace.[65]

In short, member states, as sovereign authorities and guardians of the domestic common good, possess a basic and fundamental duty to promote the international common good defined as order, justice and peace or "ordered liberty."[66]

Again, the objection I am attributing to Weigel deserves serious attention. To the extent the Archbishop's analogy between the private individual and the member state is all-or-nothing (i.e., must apply both domestically and internationally or not at all), Weigel's argument would seem insurmountable. However, I would suggest that while the international and domestic common goods are not fully severable, they are distinguishable enough to support the Archbishop's analogy.

Taking the example of September 11th suggested above, it is true that an attack against the United States by foreign terrorists supported—or at least sheltered—by a foreign state has a direct and undeniable impact on the domestic common good. However, as has been previously discussed, even though Aquinas denies that individuals have a legitimate right to use force in pursuit of the common good, he permits a limited right of self-defense even in the presence of a sovereign authority.[67] As such, events like the September 11 attacks, in which the domestic common good is directly

---
[65] Ibid.
[66] Ibid.
[67] Aquinas, note 3 supra, at 515.

threatened on an international level, may be properly accounted for as exceptions to general rule prohibiting the private use of force and permitted by the necessity self-defense (within the bounds of proportionality). Thus, in September 11th type situations, the state can be understood, on a domestic level, as acting as a sovereign authority safeguarding the common good, while simultaneously behaving as a private individual exercising its right of self-defense on the international level.

However, Weigel's objection of protecting the domestic interest does not stop at the basic level of self-defense. Indeed, as is apparent from the language quoted above, Weigel understands the domestic common good to be one and the same as the international common good. Domestic order, justice, and peace are simply part and parcel of international order, justice, and peace. In addition, to the extent that I understand Weigel's argument correctly, a sovereign authority's duties on the international level are both fully derivable and logically implied by its duties on the domestic level both "empirically and morally."[68]

This is certainly a powerful objection with a powerful central premise. In equating the domestic common good with the international common good, Weigel looks to what he terms a "national purpose," a fidelity to American—and democratic—values of freedom that extends beyond American borders.[69] Thus, my answer of self-defense is insufficient; while the private individual may only defend himself proportionately and to "withstand the injury done to him," Weigel appears to advocate a (potentially militant) proselytizing of "ordered liberty" by member states generally and the United States in particular. In the absence of "ordered liberty" the domestic common good—broadly defined—is threatened in a way that extends beyond an imminent national threat.

Of all of Weigel's objections to the member state qua private individual analogy, this may perhaps be the strongest and hardest

[68] Weigel, note 1 supra.
[69] Ibid.

to answer. I have, thus far, presupposed that national sovereign authorities may fulfill their obligations to protect the common good on an international level solely within the confines of Aquinas' self-defense exception. However, it is clear that Weigel's understanding of the domestic common good that the sovereign authority must protect extends far beyond mere self-defense. The private individual may not protect herself by imposing a value system on her neighbor by any means. But, according to Weigel, a member state may seek to advance the international common good (as part and parcel of its domestic common good) "as best [it] can," even to the invasion of another member state and violent overthrow of its government.

As an answer to Weigel, I see no choice but to simply deny his premise. To begin with my conclusion, while promoting ordered liberty may contribute to the domestic common good, and is therefore the duty of the national sovereign authority, it may and must—under my argument—do so as a private person. In short, I am denying that the duty to take *armed* action to promote ordered liberty is in anyway "morally or empirically" implied by a national sovereign authority's duty to protect the domestic common good. I do not believe this begs the question in favor of my conclusion (that member states can be sufficiently analogized to Aquinas' private individuals). I simply do not see any basis, either logical or empirical, for deriving an international duty to the common good from a domestic duty to the common good in the presence of an authority concurrently charged with promoting that good. To be sure, an ordered international system is likely to promote domestic order, peace, and justice. But similarly, domestic order promotes the good of the individual. However, to return to Aquinas' argument, that the individual would benefit from an enhanced common good does not give her the right to enforce that common good through violence. Likewise, where a larger body charged with protecting the international common good exists, the fact that states would benefit from greater international order does not logically extend a state's duty to protect the national common good to a broader duty to protect the international common good through force.

While Weigel and those sympathetic to his position may feel dissatisfied with this response, it should be noted that the position I am advocating does not deny any link between the domestic and international common good. It may well be, as Weigel argues, that promoting ordered liberty is key to national security, and therefore, as a guardian of the domestic common good, the national sovereign authority should (and must) seek to promote ordered liberty "as best [it] can." Indeed, I would agree that this connection does exist. The premise I reject is that protection of the national common good necessarily implies a duty to protect and spread ordered liberty through force. Put another way, I am arguing that that "moral and empirical" link Weigel argues for does not logically extend to the use of force to accomplish the goals he advocates. Thus, the analogy between member states continues to possess a great deal of weight as they may act as sovereign authorities domestically while seeking to accomplish international goals of ordered liberty as quasi-private individuals. In short, sovereign authorities may continue to protect the national common good up to the point of using force for reasons other than self-defense.

To the extent that I have successfully argued that a sovereign authority's duty to protect the common good is not dramatically impaired by the inability to use force outside the context of self-defense, the analogy as I have presented it remains fully coherent. However, I willingly admit that the analogy cannot be adequately supported if it is indeed "morally and empirically" true that protection of the common good on the national level requires the use of violence outside the context of self-defense.

However, accepting that the argument I presented remains both coherent and plausible, it is necessary to examine Weigel's second objection to the general analogy I have supported, specifically that the United Nations cannot properly be analogized to a sovereign authority. The following section will present Weigel's argument and my responses to it.

B. The United Nations as Sovereign Authority

Weigel's second objection, that the United Nations cannot be properly analogized to the sovereign authority, is largely an extension of the objections already presented and responded to. Generally, Weigel argues that unlike a sovereign authority charged with the protection of the common good, the United Nations is simply a tool of the states, particularly the permanent members of the Security Council.[70] Insofar as the United Nations does not concern itself with the common good, it cannot be considered a proper sovereign authority. To make use of Aquinas yet again, Weigel analogizes the United Nations more to a tyrannical government, "conducive to the private good of the ruler, and to the injury of the multitude," than a sovereign authority.[71] Consequently, the member states are permitted to wage *bellum* outside the context of the United Nations because:

> A tyrannical government is not just, because it is directed, not to the common good, but to the private good of the ruler...there is no sedition [a mortal sin] in disturbing a government of this kind, unless indeed the tyrant's rule be disturbed so inordinately, that his subjects suffer greater harm from the consequent disturbance than from the tyrant's government.[72]

Member states are freed from their obligation to refrain from violence because of the corruption of the present sovereign authority.

It is important to note the theoretical and empirical aspects of Weigel's argument. On the theoretical level, Weigel could be read as arguing that, like Aquinas' tyrant, the United Nations seeks only its own good while ignoring the common good of the member states. Additionally, Weigel may simply be arguing that, as an ineffectual

---
[70] Weigel, note 1 supra.
[71] Aquinas, note 3 supra, at 518
[72] Ibid.

organization, the United Nations does not fulfill its duties of safeguarding and promoting the common good.

While it is prudent to grant the persuasiveness of Weigel's argument; it seems tenuous to argue that the United Nations seeks only its private good. While I certainly grant that the United Nations Security Council often faces deadlock in the face of difficult issues, this is a substantively different position from saying that it is unconcerned with the international common good or so corrupt that it only seeks its own good.

Perhaps Weigel's more convincing claim is the sheer inefficacy of the United Nations. To be sure, there may be problems with the United Nation's ability to secure the international common good especially given the difficulty in reaching a consensus even between the permanent members of the Security Council. However, as I have argued above, the need to reform the United Nations does not discount the analogy I have argued for. The question of whether the United Nations perfectly promotes the common good is a distinct question from whether or not it is duty bound to protect the common good (or whether it is a tyrant). Thus, arguments for improvement are just that. They suggest a need for reform but not a case for rejecting the analogy I have set forth. While this position may seem a bit unsatisfying, it should encourage us to work towards reform rather than rejecting the United Nations because it does not always guarantee perfect justice. In short, even accepting the truth of Weigel's empirical argument—which we need not—the analogy remains sound and worthy of careful consideration if not acceptance.

In sum, this section has offered a defense against what I perceive as the most persuasive objections to the analogy I attribute to the Archbishop. To this end, I have argued that the Archbishop's analogy can adequately account for a state's obligation to protect the common good, as well as the perceived in effectiveness of the United Nations to do the same. While a great deal remains to be said, I have tried to lay out a basic analytic framework upon which an even stronger argument might be built.

CONCLUSION

In the previous three sections, this article has examined Aquinas' sovereign authority requirement in just war to determine who, in contemporary international relations, possesses the authority to wage just war. Proceeding from arguments presented by the Archbishop of Canterbury and critiques by George Weigel, this essay has attempted to defend the argument that the United Nations should be understood as supplanting member states as the new sovereign authority. To this end, I have attempted to defend the Archbishop's analogy between Aquinas' private individual and United Nations member states acting internationally. I have suggested both that this analogy is sustainable, and that it necessarily (and rightfully) implies a far stronger conclusion than the Archbishop acknowledges.

By way of conclusion, it should be noted that both Weigel and the Archbishop acknowledge the need to improve the United Nations and reduce its tendency to enshrine the interests of certain member states (notably the permanent members of the Security Council). This is certainly wise counsel. Although it has not been the purpose of this article to examine potential improvements that might be made to the United Nations, I would be remiss not to mention the continuing need for the United Nations to work to fulfill its purpose as a truly Aquinean sovereign authority and secure order, peace, and justice for all its members.

REVISITING FULLER'S CAVE: A SPELUNKER AND HIS LAWYERS

Jason Isbell

INTRODUCTION

In 1949, Harvard Professor Lon L. Fuller published a law review article entitled *The Case of the Speluncean Explorers*.[1] This unique piece of legal literature explored various schools of jurisprudential thought through the fictitious eyes of the five-member Supreme Court of the Commonwealth of Newgarth.[2] Meeting in the early months of the year 4300, the Court heard on appeal the case of four defendants sentenced to hang for violating Section 12-A of the Newgarth Statutes, which stated that "[w]hoever shall willfully take the life of another shall be punished by death."[3]

The facts surrounding the murder allegedly committed by the quartet elevated this otherwise commonplace case into an extraordinary work. Although hypothetical, Fuller's original facts paralleled two very real cases: the 1842 case *United States v. Holmes*[4] and the 1884 case *Regina v. Dudley & Stephens*.[5] Through the pen of Chief Justice Truepenny, readers of Fuller's tome learn about Mr. Roger Whetmore and his team of fellow spelunkers, who set out to explore a limestone cavern in May of 4299.[6] Traveling with scant provisions, the group faced impending death by starvation after an unexpected landslide entrapped them in the cave for weeks.[7] In formulating a survival plan, the group deduced that some could avoid

---

[1] Lon L. Fuller, "The Case of the Speluncean Explorers," 62 *Harv. L. Rev.* 616 (1949).
[2] Ibid. The opinion of Chief Justice Truepenny begins at page 616. The opinion of Justice Foster begins on page 620. The first opinion of Justice Tatting begins on page 626. The opinion of Justice Keen begins on page 631. The opinion of Justice Handy begins on page 637. The second opinion of Justice Tatting begins on page 644.
[3] Fuller, supra note 1, at 616, 619.
[4] 26 F.Cas. 360 (C.C.E.D. Pa. 1842).
[5] [1884] 14 Q.B.D. 273 (DC).
[6] Fuller, supra note 1, at 616.
[7] Ibid.

the ominous fate of death, but that such avoidance would come at a high price.[8] Mr. Whetmore, it turned out, paid such a price.[9]

Troubled by their scenario, the "unfortunate men within the mountain" sought professional advice on at least three matters before eventually emerging from the cave.[10] First, the group inquired how much longer their rescue would take (the engineers answered that they needed at least ten more days, assuming no new landslides).[11] Similarly, a committee of medical experts replied to the question of whether the group could survive ten more days without eating anything (the answer was no).[12] Yet when the trapped spelunkers requested that a "judge or other official of the government" answer a question regarding their plan for survival, they received no response . . . other than silence.[13]

David L. Shapiro labeled the work "as close to perfection as one can get."[14] Anthony D'Amato termed the original "a classic in jurisprudence."[15] William N. Eskridge, Jr. considered the opinions of Fuller's justices as a "microcosm of the [twentieth] century's debates over the proper way to interpret statutes."[16] In short, according to noted philosopher Dr. Peter Suber, *The Case of the Speluncean Explorers* is arguably "the greatest fictitious legal case of all time."[17]

The works spawned by the article, however, may best illustrate its greatness. For example, the George Washington Law Review's

[8] Ibid. at 618.
[9] Ibid.
[10] Ibid. at 617.
[11] Ibid.
[12] Fuller, supra note 1, at 617.
[13] Ibid.
[14] David L. Shapiro, "Foreword: A Cave Drawing For the Ages – The Case of the Speluncean Explorers: A Fiftieth Anniversary Symposium," 112 *Harv. L. Rev.* 1834, 1838 (1999).
[15] Anthony D'Amato, "The Speluncean Explorers – Further Proceedings," 32 *Stan. L. Rev.* 467, 467 (1980).
[16] William N. Eskridge, Jr., "The Case of the Speluncean Explorers: Twentieth-Century Statutory Interpretation in a Nutshell," 61 *Geo. Wash. L. REv.* 1731,1732 (1993).
[17] Peter Suber, *The Case of the Speluncean Explorers – Nine New Opinions* ix (Routledge, 1998).

August 1993 issue devoted over seventy-five pages to "speluncean" analysis.[18] Similarly, in their June 1999 edition, the Harvard Law Review marked the fiftieth anniversary of Fuller's original with a symposium dedicated to one of its most frequently cited pieces.[19] In all, in addition to Fuller's five opinions, the Supreme Court of Newgarth has issued twenty-four opinions directly related to the original facts: thirteen during the Court's 4300 term,[20] two during the Court's 4321 term (in a case involving the son of a spelunker),[21] and nine during the Court's 4350 term (in a case involving a mysterious, previously unknown fifth survivor).[22] Additionally, three professors of the University of Newgarth School of Law have each issued an opinion to the Chief Executive of Newgarth as part of a Special Commission constituted to provide recommendations on executive clemency.[23]

---

[18] See Eskridge supra note 16, at 1731-52; Naomi R. Cahn et al, "The Case of the Speluncean Explorers: Contemporary Proceedings," 61 *Geo. Wash. L. Rev.* 1754, 1754-1811 (1993). The opinion of Naomi R. Cahn begins on page 1755. The opinion of John O. Calmore begins on page 1764. The opinion of Mary I. Coombs begins on page 1785. The opinion of Dwight L. Greene begins on page 1790. The opinion of Geoffrey C. Miller begins on page 1798. The opinion of Jeremy Paul begins on page 1801. The opinion of Laura W. Stein begins on page 1807.

[19] *School News: Revisiting Fuller's Famous Spelunkers*, http://www.law.harvard.edu/news/bulletin/backissues/summer99/article65.html (last visited Sept. 1, 2009). See also Shapiro, supra note 14, at 1834; Alex Kozinski et al, "The Case of the Speluncean Explorers: Revisited," 112 *Harv. L. Rev.* 1876, 1876-1923 (1999). The opinion of Judge Alex Kozinski begins on page 1876. The opinion of Cass Sunstein begins on page 1883. The opinion of Robin West begins on page 1891. The opinion of Alan Dershowitz, writing as "Justice De Bunker," begins on page 1899. The opinion of Judge Frank Easterbrook begins on page 1913. The opinion of Paul Butler, writing as "Justice Stupidest Housemaid," begins on page 1917.

[20] The seven opinions that appeared in 1993 in the *George Washington Law Review* and the six opinions that appeared in 1999 in the *Harvard Law Review* were each written during the Court's 4300 term.

[21] Burton F. Brody, "Son of the Speluncean Explorer," 55 *Iowa L. Rev.* 1233 (1970). The Court's majority opinion, written by Acting Chief Justice Abner, begins on page 1233. A dissenting opinion, authored by Justice Schweitzer, begins on page 1246.

[22] Suber, supra note 17, at 33. The book contains the opinions of Chief Justice Burnham as well as Justices Springham, Tally, Hellen, Trumpet, Goad, Frank, Reckon, and Bond.

[23] D'Amato, supra note 15, at 468. The opinion of Professor Wun begins on page 468. The opinion of Professor Tieu begins on page 475. The opinion of Professor Thri begins

This paper not only introduces (or re-introduces) readers to Fuller's original piece, it also adds a unique twist to the speluncean saga. Part I summarizes for the reader the facts and opinions included in Fuller's original work. Part II explores the cases and thought experiments from which Fuller drew the facts of his original hypothetical. Part III analyzes the multiplicity of opinions that have rendered a judgment on the original's facts. Part IV "revisits" the cave using communications between a trapped spelunker and his lawyers. Finally, Part V provides a conclusion.

PART I: THE ORIGINAL

The Facts

Justice Truepenny, Chief Justice of the Supreme Court of Newgarth, set forth the facts in his opinion.[24] Five members of a Newgarth organization known as the Speluncean Society, including Mr. Roger Whetmore, set out in early May of 4299 to explore a nearby limestone cavern.[25] Shortly after entering the cave, a landslide caused heavy boulders to block the cave's only known entrance. Aware of the seriousness of their situation, the men settled near the blocked entrance and waited on a rescue party to remove "the detritus that prevented them from leaving their underground prison."[26]

Prior to their excursion, the group had provided the Society with the location of the cave they had chosen to explore.[27] When the quintet failed to come home, the Secretary of the Society promptly dispatched a rescue party to the group's location. Workmen, engineers, geologists, and other experts established a huge temporary camp just outside the obstructed entrance. Rescue efforts, however, proved extremely difficult. In fact, fresh landslides

---
on page 480.
[24] Fuller, supra note 1, at 616-19.
[25] Ibid. at 616.
[26] Ibid.
[27] Ibid.

resulted in additional delay.[28] Because the explorers carried only scant provisions inside the cave, and because the cave contained nothing edible, the rescuers feared the worst: the spelunkers would starve to death.[29]

On the twentieth day of the group's imprisonment, rescuers learned that the explorers had a wireless machine capable of sending and receiving messages.[30] After installing a similar machine at the rescue camp, communication between the explorers and the rescuers commenced. The trapped spelunkers first asked how much longer it would take to secure their freedom. The rescuers answered that it would take at least ten more days, assuming no new landslides. Next, after describing to a committee of medical experts their physical condition as well as the rations of food they had taken with them, the explorers asked whether they could survive ten more days without sustenance. Politely, the physicians answered that there was "little possibility" of survival. With that, the wireless machine remained silent for eight hours.[31]

When communication resumed, Mr. Whetmore, speaking on behalf of the spelunkers, asked whether the group could survive ten more days "if they consumed the flesh of one of their number."[32] Reluctantly, the physicians answered yes. Mr. Whetmore then asked if the group should cast lots to determine which of them should be eaten. This question, it turned out, stumped the entire rescue camp. None of the engineers would answer the question. None of the physicians would answer the question.[33] In fact, *no one*—no judge, no government official, no minister, and no priest—gave Mr. Whetmore any advice.[34] With that, the wireless machine remained silent . . . for good.[35]

[28] Ibid.
[29] Ibid. at 617.
[30] Ibid.
[31] Fuller, supra note 1, at 617.
[32] Ibid.
[33] Ibid.
[34] Ibid. at 617-18.
[35] Ibid. at 618.

As he intimated to the physicians, Mr. Whetmore had devised a method of determining who would serve as the group's sacrificial lamb. The scheme, initially agreed upon by all five explorers, involved a pair of dice that Mr. Whetmore had brought with him on the exploration. Before casting began, however, Mr. Whetmore withdrew from the arrangement, deciding that he could last at least another week before "embracing an expedient so frightful and odious."[36] Upon hearing this, the other four explorers charged him with a breach of faith. Further, they cast the dice on his behalf. When the throw went against Mr. Whetmore, his companions killed and ate him. Mr. Whetmore's death occurred twenty-three days after the spelunkers first entered the cave.[37]

For the imprisoned men, freedom came nine days later, or thirty-two days after their entry.[38] After being rescued, the four survivors underwent treatment for malnutrition and shock at a Newgarth hospital. Following their hospital stay, a Newgarth prosecutor indicted the survivors for the murder of Roger Whetmore.[39] On the basis of the jury's special verdict, the trial judge found the defendants guilty of murder.[40] As required by Newgarth law, the judge sentenced the four defendants to death by hanging.[41] The Court of General Instances of the County of Stowfield issued this ruling.[42] The defendants brought before the Supreme Court of Newgarth a petition for error. Each justice issued his own opinion.

Chief Justice Truepenny: Affirm

In affirming the lower court, Chief Justice Truepenny stated that the trial judge and jury followed "the only course that was open to

---

[36] Ibid.
[37] Fuller, supra note 1, at 618.
[38] Ibid.
[39] Ibid.
[40] Ibid. at 619.
[41] Ibid.
[42] Fuller, supra note 1, at 619.

them under the law."⁴³ The law to which he referred, Section 12-A of the Newgarth Statutes, stated "[w]hoever shall willfully take the life of another shall be punished by death." The Chief Justice, clearly sympathetic to the defendants' plight, apologized for not being able to mitigate the "rigors of the law." Joining the trial judge and jury, Chief Justice Truepenny requested the defendants receive executive clemency from the Chief Executive of Newgarth. In his opinion, involvement from Newgarth's Chief Executive would provide justice "without impairing either the letter or spirit of [Newgarth's] statutes and without offering any encouragement for the disregard of law."⁴⁴

Justice Foster: Reverse

Justice Foster began his opinion by scolding the Chief Justice's recommendation of executive clemency, calling Mr. Truepenny's position "sordid" and "shock[ing]."⁴⁵ For two reasons, Justice Foster believed that Newgarth law did not compel the conclusion that the defendants committed murder. First, he considered the positive laws of Newgarth inapplicable to the facts and instead believed that the "law of nature" governed the defendants' actions.⁴⁶ This proposition rested solely on Foster's supposition that a coexisting group may evade, either geographically or morally, the force of any legal order. Thus, "when these men made their fateful decision" to enter the cave, they removed themselves from Newgarth's jurisdiction "as if they had been a thousand miles beyond [Newgarth's] boundaries." Consequently, principles appropriate to the group's condition created the applicable law. Under *those* regulations, which Justice Foster termed a "new charter of government," the explorers broke no laws; reversal of their convictions must follow.⁴⁷ The second ground on

---
⁴³ Ibid.
⁴⁴ Ibid.
⁴⁵ Ibid. at 620.
⁴⁶ Ibid.
⁴⁷ Ibid. at 621-22.

which Justice Foster based his decision concerned the purpose of the Newgarth murder statute.[48] After disregarding, for argument's sake, his initial "state of nature" reasoning, Foster concluded that the Newgarth murder statute did not apply to cases of self-defense, even if reconciling such an exception with the plain language of the statute proved impossible.[49] Because, in his opinion, the defendants acted solely in self-defense, the Newgarth murder statute could not apply to this case. Accordingly, Justice Foster voted to reverse the defendants' convictions.

Justice Tatting: Does Not Vote (Withdraws)

Justice Tatting declared that his "usual resource" – deciding a case using his intellect alone – had failed him.[50] He further revealed both his sympathy toward the defendants and his disgust with the act they committed. But before withdrawing from deciding the case, he analyzed the opinion of Justice Foster and found it impossible to accept either part of Foster's argument. Regarding Justice Foster's "state of nature" idea, Justice Tatting questioned at what point one actually entered such a state ("when the entrance to the cave was blocked, or when the threat of starvation reached a certain undefined degree of intensity"). Justice Tatting further announced his disagreement with whatever code of laws applied in the cave since, in Justice Tatting's opinion, the explorers' code must value the law of contract as more fundamental than the law of murder.[51] Regarding Justice Foster's self-defense argument, Tatting stated that the rationale behind a self-defense argument lay not in the *purpose* behind the law but in the definition of the word *willful*, as in how Newgarth's murder statute requires a man to "willfully" take the life of another.[52] In sum, Tatting noted that Foster's opinion lacked

---

[48] Fuller, supra note 1, at 623.
[49] Ibid. at 624-25.
[50] Ibid. at 626.
[51] Ibid. at 627.
[52] Ibid. at 628-29.

any coherent or rational principles. Although he withdrew his vote, Justice Tatting nevertheless confessed that he wished the prosecutor had not indicted the defendants for any crime.[53]

Justice Keen: Affirm

Justice Keen started his argument by focusing on the sole issue before the court: whether the defendants willfully took the life of Roger Whetmore within the meaning of Section 12-A of the Newgarth Statutes.[54] Accordingly, he set aside two "irrelevant" questions not before the court: the extension of executive clemency and the "'right' or 'wrong,' 'wicked' or 'good'" characterizations of the defendants' actions.[55] Justice Keen continued his opinion by distinguishing his thoughts from Justice Foster's decision to disregard the express language of a statute if such language disagrees with the purpose of the statute.[56] In Justice Keen's opinion, Foster's purpose-based argument merely revealed Foster's propensity for judicial activism, a practice that allows the judiciary to speciously fill the "gaps" left by legislators in their statutory design.[57] When dealing with a statutory exception (self-defense, for example), Justice Keen ultimately dispensed with Foster's position by noting the importance of the *scope* of the exception, as opposed to the importance of the *purpose* of the exception.[58] And because the self-defense exception applied only to cases of resisting an aggressive threat to one's own life, the defendants clearly committed murder since Mr. Whetmore made no threat against their lives.

---

[53] Ibid. at 630-31.
[54] Fuller, supra note 1, at 632.
[55] Ibid. at 631-32.
[56] Ibid. at 633.
[57] Ibid. at 634.
[58] Ibid. at 636.

Justice Handy: Reverse

In stark contrast to his colleagues, Justice Handy called this case "one of the easiest to decide that has ever been argued" before this court.[59] He stated that government officials, including judges, should go about their daily tasks with efficiency and common sense. Applying this approach, he noted a public opinion poll revealing that ninety percent of Newgarth's citizenry believed that the defendants should *not* hang.[60] This poll, per Justice Handy, indicated that a conviction would not have resulted had a jury, rather than the trial judge, adjudicated the defendants.[61] Justice Handy also noted the Newgarth Chief Executive's firm determination to not commute the defendants' sentence.[62] Simply put, however, Justice Handy, without much discussion, based his conclusion of innocence on his "common sense" approach to the situation.[63]

The final tally showed the Court's even divide: two votes affirmed the decision below (Truepenny and Keen), two votes reversed the decision below (Foster and Handy), and one justice withdrew his decision altogether (Tatting). Thus, the Court affirmed the murder conviction and the hanging sentence imposed by the Court of General Instances of Stowfield County.[64]

PART II: THE ORIGINAL'S INSPIRATION

Professor Fuller based his hypothetical case on at least two very real cases. In one case, *United States v. Holmes*, killings occurred to lighten a badly overloaded lifeboat.[65] In the other, *Regina v. Dudley & Stephens*, the killing of a passenger created a meal for

---

[59] Ibid. at 638.
[60] Fuller, supra note 1, at 639.
[61] Ibid. at 641.
[62] Ibid. at 642.
[63] Ibid. at 644.
[64] Ibid. at 645.
[65] Holmes, 26 F.Cas. at 360-63.

starving survivors.⁶⁶ Additionally, some have compared Fuller's hypothetical to an ancient thought experiment known as the Plank of Carneades.⁶⁷

United States v. Holmes

In March of 1841, an American ship left Liverpool, England, bound for Philadelphia, Pennsylvania.⁶⁸ Along with a heavy cargo, the ship contained a total of eighty-two passengers, including seventeen crew members. After hitting an iceberg off the coast of Newfoundland, the boat began to sink. The captain immediately lowered the only two lifeboats available. On one boat, a "jolly-boat," he placed nine crew members (including himself) and one passenger. On the other boat, a "long boat," the captain placed ten crew members and thirty-one passengers. Consequently, the thirty-one passengers remaining on the sinking ship perished when the ship went down approximately ninety minutes after striking the iceberg.⁶⁹

Too overloaded to move, the long boat drifted for at least a day.⁷⁰ Once the weather picked up, water furiously spilled into the boat. In order to lighten the boat's load, Mr. Holmes tossed at least eight men and two women overboard. Another boat eventually retrieved the long boat off the coast of France. At the urging of the long boat's survivors, Philadelphia's District Attorney prosecuted all of the long boat's sailors for murder. Unfortunately, Mr. Holmes was, at the time, the only long boat sailor in Philadelphia. Although not charged with murder, Mr. Holmes faced prosecution for voluntary manslaughter.⁷¹

---

⁶⁶ Regina, 14 Q.B.D. at 274.
⁶⁷ *Plank of Carneades*, http://en.wikipedia.org/wiki/Plank_of_Carneades (last visited Sept. 4, 2009).
⁶⁸ Holmes, 25 F.Cas at 360.
⁶⁹ Ibid.
⁷⁰ Suber, supra note 17, at 1.
⁷¹ Ibid.

Mr. Holmes offered a necessity defense, stating that the survival of the long boat's passengers legally justified his actions.[72] Temporarily sitting as a Philadelphia trial judge, United States Supreme Court Justice Henry Baldwin instructed the jury that the law did not entitle sailors with any privileges over passengers unless the sailors were needed to navigate the boat. Thus, any non-navigating sailors should have stood their chances in a lottery with the passengers. Accordingly, the jury convicted Mr. Holmes of voluntary manslaughter. Although sentenced by Justice Baldwin to six months in prison and fined twenty dollars, Mr. Holmes served his prison time, but paid no fine, thanks to a pardon by President John Tyler.[73]

Regina v. Dudley & Stephens

When an Australian yacht bound for Sydney began sinking, four passengers, including Mr. Parker, a sickly seventeen-year-old, relocated to a lifeboat.[74] The quartet first entered the lifeboat with no supply of water or food, except two one-pound tins of turnips.[75] On the fourth day of their travels they caught a small turtle, which the group consumed by the twelfth day.[76] Dehydration and starvation were rapidly killing Mr. Parker, however, and the group knew that he would soon die.[77] As a result, the other three proposed to kill and eat Mr. Parker in order to stay alive. On the nineteenth day, after offering a prayer for forgiveness, Mr. Dudley, with Mr. Stephens's assent, put a knife into Mr. Parker's throat and killed him. Mr. Dudley, Mr. Stephens, and the other passenger, Mr. Brooks, fed on Mr. Parker's body until a German sailing ship rescued the group four days later.[78]

---

[72] Ibid. at 2.
[73] Ibid.
[74] Ibid.
[75] Regina, 14 Q.B.D. at 273.
[76] Ibid. at 274.
[77] Suber, supra note 17, at 2
[78] Ibid.

Captured and arrested in Falmouth, England, the three survivors defended themselves against charges for murder.[79] Public opinion in favor of the defendants resulted in the jury's issuance of a special verdict. On the facts found by the jury, however, the judge rejected the trio's necessity defense and convicted them of murder. Although sentenced to hang, Queen Victoria pardoned the three defendants on the advice of the same government official who had initially recommended prosecution.[80]

The Plank of Carneades

The Greek scholar Carneades first proposed the thought experiment known as the Plank of Carneades.[81] Deemed a standard in European legal literature, two versions of the hypothetical Plank Case exist, each centering on two men shipwrecked at sea. As the two men drown, they see a wooden plank large enough to support only one man. According to one version of the case, after one man has already managed to grab hold of the plank and lie upon it, the second man pushes the first man off the plank, causing the first man to drown. In the other version, neither man possesses the plank. As the two men race toward it, one of them pushes the other and grabs hold of the plank. What results from either version is a timeless philosophical question: whether a person may save himself at the expense of another.[82]

PART III: THE ORIGINAL'S PROGENY

Since it originally appeared in the Harvard Law Review in 1949, *The Case of the Speluncean Explorers* has spawned countless subsequent articles. The following summarizes some of those writings.

---

[79] Ibid.
[80] Ibid.
[81] Khalid Ghanayim, "Excused Necessity in Western Legal Philosophy," 19 *Can. J. L. Jur.* 31, 31-32 (2006).
[82] Ibid. at 31-32.

Son of the Speluncean Explorer

In 1970, Professor Burton F. Brody published *Son of the Speluncean Explorer* in the University of Iowa Law Review.[83] In Brody's hypothetical, the Supreme Court of Newgarth heard a challenge in the year 4321 from the son of one of the four defendants hung in Fuller's original article.[84] The law at issue in this case prohibited a person from registering to vote if he or she was a lineal descendant of a person convicted of a violent crime within Stowfield County.[85] In Brody's article, Acting Chief Justice Abner ultimately declared the spelunker's son eligible to vote.[86] The Chief Justice reached his decision, however, not based on his opinion of the county's voting prohibition ordinance, but because he thought the judges erred in convicting the defendant's father in the first place.[87] Essentially, Justice Abner believed that the only objective evaluation given to the appellant's father was the thought behind the drafting of the Newgarth statute at issue (Section 12-A) in the original case. Justice Abner noted that the Newgarth Supreme Court "swerved from the essence of the problem and devoted itself entirely to . . . tangential questions."[88] For example, Justice Abner noted that Chief Justice Truepenny merely engaged in "pontifical evasion" and "bureaucratic buckpassing" in recommending executive clemency.[89] Furthermore, Abner noted that the opinions of Justices Foster, Keen, and Handy left a reader "wanting either in reasoning or result."[90] Thus, Justice Abner would have voted to allow the original defendants to live. Incidentally, Justice Cadwallader, one of Justice Abner's colleagues, concurred with Justice Abner's decision.[91]

---

[83] Brody, supra note 21, at 1233.
[84] Ibid. at 1234.
[85] Ibid. at 1233.
[86] Ibid. at 1246.
[87] Ibid.
[88] Ibid. at 1236.
[89] Brody, supra note 21, at 1237.
[90] Ibid. at 1241.
[91] Ibid. at 1246.

Justices Schweitzer and Gabriel, however, dissented from Justice Abner's opinion.[92] According to their dissenting opinion, the Newgarth Supreme Court properly convicted the defendant's father since he willfully killed Mr. Whetmore. Specifically, Justice Schweitzer noted that if the group had waited until the first of their number perished, the explorers would have been scavengers, not murderers.[93] Incidentally, although former Justice Boedel heard oral arguments in this matter, he did not participate in the decision because he resigned from office.[94] Thus, as in Fuller's original case, two Justices have decided one way, two Justices have decided another way, and one Justice has not decided anything.

The Speluncean Explorers—Further Proceedings

In 1980, Stanford Law Professor Anthony D'Amato, himself a former student of Professor Fuller, published *The Speluncean Explorers—Further Proceedings*.[95] In his article, Mr. D'Amato imagined that, in response to the Newgarth Supreme Court's calls for executive clemency, the Chief Executive of Newgarth constituted a Special Commission of three law professors—Professors Wun (One?), Tieu (Two?), and Thri (Three?)—from the University of Newgarth School of Law. The commission's task was to recommend whether the convicted defendants deserved executive clemency.

Professor Wun considered the defendants guilty since they acted willfully and out of self-interest (to increase the odds of their individual survival).[96] Accordingly, he recommended that the Chief Executive not undercut the conviction or death sentence given to the defendants.[97] In contrast, Professor Tieu considered all four

---

[92] Ibid. at 1246-47.
[93] Ibid. at 1247.
[94] Ibid.
[95] D'Amato, supra note 15, at 467.
[96] Ibid. at 474.
[97] Ibid. at 474-75.

defendants innocent of any crime.[98] Her conclusion, however, rested on her definition of "life" in the context of the cave. Tieu labeled the trapped explorers a single collective life, akin to a "total society."[99] Since cannibalism ensured survival of the "life," no Newgarth statute was violated.[100] Finally, Professor Thri recommended that the Chief Executive commute the sentences of the defendants to several years' service in a hospital, but considered the defendants neither guilty nor innocent of murder.[101] Thus, as in Fuller's original, perfect balance existed among the collective opinion of the professors.

The George Washington Law Review Symposium

The George Washington Law Review devoted its August 1993 issue to Fuller's original hypothetical, with seven justices hearing the case.[102] While only hypothetically donning a black robe—at the time, at least, each of the participating jurists were law professors—each justice focused on different ways to interpret statutes. For example, Naomi Cahn, Mary Coombs, and Laura Stein approached their reconsideration of Fuller's original piece from the feminist perspective.[103] On the other hand, John Calmore and Dwight Greene represented conclusions reached by critical race theorists.[104] Geoffrey Miller elaborated on different facets of statutory interpretation, showing that since the Newgarth statute technically forbids the killing of "another," a murderer could include, in Miller's words, anyone who killed a horse or a fetus.[105] In fact, Miller noted, certain interpretations would indict the defendant's *executioners* for murder,

---

[98] Ibid. at 475.
[99] Ibid. at 479.
[100] Ibid. at 480.
[101] D'Amato, supra note 15, at 480.
[102] Eskridge, supra note 16, at 1731.
[103] Ibid. at 1751.
[104] Ibid. at 1753.
[105] Geoffrey C. Miller, "The Case of the Speluncean Explorers: Contemporary Proceedings," 61 *Geo. Wash. L. Rev.* 1798, 1798 (1993).

since they "willfully took the life of another."[106] Incidentally, Justice Miller's "purposive" analysis paralleled Justice Foster's original opinion.[107] And Jeremy Paul wondered how any legal system could condemn to death defendants that, in the eyes of many citizens and in the views of several members of the Newgarth Supreme Court, did not even commit a crime.[108] Paul's opinion, written on behalf of the "critical legal studies" movement, resembled Justice Handy's original opinion.[109]

In summary, Justice Cahn would remand for a more complete development of the facts of the case.[110] Justice Coombs would remand for a jury trial.[111] Justice Stein would reverse outright because the explorers acted only after authorities refused to advise them on how to cope with their dilemma.[112] Justice Calmore would set aside the death sentences of the defendants.[113] Justice Greene would affirm the defendants' convictions but reverse their death sentences.[114] Justice Miller would reverse the defendants' judgments and sentences.[115] Finally, Justice Paul would reverse the convictions.[116] Note, however, that none of these justices voted to affirm both the defendants' convictions *and* sentences.[117]

---

[106] Ibid. at 1798-99.
[107] Shapiro, supra note 14, at 1841.
[108] Jeremy Paul, "The Case of the Speluncean Explorers: Contemporary Proceedings," 61 *Geo. Wash. L. Rev.* 1801, 1802 (1993).
[109] Shapiro, supra note 14, at 1841.
[110] Eskridge, supra note 16, at 1752.
[111] Ibid.
[112] Ibid.
[113] John O. Calmore, "The Case of the Speluncean Explorers: Contemporary Proceedings," 61 *Geo. Wash. L. Rev.* 1764, 1764 (1993).
[114] Dwight L. Greene, "The Case of the Speluncean Explorers: Contemporary Proceedings," 61 *Geo. Wash. L. Rev.* 1790, 1790 (1993).
[115] Paul, supra note 108, at 1801.
[116] Laura W. Stein, "The Case of the Speluncean Explorers: Contemporary Proceedings," 61 *Geo. Wash. L. Rev.* 1807, 1807 (1993).
[117] Shapiro, supra note 14, at 1841.

The Harvard Law Review Symposium

In 1999, the Harvard Law Review solicited speluncean opinions from six noted judges and scholars as a way of celebrating the fiftieth anniversary of one of its most cited articles.[118] Judge Alex Kozinski of the Ninth Circuit Court of Appeals (currently that court's Chief Judge) voted to affirm the defendants' convictions.[119] Taking the "textualist" route, Judge Kozinski noted that the thirteen words of the applicable statute left no room for a conscientious judge to do anything other than apply the law as written by the legislature.[120] Since the common law did not apply, and since the defendants— theoretically, at least—had other options, affirming the defendants' conviction and sentence became, to Judge Kozinski, the only choice available.[121] Professor Cass Sunstein (then of the University of Chicago and now a member of the Obama Administration) also voted to affirm.[122] Sunstein considered the killing of Mr. Whetmore unjustifiable, especially since Mr. Whetmore made a timely effort to pull out of the agreement.[123] Professor Robin West of the Georgetown Law Center also affirmed the defendants' convictions, the third justice to do so.[124] Similar to Mr. Sunstein's approach, Professor West recognized the distinction between the actions of the defendants and the classic justification of self-defense, noting the difference between resisting aggression and deliberately taking an innocent life in order to save the lives of others.[125]

In voting to reverse the convictions, Judge Frank Easterbrook of the Seventh Circuit Court of Appeals (currently that court's Chief

---

[118] *School News: Revisiting Fuller's Famous Spelunkers*, http://www.law.harvard.edu/news/bulletin/backissues/summer99/article65.html (last visited Sept. 1, 2009).
[119] Shapiro, supra note 14, at 1843.
[120] Alex Kozinski, "The Case of the Speluncean Explorers: Revisited," 112 *Harv. L. Rev.* 1876, 1876 (1999).
[121] Ibid. at 1876-77.
[122] Shapiro, supra note 14, at 1844.
[123] Ibid.
[124] Ibid.
[125] Ibid.

Judge) concluded that this case did not fall within the broad language of the statute.[126] He opined that five explorers willing to take the risks associated with a dangerous expedition would rationally agree in advance to a cannibalistic arrangement that reduced the risk of death by starvation by eighty percent.[127] Similar to Easterbrook, Harvard Law Professor Alan Dershowitz voted to reverse the defendants' convictions.[128] Writing under the pseudonym of Justice De Bunker, Professor Dershowitz hypothesized that a religious war had caused Newgarth's legal system to abandon all notions of natural law.[129] De Bunker based his reversal decision on his preference for permitting all conduct not explicitly prohibited by law (Newgarth's murder statute does not address the defendants' situation, in his opinion).[130] Finally, Professor Paul Butler of the George Washington University Law School also voted to reverse.[131] Interestingly, Butler took his pseudonym—Justice Stupidest Housemaid—from Fuller's original: Justice Foster noted that "[t]he stupidest housemaid knows that when she is told 'to peel the soup and skim the potatoes' her mistress does not mean what she says."[132] Butler's reversal essentially stemmed from two points. First, no one committed a crime deserving of moral condemnation.[133] Second, Butler noted that killing someone to prove the wrongness of killing "don't [sic] make no sense to the stupidest housemaid."[134] Thus, three justices voted to affirm the convictions while three justices voted to reverse the convictions. In the spirit of Fuller's original work, the case resulted, once again, in a deadlocked Newgarth Supreme Court.

---

[126] Ibid. at 1846.
[127] Ibid.
[128] Shapiro, supra note 14, at 1847.
[129] Ibid.
[130] Ibid.
[131] Frank Easterbrook, "The Case of the Speluncean Explorers: Revisited," 112 *Harv. L. Rev.* 1913, 1917 (1999).
[132] Fuller, supra note 1, at 625.
[133] Easterbrook, supra note 131, at 1918.
[134] Ibid.

Nine New Opinions

In 1998, noted philosopher Peter Suber published *The Case of the Speluncean Explorers—Nine New Opinions*, the first book-length treatment of Fuller's original article. In it, nine (rather than five, as in Fuller's original) judges of the Supreme Court of Newgarth are sitting during their term in 4350, a half-century after hearing the original case.[135] Dr. Suber's book contained opinions issued in a case involving a previously unknown fifth surviving speluncean explorer who, like his colleagues, is indicted and convicted of the murder of Mr. Whetmore.[136] Per the opinion of Chief Justice Burnham, the now-elderly defendant escaped from the rescue camp before his fellow explorers were captured.[137]

In Dr. Suber's book, the Newgarth murder statute in the year 4350 is identical to the Newgarth murder statute fifty years prior.[138] Incidentally, according to Chief Justice Burnham's opinion, the Newgarth Chamber of Representatives twice attempted to amend the Newgarth murder statute. Neither attempt, however, succeeded. Hence, the defendant's conviction arose under the same murder statute, and for the same act, as his spelunking companions.[139]

Chief Justice Burnham voted to uphold the conviction.[140] He noted that judges must follow the law, rather than simply issue morally easy (acquittal) or legally easy (conviction) verdicts.[141] Burnham's guilty decision rested on his belief that the defendants' necessity argument failed.[142] Further, he stated that judges should never put a statute aside in order to fulfill its purpose.[143]

---

[135] Suber, supra note 17, at 33.
[136] Ibid. at 35.
[137] Ibid.
[138] Ibid.
[139] Ibid. at 36.
[140] Ibid. at 44.
[141] Suber, supra note 17, at 37.
[142] Ibid. at 38-40.
[143] Ibid. at 40.

Justice Springham voted to overturn the conviction.[144] In contrast to the Chief Justice, Justice Springham believed that this case was decidedly *not* easy, and felt that the verdict hinged on how the word "willful" in the Newgarth murder statute should be defined.[145] In his opinion, the defendants acted in response to "the strongest kind of necessity," since the only alternative resulted in death.[146] Accordingly, they did not willfully kill Mr. Whetmore.[147]

Following in the footsteps of his colleague Springham, Justice Tally also voted to overturn the defendant's conviction.[148] Tally believed that using fatal force on Mr. Whetmore became the only reasonable way to guarantee self-protection. Thus, only a preventive killing occurred.[149] Tally also believed that this necessity justification better mitigated the "rigors of the law" than executive clemency.[150] Tally's ultimate reason for overturning the defendant's conviction, however, was that one death was a "lesser evil" when compared to six deaths.[151]

Justice Hellen voted to overturn the conviction.[152] Similar to her colleagues, Justice Hellen believed that the fifth defendant, along with his four comrades, killed Mr. Whetmore with knowledge and deliberation.[153] Yet, in her opinion, the defendant did not *willfully* choose to kill.[154] Thus, no violation of the Newgarth murder statute occurred.

Justice Trumpet voted to not only uphold the defendant's conviction, but also to remand the case for re-sentencing.[155] Trumpet

---

[144] Ibid. at 56.
[145] Ibid. at 47.
[146] Ibid. at 49.
[147] Suber, supra note 17, at 49.
[148] Ibid. at 63.
[149] Ibid. at 57.
[150] Ibid. at 63.
[151] Ibid. at 62.
[152] Ibid. at 72.
[153] Suber, supra note 17, at 65.
[154] Ibid.
[155] Ibid. at 78.

based his decision on the assumption that self-defense violated the natural law principle of "turn[ing] the other cheek."[156] He concluded that the spelunkers could have obeyed the Newgarth murder statute.[157] He further concluded that the defendant and his fellow explorers merely considered disobeying the law a more attractive option than obeying the law.[158] Thus, they acted willfully. Justice Trumpet, however, considered the principles supporting the death penalty—self-protection, deterrence, or retribution—less essential to the foundations of Newgarth law than the principle of the sanctity of life.[159] Accordingly, Trumpet would nullify the provision of the murder statute prescribing a mandatory death penalty.[160]

Justice Goad voted to uphold the defendant's conviction.[161] She centered her reasoning on the fact that the spelunkers voluntarily entered into a place (the cave) where killing became necessary to avoid their own deaths.[162] She compared the spelunkers to someone who committed a criminal act while voluntarily intoxicated: the drunk bears some responsibility both for his intoxicated state and for any harm caused while in that state.[163] Thus, she considered Mr. Whetmore's death unnecessary and the defendant's conviction proper.

Justice Frank voted to acquit.[164] As his name suggests, he reached his conclusion after taking an honest look at what *he* would have done if placed in the same situation as the defendant.[165] He concluded, quite simply, that he, too, would have joined the lottery, helped to kill the loser, and eaten what he needed to stay alive.[166]

---

[156] Ibid. at 74.
[157] Ibid.
[158] Ibid.
[159] Suber, supra note 17, at 78.
[160] Ibid.
[161] Ibid. at 88.
[162] Ibid. at 83.
[163] Ibid.
[164] Ibid. at 89.
[165] Suber, supra note 17, at 89.
[166] Ibid.

As such, he "cannot condemn, let alone execute, any man for doing what [he] would have done."[167]

Justice Reckon voted to uphold the conviction.[168] Reckon considered irrelevant to this case the issue of necessity, reasoning it would still be rational for Newgarth to punish "those who did the deed" regardless of the necessity of killing Mr. Whetmore.[169] Justice Reckon, in upholding the conviction, argued that the spelunkers "kill[ed] a person who was unwilling to kill a person" and that because they "exploit[ed] a chump," they should face punishment.[170]

Finally, Justice Bond voted to abstain.[171] The reason for his recusal, however, came under fire, even from his fellow colleagues on the bench. Bond recused himself because a partner in his old law firm argued unsuccessfully against the validity of a patent on a voltage meter connected to the batteries used in the spelunkers' communication device.[172] His colleagues disagreed with his decision, citing the remoteness of the patent litigation and the irrelevance of the batteries.[173] Bond, however, adamantly believed in the relevance of the batteries' capacity to hold their charge.[174] He reasoned that the spelunkers seceded from Newgarth and created their own form of government via peaceful revolution, but based such reasoning on the fact that the spelunkers deliberately stopped using their radio.[175] Because the group formed their own "government," there still existed the question of whether the spelunkers violated Newgarth law. According to Bond, the radio's batteries were fine; the group, therefore, deliberately stopped using their communication device.[176] As they did fifty years prior, the Supreme Court of Newgarth divided

---

[167] Ibid.
[168] Ibid. at 98.
[169] Ibid. at 91.
[170] Ibid. at 96.
[171] Suber, supra note 17, at 107.
[172] Ibid. at 99.
[173] Ibid.
[174] Ibid. at 107.
[175] Ibid. at 106-07.
[176] Ibid. at 107.

evenly, as four justices voted to uphold the conviction (Chief Justice Burnham and Justices Trumpet, Goad, and Reckon), four justices voted to reverse the conviction (Justices Springham, Tally, Hellen, and Frank), and one justice (Justice Bond) abstained.[177]

PART IV: A SPELUNKER AND HIS LAWYER

The death of Roger Whetmore in 4299 generated excessive media coverage in the Commonwealth of Newgarth. From the time of his death until the execution of his killers, news accounts about the events that transpired within the cave bombarded Newgarthians from the Central Plateau to the coastal region. The general public became upset that ten workmen lost their lives trying to rescue the spelunkers, yet became enraged that the survivors' lives ended on the gallows for actions that they likely would also have committed if placed in the same situation. Six months after the tragic events transpired, the Newgarth Speluncean Society renamed the infamous cavern "Whetmore's Cave" in honor of Mr. Whetmore. Because landslides remained a possibility, however, few spelunkers explored the cave.

In the year 4399, Scott Whetmore (Mr. Whetmore's great-grandson) and four of his friends set out to commemorate the centennial of Roger Whetmore's fateful exploration. Reminiscent of his ancestor, Scott and his partners entered Whetmore's Cave carrying only scant provisions, originally planning for their hike to last no longer than three days. In the hundred years since the death of Roger Whetmore, some areas of technology had vastly improved while some had not. For example, Scott traveled with a device that allowed him to communicate wirelessly with anyone throughout the world. Yet because no technological advancements occurred with respect to boulder-moving machinery, rescuers would need the same amount of time to clear landslide debris in the year 4399 as they needed a century earlier.

[177] Suber, supra note 17, at 107.

Three days after Scott and his partners entered Whetmore's Cave, a landslide closed the cavern's only known entrance. Immediately, Scott communicated with members of the Newgarth Speluncean Society, who promptly dispatched a team of rescuers to the cave. Unfortunately, the rescuers estimated that it would take thirty additional days to dig through the debris. Faced with the thought of death by starvation, Scott made the same suggestion to his group that his great-grandfather had made a century earlier: one of us, chosen through an agreed-upon method, should be killed and eaten.

Also like his great-grandfather, Scott asked some very important questions of the rescue team. First, he wanted to know if he and his fellow explorers could survive without food for an additional thirty days. A team of medical experts responded that they could not. Next, he wanted to know if a man could survive by eating the flesh of another man. The same experts reluctantly responded that human flesh could serve as adequate subsistence if necessary. Finally, Scott wanted to know the legal and ethical ramifications that the group's survivors would face if they implemented their proposed selection method. This question, however, was not posed to the team of rescuers or medical experts. Rather, Scott requested an answer from one of Newgarth's most well-known law firms: Tottle & Ham. The firm's two lawyers, Ari S. Tottle and Ben T. Ham had advised Scott on some prior business deals and had represented one of his co-workers in a harassment suit.

Ari and Ben immediately began researching the possible legal ramifications of Scott's lottery. Based on their research, they believed that a judge would not convict the survivors of violating the Newgarth murder statute and would not sentence them to death by hanging. In their opinion, the statute—"[w]hoever shall willfully take the life of another shall be punished by death"—must obviously contain at least *some* implicit exceptions. If not, for example, then the executioner chosen to implement a death sentence would violate the same statute as the person slated for execution. Thus, Ari and Ben considered killing someone for the sole purpose of sparing a life as an act of necessity, whether you kill someone attacking you with a gun or acquiesce, as a "last resort," to the implementation of a quasi-lottery designed to (possibly) keep you from starving to death. And based on principles enunciated by the Newgarth Supreme Court in prior cases, a *necessary* killing is one unworthy of the gallows.

After dispensing with the legal question, Ari and Ben advised Scott on the ethical ramifications of his lottery proposal. While the pair agreed on the answer to Scott's legal question, Ari and Ben disagreed on the ethical question's answer. Ari believed that Scott and his fellow spelunkers should not execute their plan, regardless of its legal ramifications. Under any scenario, Ari considered the act of purposely harming someone as ethically wrong and unjust. Frankly, if he were placed in the same situation, Ari believed that voluntarily serving as the group's sacrificial lamb would be the only ethically plausible decision.

In contrast, Ben saw no ethical problem in selecting one group member to die for nutritional purposes. He based his reasoning on something akin to a cost/benefit analysis. For instance, if *no one* were chosen in the lottery to be sacrificed, then all five explorers would die. On the other hand, if only one explorer died, the selection process would result in the safety of four members of the group. Thus, as a whole, the entire group would benefit from Scott's suggested lottery method. As such, Ben had no objection to its execution.

Ari and Ben conveyed their thoughts to Scott. Scott thanked them for their research and candidness and said that dying batteries on his communication device would preclude additional discussion. As for Whetmore's Cave, the rescuers should have all of the debris removed by tomorrow afternoon.

PART V: CONCLUSION

Lon Fuller's *The Case of the Speluncean Explorers* remains a celebrated work of legal literature. In the article, Professor Fuller introduced his readers to five hypothetical spelunkers who set out with scant provisions to explore a cave in the fictitious land of Newgarth. When a landslide entrapped the quintet, the group faced the prospect of dying by starvation. To avoid their impending doom, the hikers developed a survival plan: the group would choose (by lottery) one of their own to be killed and eaten. Ironically, the lottery chose its own inventor, Mr. Roger Whetmore. Upon leaving the cave, the survivors found themselves indicted for murder under the Newgarth murder statute. Once convicted, the trial court sentenced the group to die by hanging. A (perfectly) divided Supreme Court of Newgarth affirmed the conviction.

Using these hypothetical cave explorers, Professor Fuller presented a balanced analysis of the several schools of jurisprudential thought prevalent when the article was written in 1949. While the original was drawn from real-life cases, the number of opinions written by subsequent members of the Supreme Court of Newgarth best illustrate the original article's timelessness. Legal students of any ilk would do well to introduce themselves to this seminal work and don their own black robe.

PERSUASIVE REASONING AND THE PRAXIS OF VIRTUE
Jeffrey J. Maciejewski

The idea that the operations of the mind involve some manner of persuasive discourse has been suggested with some consistency since the time of the ancients. Isocrates, Michael Billig points out, "claimed that 'the same arguments which we use in persuading others when we speak in public, we employ also when we deliberate in our thoughts.'"[1] That persuasion is somehow involved in motivating the intellect and will was a matter taken up by Francis Bacon, who believed that "the solitary thinker uses rhetoric to excite his own appetite and will in a sort of intrapersonal negotiation—that is ... to 'talk oneself into something.'"[2] Bonnie Kent has similarly remarked that the will must be moved "by *persuasion*, by presenting [it with] the good."[3] Christopher Johnstone, meanwhile, has connected persuasion and deliberation by writing that "the 'man of practical wisdom,' when he deliberates about conduct with a view toward choosing among competing alternatives, employs a kind of internal rhetoric."[4] Thus the operations involved in discursive reasoning appear to rely on some form of persuasive discourse to convince the agent to take action; in other words, to the extent that the content of our reasoning is instantiated discursively, one's ability to render action and to order the nascent influences of the passions requires a linguistically driven persuasive mechanism that the intellect and will use not only to precipitate action, but to convince the intellect to order the passions thus bringing harmony to the mind.

---

[1] Michael Billig, *Arguing and Thinking: A Rhetorical Approach to Social Psychology* (Cambridge: Cambridge University Press, 1987): 110.
[2] Thomas M. Conley, *Rhetoric in the European Tradition* (New York, New York: Longman, 1990): 164.
[3] Bonnie Kent, *Virtues of the Will: The Transformation of Ethics in the Late Thirteenth Century* (Washington, D.C.: The Catholic University of America Press, 1995): 119.
[4] Christopher Lyle Johnstone, "An Aristotelian Trilogy: Ethics, Rhetoric, Politics, and the Search for Moral Truth," *Philosophy and Rhetoric* 13 (1980): 12.

The necessity to harmonize the operations of the mind is illustrated by Plato's comparing of the different conditions of the mind (i.e., rational, spirited, appetitive) to the citizens of a city. Corresponding to the intellect, will, and the passions (respectively) these conditions of the individual soul can at times come into conflict with one another. As Stanley Rosen explains: "I can be angry with myself, not because I am two people but because my spiritedness is a function of the same unity as my reason and desire."[5] Aristotle recognized the same potential for division amid these different "selves": that is, "a man may be one self in his substance, but many and conflicting selves in his acts."[6]

That we can be "divided within ourselves in the way that a city is divided into its citizens,"[7] particularly in cases involving conflict or disagreement, requires some mechanism to ameliorate division. This is what virtue does. As Peter Simpson points out, "since the virtues accord with reason and nature, they integrate our soul with itself and its acts, and they also integrate acts with each other."[8] My premise, however, is that virtue requires a discursive mechanism that enables the agent to *convince herself* to act virtuously. This linguistic instrument, the one that is able to convincing and persuasively wield thought to bring about harmonized action, is ostensibly *rhetorical* in character.[9]

---

[5] Stanley Rosen, *Plato's Republic: A Study* (New Haven, Connecticut: Yale University Press, 2005): 156.
[6] Peter Simpson, "Aristotle's Idea of the Self," *The Journal of Value Inquiry* 35 (2001): 316.
[7] Rosen, op. cit.
[8] Simpson, op cit., 318.
[9] My conception of rhetoric here is more akin to Friedrich Nietzsche and Kenneth Burke than it is to the skeptical rhetorical tradition of Plato and Aristotle. Like Nietzsche, I see language itself as being "essentially and structurally metaphorical or rhetorical" (Samuel I. Jessling, *Rhetoric and Philosophy in Conflict: An Historical Survey* [The Hague: Martinus Nijhoff, 1976]: 113). Like Burke, I see rhetoric as being necessary to ameliorate the divisiveness inherent in Plato's "city." As Greig Henderson writes: "Although rhetoric involves the formation of identity and the establishment and maintenance of affiliation and community, it is predicated upon division and difference, for if identification and consubstantiality were really possible, there would be no need to induce them" (Greig Henderson, Kenneth

I am aware that for some readers conceiving of the linguistic operations of the mind as being rhetorical may well be disquieting, particularly if the practice of rhetoric is viewed as nothing more than an antediluvian art of image and manipulation. But given its ability to precipitate action (including its ability to instantiate virtue) I assert that it can be viewed in essentialist terms as a *natural kind* of communication, the purpose of which is to apprehend the stages of action to bring about the end of harmony.[10] Unfortunately, most existing theories of rhetoric lack such ontologies. Most notably, Aristotle's identification of three *species* of rhetoric (i.e., judicial, deliberative, epideictic) offers no visible connection to the praxis of action (aside from that which is associated with the needs of an audience).[11] Thus in what follows I offer a prefatory theory of "natural rhetoric" with an ontology that is linked to Aristotle's theory of action.

The essence of this natural rhetoric can be understood in terms of three dispositional properties all of which share a teleological orientation aligned with the human capacity for action as it is instantiated through the exercising of reason:[12] an *apprehensive property* (wherein rhetoric makes possible the apprehension or

---

Burke, *Literature and Language as Symbolic Action* [Athens, Georgia: The University of Georgia Press, 1988]: 50). As it is implicated in this discussion, as an artifact of reasoning, I conceive of rhetoric as Henry Johnstone does when he writes: "Rhetoric is the evocation and maintenance of the consciousness required for communication" (Henry Johnstone, "The Philosophical Basis of Rhetoric," *Philosophy and Rhetoric* 40 [2007]: 21).

[10] I base this conception of rhetoric as a natural kind of communication using the philosophy of St. Thomas Aquinas and his essentialist ontology. See generally Anthony J. Lisska, *Aquinas's Theory of Natural Law: An Analytical Reconstruction* (Oxford: Clarendon Press, 1996); John Finnis, *Aquinas: Moral, Political, and Legal Theory* (Oxford: Oxford University Press, 1998); Jean Porter, *Nature as Reason: A Thomistic Theory of the Natural Law* (Grand Rapids, Michigan: William B. Eerdmans Publishing Company, 2005).

[11] For more on Aristotle's conception of the species of rhetoric, see George A. Kennedy, *A New History of Classical Rhetoric* (Princeton, New Jersey: Princeton University Press, 1994): 58. I should point out that Kennedy is alone in describing Aristotle's kinds of rhetoric as being species.

[12] I rely here on Aristotle's theory of human action. See Daniel Westberg, *Right Practical Reason: Aristotle, Action, and Prudence in Aquinas* (Oxford: Oxford University Press, 1994): 119-35.

grasping of an action or object as a good); a *decisive property* (in which rhetoric is brought to bear on judging and deciding); and a *deliberative property* (where rhetoric is used to choose among means).

The dispositional properties of rhetoric can be understood to function in the following way: The apprehensive property of natural rhetoric, the end of which is apprehending the intentional stage of action, is used by the individual himself as an instrument to grasp an object (action) as a good, to direct the will toward the object (to recognize that the object or action is in some way good) and to engage in the act of ordering means toward an end; or to order means toward apprehending the object. Similarly, the decisive property of natural rhetoric is directed toward judgment and to presenting the object to the will in such a way so as to enable the will to recognize that the object tends toward the good (thus being in some way attractive). Identifying and deliberating over means is the principle aim of the deliberative property, as the intellect specifies means and the will identifies them as attractive and identifies one or more means as being the most attractive.

If the stages of action engaged in by the mind—involving the related dispositional properties of natural rhetoric—yield correct action, we can say that the agent has acted reasonably by successfully apprehending the first principles of reason. If so, we can say also that the agent has properly ordered the potentially conflicting influences of the passions in relation to the intellect and the will, thus bringing harmony to the mind. To the extent that harmony has been achieved, such achievement is indicative of virtuous action. As Simpson reminds, this harmony brings unity to the soul. He writes: "Virtue is what brings our soul to unity and makes us into single selves." But virtue brings other selves into harmony with one another; for "without virtue, individuals and communities are torn and divided."[13]

Before I begin to discuss how my conception of discursive praxis apprehends virtue, I must make an important ontological distinction:

---

[13] Simpson, 316.

that is, to distinguish between the first- and second-order operations of natural rhetoric. As much as the employment of the dispositional properties enables the agent to engage in correct action and insofar as such reasoned action characterizes distinctively human action, we can say that natural rhetoric has enabled the agent to order the operations of her mind. Insofar as this ordering is reflective of correct action we can say it embodies virtue.

I will discuss later what particular virtues are involved. For now, the salient point is that what I just described entails the first-order operation of natural rhetoric: that which enables the agent to establish an internal form of harmony. This is a necessary precondition for establishing harmony with others; for one whose mind is in disorder can do no more than engage others in disorder. For Aristotle, such disharmony is characteristic of a "bad man," insofar as "a bad man is not a self but many selves that are hostile to each other."[14] Thus one cannot foster order among and with others if he himself is in a state of disorder.

Consequently, if the first-order employment of natural rhetoric is necessary to dispose the agent to the bringing about of an *externally* directed state of harmony, then it would seem there is a second-order operation of natural rhetoric: that is, for the agent who has employed the first-order operation of natural rhetoric to then engage in the good of sharing this harmony by employing the properties of natural rhetoric communally, aiding others in discursive praxis so as to actualize virtue and achieve social harmony.[15]

---

[14] Simpson, op cit.,p. 317.
[15] Finnis writes that "harmony is the fittingness of order;" and "Good consists in order; but people are rightly ordered to other people in mutual dealings both in words and in actions, so that each relates to each as is proper; [and] this fittingness of [interpersonal] order [is a special type of intelligible good]" (Finnis, 111).

I.

Natural Rhetoric and the Praxis of Virtue

As I asserted at the outset, the dispositional properties that characterize the essence of natural rhetoric are employed discursively by both the intellect and the will so as to order the influences of the passions and to enable the agent to apprehend that which is reasonable. As a result, we can say that such an agent has achieved an inner sense of harmony; by ordering her desires and by correctly appraising the good, thereby demonstrating excellence of counsel, she has harmonized the operations of her mind.

To achieve this sense of harmony through deliberation, virtue regulates the activities of reason and the appetites. As Daniel Westberg explains: "For reason to be correct, the appetite needs to be properly ordered, seeking after proper goals, with contrary or excessive desires properly regulated, fear, anger, and so on under control, and proper regard for other persons" good held in the will. When reason and appetite are mutually regulated in this way, then the agent may be seen as virtuous."[16] By characterizing them as being directed to either reason or appetite, Westberg illustrates that virtues can be either (with the exception of prudence) moral or intellectual. Virtues involving reason are intellectual and are considered "morally neutral."[17]

Ralph McInerny broadens the distinctions, identifying understanding, science and wisdom as virtues of the speculative intellect, and art and prudence as virtues of the practical intellect. Virtues involving the appetites are more properly considered moral. McInerny writes: "The two main virtues having their seat in the sense appetite [i.e., passions] are temperance and courage. Our

---

[16] Westberg, 247.
[17] See Porter 169-70. While prudence is "strictly speaking a virtue of the practical intellect" she suggests that it takes on moral force as it relates to the properly moral virtues of justice, courage, and temperance.

concupiscible appetite bears on pleasures and pains; we tend toward the former and withdraw from the latter."[18] Justice, meanwhile, is "the virtue having to do with those actions whereby we enter into relations with other persons [and] has its seat in the will [i.e., the rational appetite]."[19] Although it is possible to make a further distinction between infused virtues (e.g., faith, hope, charity) and those that are acquired, I will be focusing on those that are acquired and are moral.

Moral virtues demand of the agent stability of disposition and are inter-related. On Westberg's view, the "role of the moral virtues is to enable practical reason to operate properly, to enable choices of particular actions to be made in light of what is truly good."[20] Enabling reason to do so requires a steadiness of disposition; or, as McInerny describes it, a "stable and settled readiness to make rational judgments bearing on emotions is what is meant by moral virtue."[21] Insofar as they are stable dispositions and insofar are they are acquired, they are subject to habit. As Jean Porter writes: "the moral virtues are *habitus*, or stable dispositions, of the distinctively human capacities for intellectual activity, judgment, and desire, through which the human person is disposed to act in good and appropriate ways, and to avoid vicious kinds of actions."[22] McInerny elaborates:

> There is, for better or worse, a predictability in our lives, a stability of choice, an ingrained disposition to act in one way rather than another. We are disposed, because of the actions we have already performed, to perform similar actions in the future. This is what is meant by habit: a disposition to perform acts of a certain kind.[23]

---

[18] Ralph McInerny, *Ethica Thomistica: The Moral Philosophy of Thomas Aquinas* (Washington, D.C.: The Catholic University of America Press, 1997): 97-8.
[19] McInerny, op cit., 98.
[20] Westberg, 223.
[21] McInerny, op cit.
[22] Porter, 163.
[23] McInerny, 91.

In addition to being stable dispositions, virtues are inter-related and inter-connected, dependent namely on prudence. McInerny describes such a state of inter-connectedness as a "virtuous circle": "The moral virtues presuppose prudence, prudence presupposes the moral virtues."[24] Westberg offers some clarification when he writes: "the virtues are truly interconnected: a prudent decision and action must be governed by justice (with due regard for relationships with others), temperance (desires for pleasure under control), and fortitude (being constant and firm in adversity)."[25] But as John Finnis observes: "[For Aquinas] there is one principal virtue, called *prudentia*" that is at the heart of the good of practical reasonableness and that extends "reason's order" into actions and emotions.[26]

Insofar as it precipitates virtues seated in the appetites, prudence is moral. Generally, Porter suggests that it has "the task of ordering diverse aims in accordance with one's overall end in acting."[27] Westberg punctuates the practical orientation of prudence when he writes: "Prudence is the developed ability to choose the right means, the disposition of mind—dependent on right appetite—to make decisions, to consider other possibilities when necessary, and to put the decision correctly into action."[28]

However, he goes on to remind us that "prudence depends on temperance and fortitude."[29] Following McInerny's assertion

[24] McInerny, 107. He goes on to describe the interaction of the virtues: "As to their interaction, the following picture is urged upon us. The moral virtues ensure an appetitive ordination to particular ends constitutive of the ultimate end. Prudence or practical wisdom determines how the moral ideal can be realized here and now; that is, thanks to prudence, we deliberate, judge, and command as to the means of realizing the end. It is here that the notion of practical truth makes its appearance. The judgment of prudence as to the means of realizing the end is said to be true, not by conformity with the way things are, but by conformity with the presupposed ordination to the end by moral virtue. Only if my judgment that courage is good is complemented by my appetitive ordination to that good as good can my deliberation, judgment, and command as to how that constituent of the ultimate end is here and now to be realized be effective."
[25] Westberg, 223.
[26] Finnis, 98-9.
[27] Porter, 130.
[28] Westberg, 188.
[29] Westberg, op cit., 255.

that "our concupiscible appetite bears on pleasures and pains; we tend toward the former and withdraw from the latter,"[30] and if we subsequently relate temperance with a predilection for pleasure and courage with a dislike for pain, it would follow that one who is intemperate is incapable of making a prudent decision because of a disposition toward pleasure and that an agent who lacks courage is prevented from doing what is prudent due to an overwhelming desire to avoid that which is painful.

While this illustrates how intemperance (or a lack of fortitude) can forestall prudent deliberation, it illustrates also how it is that "sense appetite becomes the seat of virtue insofar as our emotional life can come under the sway of reason."[31] To bring about affirmative forms of action, reason must manage the influence of the passions; to do so, Finnis observes that "in virtuous action, emotions are taken up into reason." That is, "the subjection of passions (emotions) to reason, a subjection which for Aquinas is of the essence of moral and political soundness, involves not their suppression, elimination, or even diminution, but rather their integration with reasons, i.e. with the intelligible goods instantiated in persons."[32] McInerny describes such integration with reasons as making emotions "rational by participation": "the activities of faculties other than reason [e.g., sense appetites] that come under the sway of reason are thus rational by participation."[33]

Insofar as it perfects an appetitive power, temperance is a moral virtue. To perfect the sense appetite, Porter maintains that temperance "shapes the passions of desire in such a way that the agent desires what is truly in accordance with her overall good."[34] Of course, in McInerny's view, this "shaping" ostensibly involves maintaining one's affective response to pleasure. But as it shapes our desires, our responses to pleasure, it influences our perceptions of our own

---

[30] McInerny, op cit.
[31] McInerny, op cit.
[32] Finnis, 76.
[33] McInerny, 23.
[34] Porter, 170.

happiness, or how it is we constitute our happiness. Thus as Westberg asserts, "moral virtues are required for right desires."[35] The main point is that while virtues are stable dispositions, the intemperate person—by turning away from that which reason has already prescribed as the good—demonstrates instability of character. As such, the intemperate of disposition requires the virtue of constancy in order to follow that which correct reason has identified as the true good.

We now turn to look at the virtue of courage. As the other moral virtue that perfects the sense appetite, fortitude "shapes the passions [so as] to resist obstacles."[36] But whereas temperance manages the effects of pleasure, McInerny sees courage as being necessary to manage the effects of the irascible appetite, which "has to do with goods difficult of achievement and pains hard to avoid."[37] Thus one who lacks the virtue of fortitude cannot find the means to act in adverse situations because his reason cannot effectively manage his response to fear, be it related to things hard to achieve (e.g., as in a fear of failure) or pains hard to avoid. In this way, his perception of fear colors his deliberations and subsequent judgments. Nevertheless, following McInerny's observation, if fear avails itself to the insight of reason it can be made "rational by participation."[38] By participating in rationality, the desire is made to conform to that which is reasonable.

Generally justice pertains to one's relations with others; or, as Porter maintains, it concerns the "constant and perpetual will to render to each his or her due."[39] Westberg claims that "justice is the special moral virtue of the will, but it is directed to those actions which involve relationship to another person, while the other moral virtues perfect the agent only in those things which pertain to

---

[35] Westberg, 15.
[36] Porter, 130.
[37] McInerny, op cit.
[38] McInerny, op cit., 107.
[39] Porter, 217.

himself."⁴⁰ Thus the moral virtue of justice is seated in the will, the rational appetite.

Since the will is necessarily oriented toward the good—that which has been dictated to it by reason—it carries forth a due consideration of others into human affairs: As McInerny observes, justice is the "institution into human affairs of right reason."⁴¹ This directing of right reason into human affairs predisposes the will to the good of justice by "[orienting] the will toward fairness."⁴²

II.

Virtue and the First-Order Operations of Natural Rhetoric

We now turn our attention to how the dispositional properties of natural rhetoric instantiate virtue as the individual seeks to harmonize the intellect and will, and the influence of the passions. As they enable the agent to reason well, the dispositional properties of natural rhetoric have the capacity to perfect those aspects of the mind that are stimulated to action by instantiating virtue; that is, by rendering virtue as intelligible, by making it capable of being expressed and internalized.

I would like to begin by examining what properties of natural rhetoric instantiate prudence. Insofar as Westberg notes that prudence is "involved in deliberation, decision and execution,"⁴³ it would follow that the deliberative and decisive properties of natural rhetoric instantiate prudence by perfecting the operations of the practical intellect as those operations embody excellence of counsel. That said, the use of these properties presupposes the exercise of the apprehensive property, which implicates the will and reason in a specific orientation to the good.

---

⁴⁰ Westberg, 246.
⁴¹ McInerny, 47.
⁴² Porter, 170.
⁴³ Westberg, op cit., 191.

Insofar as the apprehensive property of natural rhetoric enables the agent to apprehend the good, it brings about prudence by enabling the practical intellect to clarify intentions in the intentional stage of action. Westberg writes:

> Intention is part of the process of cognition, proceeding from apprehension to reasoning, knowledge, and wisdom. In the words of Thomas, that act which first simply apprehends or grasps an object is called the intelligence; then the second act of mind, which relates what is to be known or done to something else, is called intention. Relating data to known facts and principles is the means of building up knowledge, and relating desired objects to purposes is the key to moral agency.[44]

While he goes on to observe that "the process of practical reason (in deliberation and judgment) can be seen as a way of clarifying intentions so as to be able to act,"[45] the important point that Westberg punctuates is that the apprehensive property is used by the intellect in the first act of the mind to simply grasp an object (e.g., that this object before me now is a good). Thus the apprehensive property instantiates virtue indirectly by enabling the mind to engage in a preliminary act that ultimately has the *potential* to lead to prudence: that is, by way of the will responding to this initial grasp of the good by engaging in what Finnis describes as a "preliminary or procedural choice . . . a choice which initiates deliberation,"[46] in which the deliberative property of natural rhetoric is subsequently used by the intellect to instantiate prudence more directly in the process of deliberating and judging.

Westberg suggests how this is possible in his description of prudence in the operations of reason: "though *consilium* is not required for many actions, it is in precisely those difficult and

---
[44] Westberg, 137.
[45] Westberg, op cit.
[46] Finnis, 70.

uncertain situations requiring deliberation when it is essential for the prudent agent to be a good reasoner (*bene ratiocinativus*) so that he may then rightly apply (in the act of judgment) universal principles to particular situations which are various and uncertain."[47] Thus it should be clear that the apprehensive property enables the agent to determine that she is in a difficult and uncertain situation and to come to the realization that deliberation here and now is a good to be pursued.

Johnstone contextualizes the role of rhetoric in deliberation when he writes:

> Recall that Aristotle defines the particular excellence of the practical intellect as the ability to deliberate well about action. Practical wisdom, which determines in any particular instance the standard by which conduct is to be appraised and chosen, is a capacity to deliberate well and a disposition to choose according to the conclusion attendant upon such deliberation. Now rhetoric, as we have seen, is a practical faculty, and it is concerned with such matters as we deliberate upon. Furthermore, since rhetoric aims properly at facilitating reasoned judgment about such matters, we can say that it aims at excellence in practical deliberation.[48]

Following Westberg's and Johnstone's observations it is the deliberative and the decisive properties of *natural* rhetoric that more directly actualize prudence by enabling the agent to effectively deliberate and judge. Westberg reminds that "when the particular action to be done is not clear or intelligible to the agent, he needs to conduct an *inquisitio* through discursive reasoning."[49] As a result it is in fact the paradigmatic *quality* of the argument, as *inquisitio*, that is discernable by virtue, which is indicative of the excellence in deliberation that Johnstone refers to.

[47] Westberg, 193.
[48] Johnstone, 11.
[49] Westberg, op cit.

Joseph Pilsner writes that "contemplation is also assisted by certain moral virtues which help prevent distraction. Courage and temperance, for example, keep the passions of fear and concupiscence, respectively, from exceeding their due bounds and demanding the contemplator's attention."[50] When one engages in deliberation (i.e., as *inquisitio*), one focuses the intellect in an act of sustained attention in such a way that to demonstrate prudence the intellect must be reflexive in the coterminous act of contemplation. Although the intellect relies on courage and temperance to forestall the influence of the passions it is the manner in which the act of contemplative deliberation is obtained that instantiates of the virtue To summarize how it is that natural rhetoric brings about the virtue of prudence in order to harmonize the operations of the mind, recall that the apprehensive dispositional property of natural rhetoric apprehends the intentional stage of action and is used by the individual himself as an instrument to grasp an object (action) as a good, to direct the will toward the object (to recognize that the object or action is in some way good) and to engage in the act of ordering means toward an end; or to order means toward apprehending the object. The apprehensive property is thus used by the agent in the first act of the mind engaged in by the will to grasp the good of subsequent deliberation, a procedural choice prior to deliberation. This use of the apprehensive property does not in itself actualize prudence; instead it simply disposes the agent to the *possibility* of prudential choice.

Recall also my assertion that identifying and deliberating over means is the principle aim of the deliberative property, as the intellect specifies means and the will identifies them as attractive and identifies one or more means as being the most attractive. Thus the deliberative property more acutely brings about prudence as it is used by the intellect to speculatively deliberate in a persuasive fashion about the constituent nature of the goods in question (e.g.,

---

[50] Joseph Pilsner, *The Specification of Human Actions in St. Thomas Aquinas* (Oxford: Oxford University Press, 2006): 27.

what are the goods that can be pursued here and now). Of course, as it deliberates the intellect relies on courage and temperance to keep the passions from unduly compromising its deliberations.

Since the decisive property of rhetoric is directed toward judgment and to presenting the object of the intellect's deliberations to the will so as to enable the will to recognize that the object tends toward the good (thus being in some way attractive), the intellect uses the decisive property to affirm its deliberations in judgment. The will then uses the decisive property itself in exercising choice (e.g., that among the goods presented, this particular good must be pursued here and now). After the will chooses, the intellect again uses the deliberative property of natural rhetoric to practically consider the means necessary to secure the chosen good. In the end, it is only by the intellect and the will working in harmony, using all three dispositional properties of natural rhetoric, that a prudent choice can be made.

Perhaps an example that Finnis offers can illustrate what I have just proposed:

> Here is a group of eight students, occupying a corridor of eight rooms and a small kitchen in the college hostel. They are deciding whether or not to establish for themselves, by agreement, a curfew on cooking and kitchen conversation after 9:00 p.m. The walls are thin, the doors even thinner, voices and kitchen noises travel, some of the students find it hard to study at nights with these distractions. But they all enjoy company, and like relaxed night-time talking; and some of them get back late from libraries and would prefer to cook late. From time to time, most of them get really interested in the work, and want to read late and do the note-taking that brings comprehension. More constantly, they want to succeed in examinations, to get employment and the bundle of benefits loosely envisaged and named "a future." They see the point of getting along together, and understand how in this debate that cuts both

ways. As an individual student in this situation, what are the elements in one's deliberating and choosing?[51]

Presumably reasoning begins when a particular student thinks to himself: "Although I like my friends, there do appear to be times when I need to have some quiet time to study. And it seems like some of my roommates might feel the same way." By saying this to himself he is, in effect, employing the apprehensive property of rhetoric; that is, his intellect is grasping the good of quiet time while his will is being persuasively directed to consider quiet time as a good. Of course, what I am asserting is that by thinking these things to himself he is engaging in what Billig describes as "dialogic thinking, or the conduct of internal debate;"[52] a necessarily *persuasive* form of discursive reasoning, so as to "talk [himself] into something."[53]

Moreover, by saying these things to himself his will is employing the apprehensive property of natural rhetoric to make a procedural choice prior to deliberation. So while this instantiation of the first fact of the mind directed the student toward a particular good (i.e., that perhaps the group—like the student himself—would like to establish quiet time for study), it did not itself actualize prudence; it merely predisposed the student to the making of a prudential choice.

As I indicated, identifying and deliberating over means is the principle aim of the deliberative property of natural rhetoric. The student in Finnis' example employs the deliberative property as his intellect engages in a persuasively oriented speculative deliberation about the goods in question: "If I lived here by myself, this would not be a problem. But I have seven roommates whose needs I must consider; after all, I simply cannot mandate a curfew all by myself." By thinking this he comes closer to making some sort of prudential choice, while demonstrating that he (as Finnis describes) "[sees] the

---

[51] Finnis, 63.
[52] Michael Billig, "Rhetoric and the Unconscious," *Argumentation* 12 (1998): 203.
[53] Conley, 164.

point of getting along together, and [understands] how in this debate that cuts both ways." But it is his further use of the deliberative property in consideration of the means that more precisely apprehends prudence: "We could vote (however, some might be for it and some might be against it; are there enough in favor to weigh against those who oppose?); I could put on headphones and listen to music (but some of my roommates might think I am isolating myself; I wish to maintain good relations with them, so having them think that I am isolating myself is not very desirable); or I could simply go along with whatever decision is made (but then I would not be able to share my input)."

Since the decisive property of rhetoric is directed toward judgment and to present the object of the intellect's deliberations to the will in such a way so as to enable the will to recognize that the object tends toward the good, the intellect uses the decisive property to affirm its deliberations in judgment: "Voting is by far the most democratic way to handle things; I think our deliberations should focus on having everyone vote on a number of options for having quiet time in the kitchen."

At this point, the will uses the decisive property to exercise the choice to assent to what the intellect has just proposed: "Okay then, let us vote." Of course, after the will chooses, the intellect again uses the deliberative property of natural rhetoric to practically consider the means necessary to secure the chosen good: "We could all vote either yes or no, writing our choices on slips of paper and then count the votes for and against; or we could simply do a show of hands; but some of us might not want to reveal our vote." Thus, as I asserted, all three dispositional properties of natural rhetoric (but more particularly the deliberative property) instantiate prudential choice by effecting the constitutive *quality* of deliberations.

Following what I have just proposed, the decisive property of natural rhetoric would seem to be the instrument of courage and temperance, a mechanism that enables the intellect to avoid the distractions of the sense appetites in order to engage in focused attention on the object of contemplation. Doing so requires the exercising of temperance and fortitude, which "are both needed in order to make the right decision and to carry it out (especially if difficult or unattractive) in the right way at the right time."[54] Given that the decisive property of natural rhetoric is directed toward the cognitive act of judgment and the coterminous act of the will—choice—it would follow that the decisive property of natural rhetoric apprehends temperance and courage, so as to "make the right decision and to carry it out."

Doing so requires that the property be employed by the will, but only *after* deliberation undertaken by the intellect that enables it to grasp the good of the passions made reasonable by their ordering through the virtues of temperance and courage. Kent observes that "the sense appetite merely obeys reason,"[55] an apparent parallel to McInerny's claim that the "sense appetite becomes the seat of virtue insofar as our emotional life can come under the sway of reason."[56] What Kent and McInerny seem to suggest is that to get the sense appetite to obey reason's dictates, the intellect employs the deliberative property on itself to actively resist the influences of pleasure and pain by deliberating on the good of the passions ordered by the requirements of courage and temperance. Of course, such deliberation presupposes what McInerny describes as an "appetitive ordination to [the] good as good,"[57] as determined by the overall disposition of one's will which initiates deliberation to begin with.

Having deliberated on the goods of courage and temperance the intellect again uses the deliberative property to persuade the will of its deliberations. At this juncture, the will employs the decisive property of natural rhetoric in deciding to pursue that which exemplifies courage or temperance and in doing so, persuading the intellect to engage in further deliberation on the means necessary in order to

---

[54] Westberg, 222.
[55] Kent, 214.
[56] McInerny, 98.
[57] McInerny, 97.

bring about courage or temperance. Thus it is the act of judgment itself that in the end directly apprehends courage and temperance but only after the passions that are their subject have been taken up into reason and subjected to deliberation and subsequent ordering.

Returning to the college students, the need for courage or temperance might arise during the student's deliberations. Since the passions exert their influence indirectly on the intellect, the intellect may entertain a proposition sourced to the passions. The student deliberates: "We could vote (however, some might be for it and some might be against it; are there enough in favor to weigh against those who oppose?);" at which time the passions prompt the intellect to consider a conflicting proposition: "Brian always resists what the group wants to do—he has to be the most selfish person I know. What good is voting if he will convince everyone else to vote his way?"

To instantiate temperance, the intellect uses the decisive property of natural rhetoric to assert persuasive, contradictory propositions into deliberations so as to maintain prudential choice: "That is not a healthy way for roommates to think of one another; after all, Brian is your friend. Besides, we can all be selfish at times." The will then uses the decisive property to direct the intellect's deliberations: "Voting is still the right thing to do."

The same process might characterize the apprehension of courage. In the midst of the foregoing deliberations on voting, the intellect might find itself exposed to passion-influenced counterproposals: "I really want quiet time to study; but few are likely to agree with me. So what good is voting anyway?" The intellect counters using the decisive property: "You will not know if you do not ask; more people might want quiet time than you know." The will intervenes with a decision: "Voting is still the right thing to do." Thus, as the foregoing examples illustrate, the intellect deploys the decisive property in managing its own divergent deliberations (particularly those influenced by the passions), while the will uses the decisive property to maintain the course of deliberations. In either case, temperance or courage is apprehended and prudent choice is obtained as a result of what would seem to be Billig's "internal debate."[58]

In this discussion of how the dispositional properties of natural rhetoric actualize virtue we have but one consideration yet to make: that is, what property of natural rhetoric brings about justice? For an answer we must return to the decisive property to discover how the will uses it to grasp justice. To instantiate justice, the will must make the rational choice to dispose itself toward fairness, an ordination determined by virtue or vice. As Porter notes, "it is this general orientation which provides the field of operation for the capacity, which is presupposed by the determination of the *habitus* of virtue or vice;"[59] a parallel to McInerny's view that "the moral virtues ensure an appetitive ordination to particular ends constitutive of the ultimate end."[60] Although he notes that "the will does not need any virtue in order to be oriented to the good as such since ... the good is its natural object,"[61] the will can nonetheless tend away from the good.

Consequently the persistent qualities of the will—as predetermined by the *habitus* of virtue or vice—characterize its general orientation, its overall disposition. Thus it can be said that one's personal dispositions and overall orientation to the good can predispose the will to choose a *particular* good. So if Porter is right in claiming that "justice orients the will toward fairness,"[62] it would seem that ordination toward the good is expressed by the will using the decisive property of natural rhetoric: to say persuasively, unequivocally, that in all fairness to others (fairness being a good I am disposed to follow) a particular choice must be made now, and the basis of this choice is that criteria which concerns others, namely justice. In this way, the decisive property instantiates justice as the will convinces the intellect to order the agent's relations with others.

[58] Billig, "Rhetoric and the Unconscious," 203.
[59] Porter, 170.
[60] McInerny, 107.
[61] McInerny, op cit., 98.
[62] Porter, op cit.

Accordingly, I have asserted that to be virtuous the agent must *convince* herself (i.e., *persuade* herself) to be prudent; she must *convince* herself to be temperate in the midst of pleasure; she must *convince* herself to be courageous when confronted with pain; and she must *convince* herself to be just when considering others. This persuasion in the form of natural rhetoric instantiates virtue by expressing it to her mind, by rendering it as intelligible and thus as actionable, as something—a good—to be acted upon. Her ability to do this with a measure of consistency not only characterizes what Porter refers to as *habitus*, but as something that she does consistently, ordained toward the good, it demonstrates what McInerny refers to as a "stable and settled readiness to make rational judgments bearing on emotions ... [thereby indicative of] moral virtue."[63]

Consequently, justice is actualized by the college student in the foregoing examples each time his will uses the decisive property in such a way as to demonstrate its own readiness to render a choice that expresses fairness; for example when his will persuasively issues a countermanding decision: "Voting is still the right thing to do." As a result, justice is instantiated not only in the will recognizing that voting (in all fairness to others) is undeniably the *right* thing to do, but also in the act of employing the decisive property which—in its employment—is paradigmatic of virtue and is indicative of the perfection of the property in apprehending its end of harmony. Thus we are able to contextualize Johnstone's claim that "the "man of practical wisdom" ... employs a kind of internal rhetoric."[64] Insofar as the use of "internal rhetoric" precipitates virtue, the form of such internal debate is itself paradigmatic of virtue in action.

All this points to a second way that natural rhetoric brings about virtue: by shaping habit. Until now, I have framed discussion of the first-order operation of natural rhetoric as taking place in a given moment in time: that is, concurrent with the praxis of action. But one can, it seems, employ natural rhetoric reflectively and

---

[63] McInerny, 107.
[64] Johnstone, op cit.

this employment itself can bring about virtue through the shaping of habit. Porter alludes to such a possibility when she writes that "the reflective practice of the virtues can itself have the effect of transforming the individual's conception of what well-being looks like."[65] This "reflective practice" would seem to hinge on an ability to reconstitute one's prior discursively oriented reasoning operations historically as part of one's own personal experience (or perhaps in conjunction with shared social experience, as we will see when we explore the second-order operations of natural rhetoric).

The result of this reflection is the recovery of one's own discursive historiography, the content of which are one's reflective understandings of one's prior persuasions: that not long ago, I convinced myself to do A; upon reflection, this was not the prudent, not the temperate, not the courageous, or not the just course of action. In this way, such reflections serve as the data of one's own prior understandings along with how such understandings were situated contingently, which are then re-examined amid new contingencies. Given that these reflections are aimed backward in time and then projected forward in time, one might refer to such activity as historically informed, *a posteriori* deduction. As Janet Smith writes: "deduction about contingent matters—and human matters are very contingent—requires data acquired through empirical observation and reflection."[66] Of course, being a historical endeavor aimed at the self, the empirical observation and related reflection involved have the self as their subject.

Thus it would seem plausible that we can bring this reflective consideration of past apprehensions, past deliberations, and past decisions (i.e., past employments of the properties of natural rhetoric) to bear on similar acts that we must undertake now or that we anticipate having to undertake in the future. Consequently

---

[65] Porter, op cit.
[66] Janet E. Smith, "Character as an Enabler of Moral Judgment," edited by J. Goyette, M. Latkovic, and R. Myers, in *St. Thomas Aquinas and the Natural Law Tradition* (Washington, D.C.: The Catholic University of America Press, 2004): 21.

this traceable path of persuasive experience, situated historically, is precisely how one embarks on acquiring virtue in the act of what Porter would seem to consider as "reflective practice"; that is, by contemplating previous contemplations and understanding how it is that such prior experiences precipitated particular acts.

The main point here is that this rearward, *a posteriori* projection of natural rhetoric into past experience plays an important role in predisposing the agent to virtuous action by cultivating habit (or perhaps even by breaking it). McInerny begins to draw this out when he writes: "A human life is a history, and we dispose ourselves, by the acts we perform, to do similar deeds in the future."[67] He continues: "A character is formed from the pattern actions assume in similar circumstances. Repeated acts of a kind dispose us—they do not condition or necessitate us—to act in the same way."[68] This, he goes on to write, "is what is meant by habit: a disposition to perform acts of a certain kind."[69]

To dispose us to perform acts of a certain kind, to shape our character in a virtuous way, we reflect on our historiography in acts of contemplation. What is the place of natural rhetoric in enabling virtue to become habit? By reflecting on one's own history of action, one constitutes a narrative (i.e., a situationally conditioned understanding of one's prior actions) that becomes the exegesis that forms the basis for habit. By variously employing all three of the properties of natural rhetoric in acts of reflecting and analyzing our histories of action, we engage in a process by which we learn about what constitutes virtuous action so as to perfect the way that we convince ourselves here and now or perhaps the way we will do so in the future.[70] In this way, we reflect in order to learn so as to be able to act.

---

[67] McInerny, 91.
[68] McInerny, op cit.
[69] McInerny, op cit.
[70] Robert Pasnau underscores this point when he writes that "learned capacities ... are generally counted as dispositions (habitus)" which "need to be built up through study or exercise" (Robert Pasnau, *Thomas Aquinas on Human Nature* [New York: Cambridge University Press, 2002] p. 150).

But what links these capacities to virtue is the same thing that is required for them to be built up through study or exercise: that is, the activity of reflection. By studying or examining past actions the agent can actively situate them proximate to other actions undertaken and assess what brought them about. In this way, the agent can more effectively grasp that which is virtuous by actively considering and relating the ends of particular acts to what was involved in instantiating them. Such reflection necessarily involves an *ad hoc* assessment of how one dealt with the multifarious contingencies in which past choices were situated.

Thus reflection is an action undertaken with the proximate aim of assessing (with the intent of better understanding) the contingent nature of previous actions as well as how these actions can be understood to direct what can and should be done here and now, which is what Porter seems to have in mind when she claims that "the reflective practice of the virtues can itself have the effect of transforming the individual's conception of what well-being looks like."[71]

Consequently I assert that if the operations of the mind are carried out discursively, rhetorically, that such reflection is subject to rhetorical re-interpretation. Here, in the act of reflection, natural rhetoric is used to perfect the manner in which we reason with ourselves, to discover that which is virtuous. Thus the apprehensive dispositional property of natural rhetoric is used by the will to grasp the intrinsic good of reflection itself. To deliberate on the nature of past persuasions or on the manner in which one convinced oneself in the past, the deliberative property is employed by the intellect. Finally, the decisive property is used by the intellect to affirm these deliberations in understanding, thus culminating reflection in the acquisition of knowledge.

How this takes place, how this discursive operation is carried out and rendered as intelligible to reason so that past acts can be deliberated on, is by analyzing past actions that are constituted (i.e.,

[71] Porter, op cit.

are recalled to oneself) narratively.⁷² Such a narrative is nothing less than a cumulative discursive exchange in which one recalls one's previous actions to one's self along with the reasoning that brought the actions about. By making such recollections we encounter our historiography of action by examining previous episodes of discursive reasoning leading to action in such a way so as to shape the constitution of our actions here and now.

The link between narrative and human action enables us to discover how it is that narrative situates the content of reflection. Barbara Hardy offers a starting point when she writes: "we dream in narrative, daydream in narrative, remember, anticipate, hope, despair, believe, doubt, plan, revise, criticize, construct, gossip, learn, hate, and love by narrative. In order really to live, we make up stories about ourselves and others, about the personal as well as the social past and future."⁷³ From this, Alasdair MacIntyre asserts that "man, in his actions and practice, as well as in his fictions, [is] essentially a story-telling animal."⁷⁴

Story-telling enables us to understand action in the course of reflection. He continues: "Action itself has a basically historical character. It is because we live out narratives in our lives and because we understand our own lives in terms of the narratives that we live out that the form of narrative is appropriate for understanding the actions of others."⁷⁵ To this I might add that if narrative is appropriate for understanding the actions of others, then so too is it appropriate for understanding the actions *of ourselves.*

Insofar as stories form the content of narratives, we employ the properties of natural rhetoric not in constituting the narratives themselves, but in analyzing them. Susan Wells sees such a task

---

⁷² That this is so seems to support Finnis' claim that we "recount" reasons for action to ourselves amid the operations of the intellect. See Finnis, 74.
⁷³ Barbara Hardy, "Towards a Poetics of Fiction: An Approach Through Narrative," *Novel* 2 (1968): 5.
⁷⁴ Alasdair MacIntyre, *After Virtue: A Study in Moral Theory* (Notre Dame, Indiana: University of Notre Dame Press, 1984): 216.
⁷⁵ MacIntyre, op cit., 212.

as inherently prescriptive: "A rhetorical analysis addresses ... narratives, not to debunk them or to uncover some shortcoming in them, but to understand what they ask us to do."[76] What these recalled histories of action ask us to do, Wells suggests, is to discover how it is that a narratively understood past can be projected into the future. She writes:

> "Temporal location enacts and renegotiates the positions of reader and writer. Telling a story enables the writer to invent or take up a position relative to the past, to trace its articulation into the present: what is coherent and unproblematic in the ideology of the assumed reader can be put into crisis by relocating it to a contradictory—and counterfactual—temporal location."[77]

In other words, one can revisit what one has done in the past by recalling the action itself, the contingencies surrounding it and the desires that supported the act's execution. What MacIntyre and Wells suggest is that such recollection is narratively constituted: the act, its contingencies, and its underlying desires and motivations form a *story* of what was done. This understanding of the past orients the agent to her situation: in the past, when she faced a similar situation (characterized by the conflation of exigencies and contingencies, along with corresponding desires and motivations), she did A. Thus the recollection of the state in which A was done serves as her *story* of doing A.

As she aims this story at the current situation she is in, she can temporally relocate this story of doing A by using it as a measure of what can or should be done here and now. Perhaps the situation she now finds herself in will be more or less the same; in which case she can easily envision using the story of doing A as a prescription for her action now. But perhaps the situation will not be identical to

---

[76] Susan Wells, *Sweet Reason: Rhetoric and the Discourses of Modernity* (Chicago, Illinois: The University of Chicago Press, 1996): 43.
[77] Wells, op cit., 51.

that which earlier involved doing A; perhaps she now faces a new variable, or perhaps her understanding of the exigencies involved now are different, as might be the contingencies.

How can one determine what can or should be done in the midst of this temporally induced, narratively characterized crisis? By subjecting the narrative of one's recollections to rhetorical analysis. First, it would seem that one recognizing a state of presumed crisis would necessarily involve the apprehensive property of natural rhetoric in recognizing that there is an apparent crisis of action and there is good in resolving it. Second, the deliberative property of natural rhetoric is deployed in deliberating on the narrative of doing A and how such a narrative can be understood to apply contingently to action here and now. As I alluded to earlier, the aim of such deliberation is to orient the agent to virtuous action; that in the past when A was done, it seemed to involve temperance, or courage, or justice, and as such was constitutive of prudent action. Finally, the decisive property of natural rhetoric is used persuasively to culminate deliberation in judgment: that with some modification to the present situation, doing A should be done again and this instance of doing A again is indeed a good.

Such a rhetorical analysis involving the dispositional properties of natural rhetoric reveals to the agent that a narrative understanding of past actions is instructive, insofar as one can learn from one's past actions and this process of learning by observation is itself a good that is instrumental in the instantiating of virtue. James Kastely links such instruction to responsibility when he writes: "To become a judge of one's own discourse and ultimately to one's own life is to adopt a critical posture toward oneself, to make oneself the subject of an inquiry. In the move from unreflective self-contentment to a reflective self-doubt, one's relationship to the world changes, for one assumes a new responsibility for both tongue and soul."[78] MacIntyre seems to underscore this very point when he writes: "a good deal of

---

78 James Kastely, *Rethinking the Rhetorical Tradition: From Plato to Postmodernism* (New Haven, Connecticut: Yale University Press, 1997): 65.

our knowledge of the virtues is ... empirical: we learn what kind of quality truthfulness or courage is, what its practice amounts to, what obstacles it creates and what it avoids and so on only in key part by observing its practice in others and in ourselves."[79]

Thus, as we constitute a narrative of past action and analyze our understanding of that narrative, we encounter the situation in which the act was done in its fullest sense: what exigencies were involved and what contingencies were accounting for, both of which characterize the "position" that Wells refers to, or the position assumed by the author of the narrative. And by reconstituting our understanding of such a narrative, we are able to learn from it,[80] speculatively adding to our knowledge of the action, including its conformity to virtue. Consequently, as Wells suggests, we can trace the path of a narrative and articulate it into the present. But the main point here is that when such an articulation involves a reflective engagement of virtue, we can say it was the narrative itself (subjected to rhetorical analysis so as to permit understanding) that provided the impetus for virtuous action.

Robert Sokolowski helps to emphasize this point in this extended passage:

> Philosophy can show the intricacies of human action and choice, the relations among the virtues of courage, temperance, and justice and friendship, and other dimensions of the moral life, but it always assumes that these things have been achieved by practical reasoning, which is where human excellence and human failure first come to light, where we first come to see what it is to be human. These achievements are then capsulated, polished, and trimmed in moral traditions, in poetry and narratives, in exemplars, maxims, and customs, where practical and

---

[79] MacIntyre, 178.
[80] As MacIntyre writes: "What the agent is able to do and say intelligibly as an actor is deeply affected by the fact that we are never more (and sometimes less) than the co-authors of our own narratives" (MacIntyre, 213).

theoretic reason join forces with literary skill to present a picture of how we can be.[81]

Thus it is that natural rhetoric—as an embodiment or manifestation of Sokolowski's "literary skill"—that instantiates virtuous action by presenting "a picture of how we can be." By reconstituting past action narratively we are able to discover *how to act virtuously*.[82] That we can present this picture to others in order to lead *them* to virtuous action is a possibility to which I now turn.

III.

Virtue and the Second-Order Operations of Natural Rhetoric

Having described the first-order operations of natural rhetoric as they enable us to bring about virtuous action, how and in what ways we share this reasoning with others by asking them to partake in action with us leads us to consider the second-order operations of natural rhetoric: that is, how the dispositional properties of natural rhetoric are constituted with others and how such constitution can harmonize society.

Pamela Hall writes: "The forms of community in which we participate and are educated will have serious consequences for the extent of our practical reasoning's excellence."[83] What this passage reveals is that we have the capacity to lead one another in such a way so as to dictate whether we reason well or reason poorly. The state of this reasoning, as we engage in it ourselves and as we engage in it

---

[81] Robert Sokolowski, "What is Natural Law? Human Purposes and Natural Ends," *The Thomist* 68 (2004): 528.

[82] I should point out that in this discussion of narrative and virtue that narrative is prior to virtue, that by employing narrative to recover our past actions that we are able to determine what amounts to virtuous action. I can, for example, narratively examine what I did in the past and come to the conclusion that a particular action was not virtuous. In this way narrative is used to determine that which is virtuous.

[83] Pamela M. Hall, *Narrative and the Natural Law: An Interpretation of Thomistic Ethics* (Notre Dame, Indiana: University of Notre Dame Press, 1999): 35.

with others, seems to be what Finnis has in mind when he discusses "rationalizations" or the reasons that we recount to ourselves or to others for doing particular actions.[84] While we can and must do such recounting individually, we must do so also with others: that is, with other persons with whom we can share our reasonings, our rationalizations for action, and through this sharing bring others to cooperate in action, whether such action is an invitation to partake in acts of cognizing that are affirmed in judgment and that lead to knowledge, or if such action involves practical matters.

Of course, the mechanism by which we seek to lead one another or to convince one another to reason in a particular way and to render our rationalizations intelligible to one another (so as to bring about virtue) is the same mechanism used to establish harmony within ourselves: natural rhetoric. Natural rhetoric has the potential to be employed well or employed badly: when it is used badly it can bring about defective action; but so too can it bring about acts of virtue.

These same uses of natural rhetoric that manifest its first-order employment characterize its second-order employment. As the individual conjoins his reasoning with the reasonings of others, natural rhetoric can be used badly in bringing about communally sourced defective action. Recall that for Porter, virtues rely on a steadiness of disposition: "[They] are *habitus*, or stable dispositions, of the distinctively human capacities for intellectual activity, judgment, and desire, through which the human person is disposed to act in good and appropriate ways, and to avoid vicious kinds of actions."[85] Thus, McInerny asserts, "we are disposed, because of the actions we have already performed, to perform similar actions in the future. This is what is meant by habit: a disposition to perform acts of a certain kind."[86]

To bring about defective action the properties of natural rhetoric are employed so as to destabilize the dispositions of

---

[84] See Finnis, p. 74.
[85] Porter, p. 163.
[86] McInerny, p. 91.

others and to inculcate pernicious desires, thereby corrupting the reasoning processes of others and fostering collective disharmony. To destabilize the dispositions of others, the properties of natural rhetoric are used (or, more accurately, are *misused*) in such a way so as to encourage the cultivation of bad habits, which ultimately lead to a disharmony between the intellects and wills of others by conditioning the responses of their passions and by suggesting how these responses are to be construed discursively.

How this is done is by influencing the overall shape and direction of the discursive reasoning processes of others.[87] Following what I have proposed, it would seem that the apprehensive property (insofar as its end is the apprehending of the good) is used in such a way so as to present a particular good to others in a particular way in order to convince them to see the good as a good. Similarly, the deliberative property of natural rhetoric (in keeping with its orientation toward permitting the good of deliberation) is used communally to influence the deliberations of others, to get others to deliberate on a particular good in a particular way. Finally, the decisive property (given its orientation toward judgment) is used in such a way so as to prompt others' wills to make particular judgments and related decisions regarding particular goods.

What should be emphasized at this point is the potentially insidious inter-relatedness of the first- and second-order operations of natural rhetoric. As I indicated, once one has employed natural rhetoric on oneself in a first-order operation, one can employ it socially in a second-order operation. Insofar as one's first-order employment is shared with others, it is in and through such sharing that others can constitute for themselves what was one's private first-order operation into their own discursive reasoning, their own first-order operation. This is how disharmony is spread. Thus we can say that such a society is bad intrinsically specifically for the

---

[87] Porter illuminates this point at 60 when she writes: "no one denies that our knowledge of the world, together with the congeries of inquiries, arguments, and speculations informing that knowledge, are socially mediated, at least to some extent and in some ways."

way in which it actively corrupts what would otherwise be the good counsel engaged in by others and prompts others to be divided within themselves.

Obviously, the second-order employment of natural rhetoric need not result in defective action. As I have indicated, natural rhetoric may be used in a desirable way so as to encourage the cultivation of good habits that are invariably virtuous. So it is that the virtuous use of natural rhetoric may be carried out in its second-order operations to stabilize dispositions, to encourage well-formed desires and to likewise encourage prudent reasoning, all of which is intended to bring about social harmony in its fullest sense, enabling us not only to live with one another, but to live with one another well.[88]

This fairly straightforward notion—that insofar as reasoning processes can be shared, that they are capable of instantiating virtue, and that they are constituted in the form of natural rhetoric—might well obfuscate a few important points. First, insofar as the foregoing is parsimonious with Aquinas' conception of human nature, I must point out his abiding belief that we must live in society with one another. Anthony Lisska situates this belief as being among the third of Aquinas' human dispositions: that is, as "dispositions or inclinations towards rational cognitivity," including the disposition "to understand (rational curiosity)" and the disposition "to live together in social communities."[89]

Porter elaborates on this social disposition when she writes:

> It is apparent that patterned social interaction *is* our species-specific way of life. We pursue, attain, and enjoy the basic components of animal well being—food and drink, shelter, security, mating and reproduction, protection while ill or infirm—in and through structured interactions with our

---

[88] Sokolowski makes this point well when he writes: "When we say that man is a rational animal, we do not just mean that he is an animal that calculates and draws inferences; we mean, more substantially, that he is an animal that is concerned about living well and not just living" (Sokolowski, p. 508).

[89] Lisska, 101.

> fellows. It is possible to [imagine] someone surviving in complete isolation from her fellows, but only under very unusual circumstances. And it is almost impossible to regard such a life as a life of well-being, any more than we could regard someone who was ill or deprived of basic necessities of life as enjoying well-being.[90]

Porter's reference to a socially instantiated life of well-being is echoed by McInerny who writes that this societal disposition carries with it a prescriptive requirement:

> man's natural condition ... is as a member of community. The good for man must of necessity concern his fulfillment or perfection as a member of society. The moral dimension then is not some putative choice to live or not to live in society, but how to this well.[91]

Living together well is no easy task. Complicating matters is that—according to Kenneth Burke—estrangement is an inescapable element of human social life. He writes that there is a need then to bridge "the perception of generic divisiveness which, being common to all men, is a universal fact about them, prior to any divisiveness caused by social classes."[92] The divisiveness that Burke refers to is manifested in discourse. Iris Young claims this particular problem to be one of "privileging argument" whereby shared, linguistically driven premises and discursive frameworks, situated in the heterogeneity of human life, are used as instruments to affect domination or oppression. In this way, she writes, "the effort to shape arguments according to shared premises within shared discursive

---

[90] Porter, 212.
[91] Ralph McInerny, "A Bracelet of Bright Hair About the Bone," edited by A. Ramos, in *Beauty, Art, and the Polis* (Washington, D.C.: The Catholic University of America Press, 2000): 4.
[92] Kenneth Burke, *A Rhetoric of Motives* (Berkeley, California: University of California Press, 1969): 146.

frameworks sometimes excludes the expression of some needs, interests, and suffering of injustice, because these cannot be voiced with the operative premises and frameworks" employed by certain groups.[93]

Thus, if the second-order employment of natural rhetoric has the ability to bridge the different affections and affiliations, interests, and identities that result from the formation of human social groups it is due to its ability to coordinate the imparting of meaning with the intent of establishing both inter- and intra-group understanding with the objective of apprehending harmony. Young conceives such an imparting of meaning as a "translation:" "Insofar as the many sub-publics in a large and free society themselves must communicate with one another to solve problems or resolve conflict ... rhetoric aims to help translate across them."[94] By imparting meaning through "translation," Young believes that rhetoric deprivileges expression, revealing the social and historical contexts that inhere in assertion, deliberation, disputation, and refutation. As such, "rhetoric is an important means by which people situated in particular social positions can adjust their claims to be heard by those in differing social situations."[95] This, I believe, follows Robert Scott's observation that "rhetoric lies with the contingencies of life; rhetoric is at least part of the social negotiation necessary for living together"[96] and Kastely's view that "rhetoric is ultimately justified as central to the necessary human task of self-invention ... that is at the heart of communal life."[97] As one might expect, my thesis throughout has been that the rhetoric that Young, Scott and Kastely refer to—what is needed in order to remedy divisiveness to secure social harmony—is *natural rhetoric*.

---

[93] Iris Marion Young, *Inclusion and Democracy* (Oxford: Oxford University Press, 2000): 37.
[94] Young, op cit., 69.
[95] Young, op cit., 12.
[96] Robert Scott, "The Forum: Between Silence and Certainty: A Codicil To 'Dialectical Tensions of Speaking and Silence,'" *Quarterly Journal of Speech* 86 (2000): 109.
[97] Kastely, 13.

The second point that might get obscured is how the good of instantiating virtue can be characterized, aside from the simple act of engaging in virtuous action. Following Aquinas' ontology of natural kinds, as dispositions apprehend their ends, they reach their full development, their actualization, and are perfected. Thus as the dispositional properties of natural rhetoric apprehend their respective ends (apprehending the good, deliberating on the good, and deciding on the good) they are perfected. With perfection, these properties (as capacities) demonstrate *virtue*. As Finnis writes: "virtue simply is the perfection of the human capacities involved in action, i.e. the powers of understanding and responding to intelligible goods and of choosing and carrying out one's choices well—a perfection which involves bringing those powers of intelligence, will, and (as sharing in rational choice and action) emotion into cooperative harmony with each other and with the human goods."[98]

Insofar as *societas* is "a basic human good ... [a] harmony among human persons" that is contingent upon a fittingness of order so that "people are rightly ordered to other people in mutual dealings both in words and in actions, so that each relates to each as is proper,"[99] achieving this form of harmony requires the perfection of the person as a dynamic, contributing member of a community; or as a person who, in reality, is implicated in overlapping pluralities of communities, be they geographic, cultural, political, economic, religious, or some combination thereof. This is a particularly important element of apprehending *societas* because living amid such a complex network of pluralistic communities (which, because of their pluralism, can perpetuate the divisiveness that Burke refers to), groups must in some way deal with matters of equality in order to establish right relations with other individuals (or with other groups) so as to live in harmony.

Establishing right relations is far from a passive activity; it requires the human person, as an agent, to take an active role in

---

[98] Finnis, 107-8.
[99] Finnis, op cit., 111-2.

not only recognizing inequalities (thereby engaging the first-order operations of natural rhetoric), but in making the choices necessary to rectify them and to remediate them socially (thus employing the second-order operations of natural rhetoric). Furthermore, it is the concurrent recognition among members of society that justice (being co-dependent on prudence, courage and temperance) is a good that is worth pursuing, that is but one measure of us living together in harmony, and revealing how it is that the dispositional properties of natural rhetoric are perfected and how it is that social harmony is achieved.

IV.

Conclusion

In this paper I have asserted that natural rhetoric is the vehicle the agent uses to express virtuous action to himself. Natural rhetoric is expressive of virtue; it renders the good of virtue as intelligible to the intellect and to the will so as to make it actionable. To act upon virtue, one convinces oneself in an act of persuasion to be prudent; to be temperate in the midst of pleasure; to be courageous in the face of pain; and to be just when considering others. These are, it should be clear, two complementary acts: In the act of realizing that one must do these things and in the act of convincing oneself to do them, virtue is not only fully expressed, it is formally apprehended.

In the first-order operation of natural rhetoric, the will uses the apprehensive property to present the good to the intellect. The intellect in turn uses the deliberative property to deliberate on the good as a good. Insofar as it is able to regulate the influences of the passions by subjecting them to the light of reason, the intellect is able to order them, thus instantiating courage and temperance. If the will stands ready to consider the agent's relationship to others as it apprehends the good, it will instantiate the virtue of justice by engaging the intellect to use justice as a criteria of its subsequent deliberations. Given that a prudent decision will depend upon differing degrees of courage, temperance and justice, if the intellect effectively orders the influences of the passions, and the will is disposed to just desires, prudence is actualized.

Virtue is not only enacted in singular acts; as Pilsner reminds, it is developed through repeated actions over time. He writes: "virtues are themselves typically developed through human actions; for instance, courage and temperance are formed through repeated actions where fears are overcome and concupiscences checked."[100] McInerny seems to agree when he writes: "It is not just knowledge of virtue we seek, but the acquisition of virtue, and virtues are acquired, not by the study of moral philosophy, but by repeated acts of a given kind."[101] So if natural rhetoric is coterminous with action and if virtue is acquired by repeated acts of a given kind, then it is possible to claim that the use of natural rhetoric is coterminous with virtue particularly as first- and second-order uses of natural rhetoric constitute repeated acts over time.

As I indicated, one way we instantiate virtue over time is through the reflective practice of examining our past histories of action. The main way that these examinations are constituted is through narrative in which one recalls the practical exigencies that underscored an act, as well as the act's accompanying motives and desires, in addition to the discursive processes that considered the exigencies, motives, and desires and that codified them in action. The important point is that this reflective examination has the potential to shape habit, which then affects the potential for acts to be repeated over time. The aim of this reflective deliberation is to orient the agent to virtuous action. This is how, as MacIntyre suggests, we edify our knowledge of the virtues: "by observing its practice in others and [more particularly] in ourselves."[102]

---

[100] Pilsner, 27.
[101] McInerny, 101.
[102] MacIntyre, 178.

Once the agent has employed the first-order operation of natural rhetoric, thus bringing about harmony to her own mind, she can engage in the second-order operation in which she employs the properties of natural rhetoric socially in order to bring about social harmony or *societas*. When it brings about defective action, natural rhetoric destabilizes the dispositions of others and in so doing cultivates bad habits (or breaks good habits) by shaping the way in which others apprehend and deliberate upon goods. To instantiate virtue, the properties of natural rhetoric are employed so as stabilize dispositions, to encourage well-formed desires and to encourage also prudent reasoning by helping others to order the influences of the passions.

It is, perhaps, the way in which we help others to instantiate virtue for themselves that perfects us as members of society. Aquinas underscores this point by warning of the "dangers of solitary life and lonely thinking:" To avoid such dangers it is necessary that "people give each other mutual help in acquiring knowledge; one stimulates another to good or pulls the other back from bad. Hence the proverb, 'Iron sharpens iron; friend shapes up friend.'"[103] Thus by employing the dispositional properties of natural rhetoric in their second-order operations social harmony can not only be secured, but members of society can strive toward some form of love. This striving, as it apprehends virtue, perfects not only the individual herself, but also the community at large. As Simpson writes: "in the pursuit of communal goods, each self is perfected as a self and finds itself again and again in other selves."[104] And this perfection, as a good to which we must strive, is edified not only with the help of others, but with the second-order operations of natural rhetoric that apprehend the virtuous community, thus establishing what might well be the highest form of harmony.

---

[103] Finnis, 12.
[104] Simpson, 322.

CONTRIBUTORS

Michael P. Boulette is a J.D. candidate, University of St. Thomas School of Law (2010), A.B. Bowdoin College (2007). His primary research interest in is the field of conservative political theory, and he is currently devoting his time to a manuscript on the subject. The author also has forthcoming articles in the area of multicultural and feminist jurisprudence. He is currently finalizing his J.D., and intends to practice in the area of family law. The author would like to thank his fiancée, Tyler Davis, and Professor Robert Delahunty for their invaluable contributions. His ongoing research can be accessed at http://ssrn.com/author=1326894.

Matthew Jordan Cochran received his B.A. degree from the University of North Carolina at Chapel Hill. He is currently attending Campbell University – Norman Adrian Wiggins School of Law and is a candidate for J.D., May 2010. He is the executive editor of the *Campbell Law Review* and recently presented "Acknowledging Fair Disparities: Why the Title VII Standard for Disparate Impacts Should Not be Applied in Fair Housing Act Claims Against Insurers," at the Law Faculty Colloquium, February 17, 2010 (Raleigh, N.C.). He has a comment, "A Fighting Chance for Outlaws: Strict Scrutiny of North Carolina's Felony Firearms Act," 32 forthcoming (2010) in the *Campbell Law Review*.

Bryan Druzin, Attorney at Law, is a Ph.D. candidate and visiting lecturer at King's College London. In 2005 he obtained his LL.B. from the University of British Columbia in Vancouver, Canada, where he went on to complete a LL.M. in 2008. He is fluent in Mandarin Chinese, having resided in China for roughly ten years, working as a translator and interpreter, as well as completing a portion of his LL.B. at National Taiwan University in Taipei, Taiwan. His master's dissertation focused on the area of spontaneous law theory. His doctoral work relates to law and social norms, and the idea of decentralized legal order. His publications include: "Law Without The State: The Theory Of High Engagement and the Emergence of Spontaneous Legal Order within Commercial Systems," 41 *Georgetown Journal of International Law* (Spring 2010 [forthcoming]); "Buying Commercial Law: Choice of Law, Choice of Forum, and Network Effect," 18 *Tulane Journal of International and Comparative Law* 131 (2009); "The Theory of High Engagement," *Consumer Finance Law Quarterly Report* (Fall 2010 [forthcoming]).

Jason Isbell is a part-time student at Faulkner University's Thomas Goode Jones School of Law, which is located in Montgomery, Alabama. He received a B.S. in Business Administration from Faulkner University's Harris College of Business (2002) and a Masters in Business Administration from the College of Business at Auburn University Montgomery (2004). Since starting law school in 2006, he has been elected to the Student Bar Administration, appointed to the *Faulkner Law Review*, and chosen as a Pupil Member of the Hugh Maddox Chapter of the American Inns of Court. He has also been active in moot court competitions, from winning Faulkner's inaugural intra-school moot court competition in 2007 to being a national quarterfinalist in the 2010 National Moot Court Competition. Since 2002, he has worked for the Alabama Legislative Fiscal Office and currently serves as the office's Education Analyst. This article was written as part of a Jurisprudence Seminar taught by Professor Thurston Reynolds. The author is indebted not only to Professor Reynolds but also to Professor Adam MacLeod and Mr. Justin Aday for their capable assistance.

Laura S. Johnson completed her B.A. at Columbia University in Sociocultural Anthropology (Specialization: Social and Cultural Theory), and her M.A. in Law and Diplomacy from The Fletcher School of Law and Diplomacy, Tufts University, writing her thesis in public international law examining legal mechanisms to provide assistance and protection to victims of human trafficking who face deportation from the European Union. Ms. Johnson is a candidate for J.D. at University of Iowa College of Law in May 2010.

Jeffrey J. Maciejewski earned his M.A. and Ph.D. from Marquette University. He has more than ten years of professional experience and has worked as a marketing communications manager and marketing manager. He has been teaching at Creighton University, where he is an associate professor, since 1999 and is the author of numerous journal articles on media ethics. His research specialties include applied natural law moral philosophy and the philosophical foundations of media ethics. His awards include a regional American Advertising Federation "Educator of the Year" citation and "Outstanding Faculty Member of the Year" honors from Creighton University's Order of the Omega (Greek honor society).

Brian M. McCall holds a B.A. from Yale University (*Summa Cum Laude*, Phi Beta Kappa, with distinction in the Major, McLaughlin Award English, in 1991), an M.A. from Kings College University of London (Fulbright Scholar English Language and Literature Before 1525, 1992), and a J.D. from the University of Pennsylvania (*Summa Cum Laude*, 1997). He has been an Associate Professor of Law at the University of Oklahoma College of Law since 2006. He is grateful to the Roman Forum, Gardone Italy, for the opportunity to present a lecture in July 2009, part of which eventually became this article. He is also grateful to J. Budziszewski, Bradley Lewis and John Rziha for reviewing and commenting on an earlier draft of this article.

CALL FOR PAPERS

In their article "The Federal Marriage Amendment and the Strange Evolution of the Conservative Case against Gay Marriage," [*PS: Political Science and Politics* © 2005 American Political Science Association] authors Frederick Liu and Stephen Macedo claim that natural law theory "remains the most elaborate intellectual case against same-sex marriage based on the intrinsic immorality of homosexual relations."

Has natural law influenced the debate on the gay marriage issue and how may it influence the issue in the future? Is natural law theory necessarily opposed to the idea of gay marriage or could it, in light of an updated view of normal human sexuality, be used to argue for gay marriage? Do Aristotelian and Thomistic views of sexuality, and the teleology of male-female unions as found in the opening of Aristotle's *Politics* (1252a24), still have something important to say about gay marriage in the 21st century, or do modern understandings of human sexuality invalidate these views?

***

Deadline for submission is June 30, 2010. Please address all manuscripts to

Richard Connerney, Editor, *Vera Lex*
Department of Philosophy and Religious Studies
Pace University
41 Park Row
New York, NY 10038

Creating Sustainability Within Our Midst
Challenges for the 21st Century

EDITOR
Robert L. Chapman
Pace Institute for Environmental
and Regional Studies,
Pace University

ISBN 0-944473-91-1

Pages: 308

Price: $45.00

The United States Society for Ecological Economics (USSEE) hosts biennial meetings to provide a national and international forum that focuses on the latest issues and shares the latest developments in Ecological Economics.

The Fourth Biennial Conference of the USSEE, "Creating Sustainability Within Our Midst: Challenges for the 21st Century," took place in June 2007 in downtown New York City on the campus of Pace University.

Partnering with the Pace Institute for Environmental & Regional Studies as a co-sponsor, the conference offered a variety of themes and special symposia featuring collective interests as well as regional issues and amenities.

Topics at the conference included the ecological economics of climate change, energy, biodiversity, ecosystems, and resource systems; valuation methodologies and issues thereof; population concerns; regional studies of sustainable development; greening the building industry; green entrepreneurship; and education in ecological economics and sustainability.

http://www.pace.edu/press

International Philosophical Quarterly

For Over 40 Years
An International Forum
For the Exchange of Philosophical Ideas
between
America and Europe
between
East and West
Sponsored by

Fordham University **Facultés Universitaires**
New York **Namur**

Subscriptions:

$25.00* ($22.00 APA, $20.00 student)
$42.00* (institutions)
$20.00* (S. America, Mid. East, India, Asia and
Africa—except in Japan and S. Africa)

*All Subscriptions outside the U.S. and Canada, add $5.00 postage.

Subscriptions or inquiries should be sent to:
International Philosophical Quarterly
Fordham University

Environmental Values

EDITOR:
Alan Holland
Dept. of Philosophy, Furness Coll.,
Lancaster University, LA1 1YG, UK

ASSOCIATED EDITORS:
Michael Hammond
Lancaster University
Robin Grove-White
Lancaster University
John Proops
University of Keele

Reviews Editors:
Clive Spash
University of Cambridge
Jeremy Roxbee-Cox
Lancaster University

ENVIRONMENTAL VALUES is concerned with the basis and justification of environmental policy. It aims to bring together contributions from philosophy, law, economics and other disciplines, which relate to the present and future environment of humans and other species; and to clarify the relationship between practical policy issues and more fundamental underlying principles or assumptions.

The White Horse Press, 10 High Street, Knapwell, Cambridge CB3 8NR, UK
ISSN: 0963-2719 Quarterly (February, May, August, November)
Vol. 9, 2000, 144 pages per issue. Includes annual index.

Institutions: (1 year) £96 ($155 US)

(Institutional Rate Includes ELECTRONIC ACCESS)

Individual (1 year) £40 ($65 US)

Student/unwaged (1 year) £30 ($50 US)

Official Journal of the International Association for
Environmental Philosophy

Environmental Philosophy

$40 ($25 for students) annually with membership to International Association for Environmental Philosophy

$25 individual non-membership subscription

Send payment to:
Kenneth Maly
Department of Philosophy
University of Wisconsin-LaCrosse,
LaCrosse, WI 54601

Published by the International Association for Environmental Philosophy, the University of Wisconsin-LaCrosse and the Division of the Environment, University of Toronto

www.ingramcontent.com/pod-product-compliance
Lightning Source LLC
Chambersburg PA
CBHW061440300426
44114CB00014B/1768